P9-CLJ-376

Microcontroller Projects Using the Basic Stamp

Second Edition

Al Williams

CMP Books
Lawrence, Kansas 66046

CMP Books
CMP Media LLC
1601 West 23rd Street, Suite 200
Lawrence, Kansas 66046
USA
www.cmpbooks.com

Designations used by companies to distinguish their products are often claimed as trademarks. In all instances where CMP Books is aware of a trademark claim, the product name appears in initial capital letters, in all capital letters, or in accordance with the vendor's capitalization preference. Readers should contact the appropriate companies for more complete information on trademarks and trademark registrations. All trademarks and registered trademarks in this book are the property of their respective holders.

Copyright © 2002 by Al Williams, except where noted otherwise. Published by CMP Books, CMP Media LLC. All rights reserved. Printed in the United States of America. No part of this publication may be reproduced or distributed in any form or by any means, or stored in a database or retrieval system, without the prior written permission of the publisher.

The programs in this book are presented for instructional value. The programs have been carefully tested, but are not guaranteed for any particular purpose. The publisher does not offer any warranties and does not guarantee the accuracy, adequacy, or completeness of any information herein and is not responsible for any errors or omissions. The publisher assumes no liability for damages resulting from the use of the information in this book or for any infringement of the intellectual property rights of third parties that would result from the use of this information.

Acquisition Editor:	Robert Ward
Editor:	Madeleine Reardon Dimond
Layout Design & Production:	Michelle O'Neal and Justin Fulmer
Managing Editor:	Michelle O'Neal
Cover Art Design:	Damien Castaneda

Distributed in the U.S. and Canada by:
Publishers Group West
1700 Fourth Street
Berkeley, CA 94710
1-800-788-3123
www.pgw.com

ISBN: 1-57820-101-2

CMP**Books**

Table of Contents

Introduction

Do you know who Rube Goldberg was? He was the cartoonist made famous by his drawings of outlandish inventions. You know the type: Sunrise causes light to fall on sleeping cat (a) causing it to wake and yawn, pulling string, (b) which tips perch, (c) startling canary, (d)... You remember. The end result would be something mundane, like flipping pancakes or applying shaving cream.

Although Mr. Goldberg's inventions were supposed to be funny, most of us engineers, scientists, and inventors actually had a sneaking desire to build things that did simple mundane tasks (but without the cat and the canary, of course). For many years, these mundane things went without automation, but Mr. Goldberg's name became synonymous with something that was a hodgepodge of parts using maximum effort to achieve a minimal result. There are even Rube Goldberg competitions where students compete by constructing egg crackers, chin wipers, and other exotic machinery.

Not that real Rube Goldberg machines didn't exist. I remember when my parents bought an early phone answering machine for their business. This was before the days when you could legally connect things to the phone line. The machine took a small endless-loop tape and also connected to an ordinary cassette recorder. It also had a large cradle that went between the phone and the phone's handset (remember, in those days there were only a few styles of phones).

The machine's cradle would detect shaking and signal the main unit that the phone must be ringing. The main unit would start a motor turning that drove a set of cams. The first cam signaled a solenoid in the cradle that allowed the phone's hook to rise, thereby answering the phone. The next cam allowed the endless-loop tape to play the outgoing message (for exactly 15 seconds). The third cam then turned on the cassette recorder for exactly 30 seconds to record the incoming message. Finally, the first cam released the solenoid so the phone would hang up. This also shut down the motor so that the entire system was ready to go again.

That system was quite expensive and it was prone to answering the phone when you slammed the door, or otherwise shook the device. Today, machines like this are compact, reliable, and cheap. Why? Microprocessors.

The microprocessor is truly the universal machine. It does nothing unless you tell it what to do, but that's the good part: it will do whatever you tell it. Once an expensive component, volume and technological advances have made microprocessors inexpensive enough to be in practically everything.

The Challenge

What does this mean? If you want to design, build, or troubleshoot modern electronic equipment, you must understand microprocessors. Not too long ago, microprocessor development was an expensive undertaking requiring special equipment (certainly more than most hobbyists were willing to spend and even more than some small companies were willing to commit). Today, however, there is an alternative that allows you to start working with microcontrollers with just a PC. No special programming hardware, no expensive cross-compilers, no ultraviolet erasers required! Just an ordinary PC, a simple to construct cable, a Basic Stamp (often called a Stamp; from Parallax Incorporated), and a nine volt battery will get you started.

Basic Stamps are simple to use, but they are very powerful. Better still, the principles you'll learn to master Basic Stamps will apply to all kinds of microprocessors, regardless of the type.

Is This Book for You?

You'll enjoy this book if you want to build things. Maybe you want to build a robot. Or you might have an idea about automating a manufacturing process. Maybe you just want to build an electronic game, or animate your Christmas lights. That's what this book is all about: solving problems with microprocessors in general and with the Basic Stamp in particular.

If you've never worked with Stamps before, you'll find everything you need to get started here. Chapters 1 and 2 will introduce you to the Stamp and the basic electronics you'll need to get started. If you have worked with Stamps before, you'll find practical advice for PC interfacing, using serial EEPROMs and other devices, analog I/O, and a host of projects that will help you realize your own designs.

What's New in the Second Edition?

Writing a book about something as dynamic as Basic Stamps is like trying to hit a moving target. Between Parallax's rapid product development and the vibrant user community of Stamp developers, there is always something new to talk about.

Luckily, many of the foundations I talked about in the first edition of this book still apply — even to the newest Stamps. However, there are several new Stamps (including the powerful BS2P) and many more peripheral options that expand the power of the Stamp. For example, the BS2P can drive LCD displays and work with I2C devices directly.

In this second edition, I've covered these new advances in Stamp technology. In addition, I've added several new projects including an RS232-controlled power supply, a bridge that lets a Stamp connected to a PC communicate via the Internet, and several new robotics projects, as well.

What You Need

Before starting this book, you should have some understanding of basic electronics. That is, you should be able to read schematics, know the difference between voltage and current, and be able to apply Ohm's law. If you are rusty on some of these things, you can still wade through by reading the first chapter. Some of the projects later in the book will assume you know quite a bit more that this, but you'll be able to get a lot from this material with just that basic background.

You also need a PC, ideally one that can run Windows 95, or Windows 98. Windows NT will work for most things too. That is all the hardware you'll need to get started. The CD-ROM contains enough software that you can do some Stamp experiments "virtual reality-style." Of course, to really get your hands dirty, you'll need a bit more than just a PC.

The first thing you'll need if you want to really build something is a Stamp. These are available from a variety of sources (see Appendix A). Even Radio Shack can order them for you. At the time of writing, you could pick up a Stamp D or Stamp I for about $35. However, if you can spare around $50, you'll be better satisfied with the Stamp II. There are a few other types of Stamps you can buy, but one of these will certainly get you started. If you want the top of line Stamp (at the time of this writing, anyway) get a BS2P. The 40-pin version has plenty of inputs and outputs although the 28-pin variant will work in any circuit that expects a Stamp II.

You also need a way to build circuits using the Stamp. The Stamp D comes with a small area where you can wire wrap or solder circuits directly to the Stamp. The others require some sort of wiring assembly. This can be as simple as a piece of perf board from your local Radio Shack where you can solder or wire wrap your circuitry.

However, you can also buy small PC boards specifically for the Stamp from Parallax. My company, AWC, makes several solderless breadboard adapters that work with the Stamp also. You can also use a plain, solderless breadboard but you'll have to wire it up yourself, which can get messy. Solderless breadboards make it very easy to experiment and try different circuits with a minimum of expense. There are other prototyping options available that you will read about in Chapter 1.

The last piece of the puzzle is a cable. Exactly what you need here depends on what kind of Stamp you will use and how you are building your circuits. For example, the Stamp D or the Stamp I require a special cable you can build or buy from Parallax. The Stamp II boards from Parallax and the AWC ASP-II require regular cables that you can find nearly anywhere.

If you plan to build your own cables, be aware that the Stamp I and Stamp D plug into the PC's printer port. The other Stamps plug into the serial port. You'll find more details about the various Stamps, their boards, and cables in Chapter 1.

The only other essential requirement is some way to power the Stamp. This can be a 9V battery (which works very well), an AC adapter, or a lab power supply. You could even draw the power from a PC power supply, if you don't mind breaking into your PC. The Stamp is not picky. You can feed it regulated 5V, or supply it with a higher voltage and let its onboard regulator provide 5V.

You don't need anything else to get started. You don't need any manuals or software — that's on the CD-ROM (and you can get updates on the Internet at www.parallaxinc.com). You don't need special programming hardware — that's on the Stamp itself. You don't need a special eraser — the Stamp knows how to erase itself!

How to Proceed

If you are experienced in the ways of electronics and computers, you might want to read just the beginning of Chapter 1 and then move on to the later chapters. If you've used the Stamp before, you can probably skip right to the chapters that interest you the most.

Everyone will probably browse Chapter 2. It contains all the Stamp's programming commands along with explanations about them and the differences between the versions of the Stamp. Browsing through this chapter will give you lots of ideas about what you can make a Stamp do.

The simplicity of the Stamp makes it ideal in a teaching environment. I've personally taught some Stamp programming to sixth graders who were in a robotics competition! Because many high school and college courses make use of the Stamp, most of the chapters include exercises and their solutions. Comparing your solutions to the answers at the end of the book can be very enlightening. In microcontroller design, there are always many ways to accomplish any task. If your way works, it is probably just as good as the book's solution. Perhaps it is even better. You can evaluate the relative merit of different solutions in a variety of ways, so rating one answer over another is fraught with peril when both give the same results.

As the old adage goes, "the longest journey begins with the first step." If this is your first step into microprocessors, you'll find it to be one of the most fascinating and enjoyable journey's you've made. If you are already walking that road, I want to show you some of the interesting spots I've found on my trip. Either way, get ready to get addicted. Microcontroller projects are like potato chips: I'll bet you can't do just one!

Chapter 1

Jump Right In

For many years, I've been an avid Star Trek fan (as are many engineers, I suppose). But no matter how much I enjoy the show, I still can't help but find fault with it on occasion (perhaps that's the part I enjoy). Take Mr. Spock. Spock has one thing in common with many scientist-types on TV. He knows about everything. Remember the professor on Gilligan's Island? Same thing. He isn't a biologist, or a chemist, or a metallurgist. Nope. He is all of those things and more.

In real life, we aren't so lucky. We have to specialize in something. I have a lot of friends who are chemical engineers, for example. I know a few astronomers. I only know a cursory amount about what they do, and for the most part, they don't know much about computers.

The catch is that computers are the universal machines and no matter what your field of endeavor, you probably have some ideas about how a computer could help you do it better. Maybe you want to control a chemical process, or move a telescope by remote control. Spock or the professor would have no trouble. But in real life, many people have to turn to specialized engineers to make these ideas a reality.

Of course, computers are ubiquitous, and many people from many different disciplines now understand the ideas behind writing a program and routinely write software that helps them do their job. Sometimes these programs will help many people in the same field do their job. But there seems to be a difference between writing some PC software in, say, Visual Basic, and designing a dedicated computer to move a telescope, right?

In the past, that has been true. Dedicated microcontrollers were the province of experts that understood digital hardware and programming. With the advent of Basic Stamps, however, all this is changing. The Basic Stamp is a special microcontroller that requires very little (if any) supporting hardware. As the name implies, you program it using a special dialect of Basic — a language that many people know and is considered easy to learn.

The Basic Stamp is opening up microcontroller design to a whole range of people who want to build *solutions*. Even electronic specialists who know how to use the more arcane microcontrollers find that Basic Stamps are easy, productive, and fun to use. In a few minutes you can develop something that would take days or even weeks using conventional techniques. Little jobs that would be too much trouble to solve with a common microcontroller are simple with Basic Stamps.

In fact, the Basic Stamp is so much fun that is has a fan club — sort of. There is a very active mailing list, maintained by Parallax (the company that makes the Stamp), where over 1,000 Stamp users ask questions and offer advice. The users of this list generate an unthinkable amount of mail each day with problems that range from the simple to the complex. (See Chapter 11 for more about this mailing list and other resources).

Another reason the Stamp is so popular is that it doesn't require much investment to get started. If you are a resourceful scrounger, you'll only need the Stamp itself (and a PC, of course). Even if you want to buy everything ready-made, you'll only wind up spending a few dollars more, depending on what choices you make.

Getting Started

So your first step is to select a Stamp and buy it. Using software on the CD-ROM, you can actually get your first taste of the Stamp without buying anything (sort of a virtual reality Stamp). Of course, that Stamp only runs on your PC. To control the real world, you will have to get a real Stamp.

You can order Stamps directly from Parallax, buy them from Radio Shack (they order them for you), or get them from most major electronic catalogs (see Chapter 11). The question is: what kind of Stamp should you get?

There are several when it comes to Stamps. Each one is a bit different, and you'll have to decide for yourself which best suits your needs. You'll find a summary of your choices in Table 1.1. You can also find the specifications for each in the datasheets on the CD-ROM. For the purposes of most of this book, the Stamp I and the Stamp D are the same, so I'll usually refer to the Stamp I, and you can assume the Stamp D is the same. The only difference is in the packaging.

By the same token, many of the Stamp variants have different packaging (for example, the OEM Stamp II or the BSIIP/40). From a software point of view, these parts are the same, so I will treat them as equivalent.

Table 1.1   Types of Stamps.

Name	Program size (bytes)	Data memory (bytes)	Speed (instructions /sec)	Notes
Stamp D	256	14	2,000	Same as Stamp I, except for package
Stamp I	256	14	2,000	
Stamp II	2,048	26	4,000	
Stamp IISX	16,384	26/63	10,000	Holds eight programs of 2,048 bytes each
Stamp IIE	16,384	26/63	4,000	Low-power version of Stamp IISX
Stamp IIP	16,384	26/63	12,000	28- and 40-pin version; each holds eight programs of 2,048 bytes

Don't be alarmed at the Stamps' apparently small sizes of memory. You'll find that it is often more than enough for the types of jobs you'll tackle with the Stamp. If you are used to dealing with PCs with dozens of megabytes and high-speed Pentium processors, you'll have a bit of culture shock. But for embedded microcontrollers, the Stamps have plenty of memory and speed.

Hardware

Once you have your Stamp, you'll need some way to program it. Here's the good news. The only thing you really need is a 9V battery and a cable. What kind of cable you need depends on the Stamp you select. The Stamp I and Stamp D connect to your PC's printer port, and therefore require a DB25 cable. For the Stamp D, the other end of the cable connects to some pins (like jumper pins) on the Stamp's PC board. You can buy the cable ready-made from Parallax, or build your own using the instructions in Appendix C. Because printer cables are cheap, you can easily buy one, cut the end off, and wire the correct end. The other Stamps require a connection to your serial port.

All of the Stamps except for the Stamp D and the OEM Stamps resemble integrated circuits (ICs). The Stamp I has a single row of pins (a Single Inline Pin or SIP package). The other Stamps utilize a DIP (Dual Inline Pin package). In either case, you'll find you need something to hold the Stamp while you work.

The simple approach is to get a piece of perfboard (often known as *Vector Board* or *Vero Board*) with holes on 0.1-inch centers. You can then use solder or wire wrapping techniques to make connections between your cable and the Stamp (as well as other circuit components).

While this approach is simple, it isn't ideal. Of course, you'd want to solder to a socket, not the Stamp directly, but the soldering makes it tedious to make changes and experiment.

If you prefer, you can buy a small PC (printed circuit) board (known as a *carrier*) from Parallax. These boards have a socket for the Stamp and a connector for the cable. The Stamp I carrier uses the same cable as the Stamp D. The carrier for the other Stamps use a standard 9-pin serial cable connector. These carriers offer a small area where you can solder or wire wrap your creations. They also provide for a 9V battery to connect to the Stamp. However, they also require major surgery if you want to build something different or even change your existing design. Also, the area for your circuits is small. You can find a picture of the carrier boards in Figure 1.1 and 1.2.

Figure 1.1 This carrier board holds the Stamp I for prototyping.

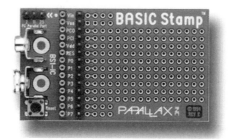

The best way, in my opinion, to work with Stamps is with a solderless breadboard. The breadboards themselves are available from a variety of vendors and are quite common. The breadboard provides holes that have spring contacts beneath them. You insert components (including the Stamp) into the holes and the springs grab the wire leads and grip them. The holes connect in certain patterns, so inserting wires in particular holes make connections between parts of your circuit.

The only problem with breadboards is that it is not very handy to connect cables to them. You can always make up something that will connect the cable to the breadboard, or you can get adapters especially designed for this purpose from AWC (see Chapter 11). If you want to roll your own, you might consider soldering wires to a socket, plugging the socket into the breadboard, and then plugging the Stamp into the socket.

Figure 1.2   The Stamp II carrier board.

Another advantage to breadboards is that they naturally decouple high-frequency noise. If you don't use a breadboard, you'll want to include small capacitors (0.01μF, for example) with short leads between the power and ground connections of your chips. The Stamp has a filter capacitor (22μF) built in, but when dealing with high-frequencies you may still need a small decoupling capacitor even on the Stamp. With a breadboard, the entire breadboard acts like a capacitor. The downside to this is that it makes it tough to prototype high frequency designs on a breadboard. However, with the Stamp, you won't be able to deal with frequencies that high anyway.

Another offering from Parallax is the Stamp Experiment Board. This board is like a super-carrier board that not only holds a Stamp, but also has a variety of switches, LEDs, and sockets for other parts onboard. This is the next best thing to a solderless breadboard as long as the circuits you want to build are already on the experiment board.

Parallax also offers the "Board of Education" which is a carrier board and a very small solderless breadboard. Unfortunately, the breadboard is very small, and it isn't connected to the Stamp at all. It is just mechanically attached to the board.

Regardless of your choice in prototyping boards, it all boils down to about the same thing. You need a way to connect a battery, a cable, and whatever parts you need to the Stamp. The battery, by the way, isn't critical. The Stamp can run off a 5V regulated voltage supply or you can feed in an unregulated voltage (like a battery) and the Stamp will regulate it. Except for the Stamp IISX, the regulator is beefy enough that you can power simple circuits that need 5V from the Stamp's regulator, if you like. The Stamp IISX, however, uses almost all the juice its regulator can provide. Because the Stamp has a built-in regulator, you can use nearly any power source — an AC adapter, a battery, or a lab supply. Just make sure the output is DC and doesn't exceed the maximum voltage the Stamp can take.

Figure 1.3 shows the breadboard I use most often. It is a large breadboard from Elenco that I picked up at a hamfest (a swap meet for ham radio operators) for $5. I permanently built a 5V regulator circuit and wired a socket for a Stamp II. The cable plugs in with an AWC ASP-2 adapter. You can build some very large projects on a board this big.

Figure 1.3   The AWC ASP-II cable adapter attaches to a standard breadboard.

Other Prototyping Needs

Of course, to make your Stamp do anything interesting, you'll need some external parts. To start with, you'd like a few LEDs, some momentary contact switches, and an assortment of resistors and capacitors. The Stamp can produce sounds, so you'll probably want a piezoelectric speaker or a 32Ω (32 ohm) dynamic speaker. Exactly what you want depends on what you want to build.

If you are using a solderless breadboard, Radio Shack sells some switches that will plug directly into the board. Look for part number 275-1571. While you are there, you might want to look at buying some 5V (5 volt) LEDs. These are LEDs that operate with 5V (the same voltage the Stamp uses). Most LEDs operate on lower voltages and require a resistor to prevent the LED from burning out at 5V. These LEDs simply have the resistor built-in. They are a bit more expensive than ordinary LEDs, but they are very handy.

Just as a starting point, here is the list of parts that AWC supplies with the ASP-A lab kit. You can find nearly all of these parts at Radio Shack (the part numbers are in parenthesis). The only parts that are odd are the 32Ω speaker and the 10K resistors. If you can't find a 32Ω speaker, use a piezoelectric speaker (or liberate one from a cheap radio). Don't use a common 8Ω speaker unless you solder a 22Ω resistor in series with one of the leads (which will make the speaker have a very low volume). In the ASP-A, the 10K resistors are in a single package that plugs directly into the breadboard. However, you can just as well use a handful of individual 10K resistors if you can't find them packaged.

- Four 5V LEDs (RS 276-208)
- Four switches that directly plug directly into the breadboard (RS 275-1571)
- Nine 10K resistors (RS 261-1335; see text)
- 10 22K resistors for various functions (RS 271-1339)
- One 32W Speaker (use a piezo speaker instead; RS 273-091)
- One 0.1mF capacitor (RS 272-1069)
- Two 10mF capacitors (RS 272-1025)
- One 10K pot that mounts on a breadboard (RS 271-282)
- One LM339 quad comparator (RS 276-1612)

Many of the projects in this book will use these parts. Of course, you can scrounge around if you have a well-stocked junk box. None of the values are especially critical. You can use ordinary LEDs if you include a dropping resistor (a topic covered later in this chapter).

If you are planning on using the Stamp IISX, you'll also want a source of 5V regulated power for the rest of your circuitry. This is easy to do with a 7805 or 78L05 voltage regulator (see Figure 1.4). You can also use a regulated bench supply. You may want to use this even with the other Stamps. Although most Stamps can supply 5V to your circuit, if you draw too much current you might blow the regulator and damage the Stamp. Since a 7805 costs about $1.50 at Radio Shack, and the least expensive Stamp is about $39, it is well worth a 7805 for a little protection. Besides, a 78L05 can supply up to 140 mA and the 7805 over 1 amp (with a heat sink).

TIP

No more batteries
You can run a Stamp for quite some time on a single 9V battery. However, it seems the battery will die just as you are about to finish a project. One simple solution is to buy a 9V battery eliminator (available nearly everywhere). This is a usually a small wall transformer that has a 9V battery connector on the end of the wire. This allows you the most flexibility since you can use a 9V battery when you want to be free of the wall outlet, or plug in when you don't want to use batteries.

Because the Stamp has its own regulator (or if you use the regulator in Figure 1.4), you'll have no problem with your 5V supply. However, don't assume that the battery eliminator's output will really be 9V. Usually, it will be higher and drop as you draw more current from it. Make sure and measure the output if you have any doubts and you are connecting a component to the supposed 9V power.

Some cheaper eliminators might have some hum (residual noise from the AC power line) that could affect your circuits. If you think this might be a problem, just put an electrolytic capacitor across the input (in addition to the .33uF unit in Figure 1.4). This won't affect your battery operation, but will filter out any hum.

Figure 1.4   A regulated 5V supply.

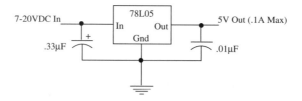

Another handy thing to have is a volt ohm meter (VOM). Digital VOMs (also called DVMs) are quite inexpensive now and you really need one for any electronic work. If you have access to an oscilloscope or other expensive test gear, good for you! However, you'll find that just a VOM will be all you really need for most Stamp projects.

The No-Hardware Approach

Of course, everyone likes to go shopping, but you also want to get started right away. Well, you can go shopping a little later if you like. On the CD in the back of this book is BS1EMU, an emulator that run on the PC and behaves like a Stamp I (see Figure 1.5). To install the program, run the SETUP program you'll find in the BS1EMU subdirectory of the CD.

Figure 1.5   Windows software simulation of the Basic Stamp.

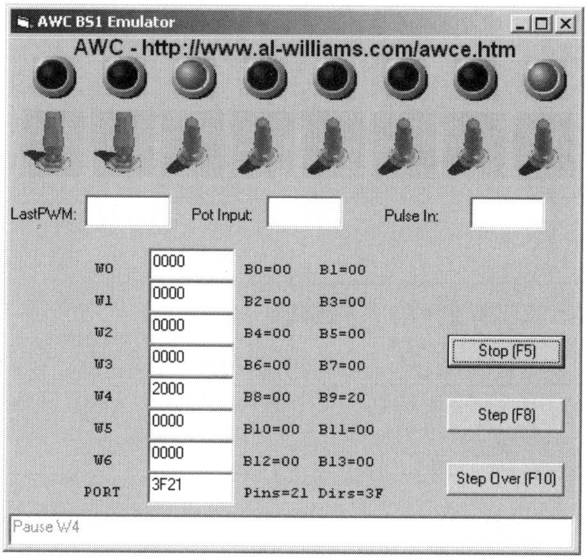

You'll find complete details on using BS1EMU in Appendix A. The simulator does not handle all the Stamp I instructions, but you can still perform many interesting experiments just using BS1EMU.

The Software

So you've either got your hardware together, or you've installed BS1EMU. The next step is to install the Parallax programming software. This software is free on the Web at www.parallaxinc.com, and you can find it on the CD in the back of the book. You'll find more details about the software in Appendix A.

If your PC is an older one, you may prefer to run the older DOS-based software. However, if you are running Windows, you'll prefer the newer Windows-based software. This book will usually assume you are using the Windows software.

You might wonder what the software actually does. The Parallax Stamp software translates your program into a special language that the Stamp understands, but would be very hard for humans to read and write. Then the software sends the program in this processed form to the Stamp. Doing it this way allows the more difficult processing to reside on the PC, while the Stamp is free to focus on the actual task.

Once the PC software downloads the program to the Stamp, you don't have to have the PC connected anymore. Because the Stamp's program memory stays programmed until you erase it, you only need to program a Stamp once. Then it works as it is supposed to until you program it again. That's true even if you turn the power off, or store the Stamp in the back of your closet for a month (or a year). I suppose that eventually the Stamp's memory will fail, but that would take many, many years.

The software checks your program for basic mistakes as it converts it into Stamp lingo. If you've made a mistake it can catch, it will tell you about it and refuse to program the Stamp until you fix the problem. Of course, the program can't catch logic errors — that's your job when you debug your program. The software also allows you to monitor the program as it executes, as you'll see shortly, which can greatly aid the debugging process.

Your First Stamp Program

Enough already! Let's try our first Stamp program. A program is nothing more than a list of instructions that tells the Stamp what to do. Our first program will use two instructions: DEBUG to write to the debug window and END, which stops the program. Run the Parallax software and enter this program:

```
DEBUG Hello Stamp Programmer!
END
```

If you are using the DOS software, press Alt+R to download the program to the Stamp. Windows users can use the Run menu selection. The power should be connected to the Stamp and the cable should also be connected. If you get an error, check your spelling and make sure everything looks like the sample. If the software reports it can't find the Stamp, make sure your cable is correct, the power to the Stamp is good, and that the cable is connected correctly at both ends. If you are using the DOS software and running Windows, try exiting to DOS or switch to the Windows software.

If you are using the BS1EMU program instead of a real Stamp, this program won't do you any good because the simulator doesn't work with the DEBUG command. Just keep reading for now.

If everything worked, a window should pop up and you should see the debugging message on the screen. If it doesn't work, you should stop and figure out why before going any further.

So, this is your first Stamp Program. Ho hum, right? Well, it isn't very exciting, but just getting the hardware connected and working is half the battle. If you yearn for something more interesting, try this:

```
W1=10*33+71
DEBUG The answer is, DEC W1
END
```

W1 is a variable — a place the Stamp stores a number. The DEC instructs the Stamp to show the W1 variable as a decimal number. You'll learn more about that later.

So this isn't going to replace your calculator, but it is a start. Of course, the real fun is connecting the Stamp to the real world. But before you can do that, you need to understand a bit about how the Stamp (and the outside world) work!

The Outside World

The Stamp talks to the outside world via its Input/Output (I/O) pins. These pins make up the majority of the Stamp's pins, in fact. The Stamp I (and Stamp D) have eight I/O pins. The other Stamps have 16. Each pin can be an input or an output and you can control them all.

TIP

Pin numbers

It is easy to get confused between software pin numbers and physical pin numbers on the Stamp. In software, you might talk about P0, the first I/O pin. However, this is not the first pin on the Stamp. On the Stamp I, for example, P0 is really pin 7. On the Stamp II, it is pin 5.

When a pin is an input, it looks like an open circuit for practical purposes. However, if the outside world connects the pin to ground, the stamp will read the pin as a zero. This is known as a *zero input* or a *logical low input*. If the outside world increases the voltage on the pin, (theoretically to 5V, but in reality to some threshold voltage below 5V) the Stamp perceives this as a high or a one. In theory, the external circuits only generate 0V and 5V (this is known as a *digital circuit* because the circuit is always in one of two states: 0V or 5V). You'll often hear these states known as low (0V) and high (5V).

When you make a pin an output, then the Stamp generates either 0V or 5V. If you send a zero to an output, it places 0V on that pin. If you send a one to an output pin, the Stamp will generate 5V at that pin. You can switch a pin from input to output at will in your program.

Besides I/O pins, the Stamps have one pin (PWR) that accepts an unregulated DC voltage, e.g., a 9V battery. If you connect a voltage here, the Stamp will generate 5V and make it available on another pin. However, you can also allow the PWR pin to float, and provide the Stamp a regulated 5V supply on the 5V pin. The Stamps all have a RES pin as well. If this pin is low, the Stamp resets. Normally, you'll tie this pin high, or leave it open. The Stamp I has a single ground pin, but the other Stamps have two (one for power ground and another for the programming cable ground — the pins are tied together internally).

The Stamp I has two pins for programming via the printer port or a PC, and the Stamp II has three pins that connect to a serial port. Aside from the reset pin, the power pins, and the programming pins, all other pins are dedicated to input and output.

Digital Basics

You can segregate the electronic business into two broad categories: analog and digital. Analog electronics has to do with signals that can change by any amount. For example, a radio's audio is an analog signal. Not only is it constantly changing, but it you can adjust its volume arbitrarily. Digital electronics only has two states: 1 and 0 (or on and off, if you prefer). There is nothing in between.

The classic examples of this are clocks. Clocks with hands are analog. If the clock is accurate enough, and your eyesight is keen enough, you can tell time to any fraction of a second you wish. The second hand sweeps from one second to the next, crossing all the subdivisions between the seconds. A digital clock, on the other hand, shows time as discrete steps. If the clock only shows seconds, then you can only gauge the time to the nearest second. There is no midpoint. The time flows from one second to the next with no intervening steps.

Modern computers are inherently digital. The Stamp operates its I/O pins in this manner. However, there are a few things you should know about digital systems before you can effectively use the Stamp.

Number Systems

Since early times, man has counted using base 10 (matching the number of fingers, most likely). The ancient Phoenicians used base 12, which is why we still deal in dozens, 12-hour clocks, and have special words for eleven and twelve (you don't say *oneteen* and *twoteen*). However, the Phoenician's system didn't really catch on, so we count by tens.

For computer use, decimal numbers (or base 10, if you prefer) are a bad idea. Computers don't have fingers. They do use digital electronics, which has two states: 1 and 0. This lends itself to the use of binary (or base 2) numbers.

In grade school you probably learned (and maybe forgot) that when you write the number 327, it really means:

$$3 \times 10^2 + 2 \times 10^1 + 7 \times 10^0$$

or:

$$3 \times 100 + 2 \times 10 + 7 \times 1$$

When you use binary notation, you use 2 as the base instead of 10. That means the digits must be either 0 or 1, just like digital logic! So in binary, if you write 1101 it really means:

$$1 \times 2^3 + 1 \times 2^2 + 0 \times 2^1 + 1 \times 2^0$$

or:

$$1 \times 8 + 1 \times 4 + 0 \times 2 + 1 \times 1$$

Solving all of that, you wind up with 13. With a little experience you realize that as you move to the left, each digit is worth twice as much as the one before it (or conversely, that moving to the right, each digit is worth half as much as the one ahead of it). This makes the math simple to do. Looking at 1101 again, you start at the left (the 1 position) and write down 1. Moving to the left, you know the position is worth 2 (1 doubled), but the digit is 0, so you won't write anything down. Moving again to the 4 position, there is a 1 so you write down 4 and then moving again, write down 8. You've written down 8, 4, and 1. Add them together and you do get the correct answer of 13.

Going the other way is a little more complicated. If you started with 13, you'd first want to know how many binary digits (or bits) the binary number will need for the answer. Starting at the right, you realize that the only numbers you can represent with one bit are 0 and 1. The next bits to the left are worth 2, 4, 8, and 16. Because 16 is larger than 13, you won't be using that digit or any of the ones further left. In most computers, numbers have a fixed size (for example, 8 or 16 bits) so you'll just fill the unused digits in with zeros. Moving back to the right, you can place a 1 in the bit that has the value of 8. Then subtract 8 from the original number (13) which leaves 5. The next bit has a value of 4. Because 5 is greater than 4, you'll write a 1 here also and subtract 4 from 5, leaving 1. The next bit is worth 2, but 2 is greater than 1, so write a zero in this position. Finally, the last bit gets a 1 and subtracting 1 from 1 leaves zero, so you are done.

If you aren't familiar with this process, try a few numbers and see if you get the right answer. For example, 100 decimal is 01100100 binary and 19 is 00010011. You can try your own numbers. Convert from binary to decimal and back again (or vice versa) and you should get the same number you started with. Of course, many modern calculators will do these conversions for you, but you should understand the process anyway.

It is common to call binary digits a *bit* (literally an acronym for Binary digIT, although people don't usually treat it as a real acronym). Groups of eight bits are known as a *byte*. A 4-bit number is often called a *nybble* or a *nibble*. Many people refer to a 16-bit group as a *word*, and this convention is often used when working with Stamps. However, on some other processors, it is common to refer to a word as some other length (typically the natural length of the computer's numbers). By convention, the Stamp considers a number with a % prefix as binary. So %1111 is a binary number (15 decimal).

Other Bases

Just as decimal is not good for computers, binary is not very handy for human beings. The problem is that there is no handy way to instantly convert decimal to binary and vice versa. Often programmers use another number bases to make life easier for them. Any number base that is a power of 2 will work out nicely, but most programmers today use hexadecimal (base 16).

With hexadecimal, you'll use the normal digits 0–9, but you'll also use six new digits: A, B, C, D, E, and F. These stand for digits that have decimal values of 10 through 15. So the hexadecimal number 6F is really:

$$6 \times 16^1 + F \times 16^0$$

or:

$$6 \times 16^1 + 15 \times 16^0$$

or:

$$96 + 15 = 111 \text{ (decimal)}$$

Converting between hexadecimal (usually just called *hex*) and decimal is still troublesome. You use the same approach you use for binary, but you use base 16 instead of base 2. However, the advantage is when you wish to go between hex and binary (or the other way around). Stamps assume any number with a $ prefix (like $A1 or $FF) is a hex number.

Because hex uses a power of 2 as a base, you can easily convert between hex and binary by simple inspection. The trick is to realize that each hex digit will correspond to four bits in a binary number. So 6F hex will require no more than eight bits to represent (two groups of four bits). What's more, each 4-bit group will correspond to the hex number as you'll see in Table 1.2. This makes it quite simple to convert from hex to binary and back again. Humans usually prefer hex notation because it is much more compact than binary.

Table 1.2   Hex digits to binary.

Hex	Binary	Decimal
$0	%0000	0
$1	%0001	1
$2	%0010	2
$3	%0011	3
$4	%0100	4
$5	%0101	5
$6	%0110	6
$7	%0111	7
$8	%1000	8
$9	%1001	9
$A	%1010	10
$B	%1011	11
$C	%1100	12
$D	%1101	13
$E	%1110	14
$F	%1111	15

Boolean Algebra

When dealing with digital logic circuits, you'll often hear references to *Boolean operators* (named for the mathematician George Boole). The normal set of operators you will find are NOT, AND, OR, and XOR. These operations form the basis of digital logic.

The simplest operator is NOT. It takes one bit and inverts it. If the bit is 1, the result is 0. If the original bit is 0, the result is 1. You can apply NOT to binary numbers, in which case the NOT operator flips each bit in the word independent of all other bits. I'll use the ~ notation for the NOT operator in this way:

~ %1011 = %0100

The OR operator (denoted by the | symbol) examines two bits. If either bit is a 1, then the result is also 1. The result is also a 1 if both input bits are in the 1 state. Again, you can apply this simply to a string of bits, so:

%1001 | %0101 = %1101

The XOR (exclusive OR, denoted by the ^ symbol) operation is the same as the OR operator, with one difference. If both input bits are 1, then the output is 0. You can think of XOR as a function that makes the output 0 if both bits are equal. For example:

%1001 ^ %0101 = %1100

An interesting property of XOR is that in applying XOR to a number and a string of 1 bits, the inversion of that number (just like the NOT operator) results.

The final operator, AND (&) is probably what you'd expect. The AND operator only provides a 1 result if both input bits are 1. Therefore:

%1001 & %0101 = %0001

Why are these operators important? They form the basic way that computers manipulate binary numbers. We use these numbers in calculations, but we also use them to represent real-world events, control the outside world, or even to stand in for letters of the alphabet.

Of course, you'll also find that the Stamp has the more familiar operators +, -, *, and / along with a few others you might not usually use. You'll find more about all of the Stamp's operators in Chapter 2.

Connecting Hardware

Working with microcontrollers involves both a program (the software) and hardware. There are only a few components you'll use for most Stamp projects. You can find more about these components in the following note "Electronic components," page 17. When we talk about hardware, we usually draw a schematic diagram of the circuit in question. These are symbolic representations of a circuit and they use special standard symbols (see Figure 1.6).

Don't confuse the physical layout of your circuit with the schematic diagram. It is unusual to place your components exactly where they appear on the schematic. The important part is the connections between the parts.

Figure 1.6   Standard schematic symbols.

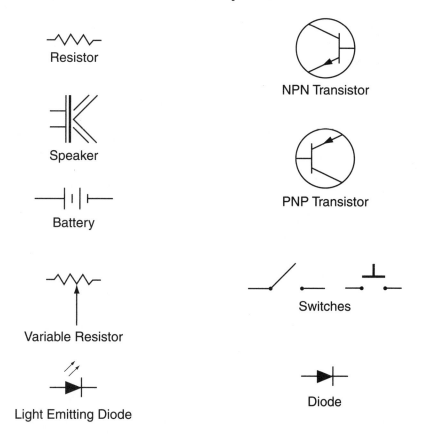

Resistor

Speaker

Battery

Variable Resistor

Light Emitting Diode

NPN Transistor

PNP Transistor

Switches

Diode

Electronic components

There are many different kinds of electronic components available. However, for most microcontroller projects, you'll only use a handful of these. Of course, the Stamp itself is a form of integrated circuit (IC). If you aren't familiar with these components, here's a brief rundown of the basic elements. This is just a quick review — any basic electronics book will have more information.

- **Resistors** — A resistor is a circuit element that impedes current flow. In this chapter, you'll see resistors used to regulate the current through an LED (light-emitting diode) and to function as a pull-up resistor that allows you to set a default state for a microcontroller input. You measure resistance in ohms represented by the Greek letter Ω. The higher the resistance, the more the resistor blocks current.

- **Capacitors** — Capacitors are complex devices that store electrical charge. This allows them to perform many important functions. For example, they block direct current (DC; like that from a battery) and work like resistors for alternating current (AC; like voltage from your wall outlet). For Stamp circuits, capacitors are mainly used to filter rough pulses into smoother voltages.

- **Diodes** — Diodes are semiconductor devices that only conduct current in one direction. Diodes have two terminals, an anode and a cathode. If the anode has a higher voltage then the cathode, the diode acts (more or less) like a short-circuit. That is, current flows through the diode without interference. If the voltage measured across the diode is less than some value (which depends on the type of diode), the diode stops conducting and appears, practically, like an open circuit. A typical diode's voltage threshold (known as the junction voltage) is about 0.7V. However, light-emitting diodes typically have higher voltages (perhaps 1.2V). Diodes can convert AC current into voltage pulses that a capacitor can filter into DC current. Diodes can also act as an electrical switch in certain cases. This book mainly uses light-emitting diodes as indicator lamps.

- **Transistors** — Transistors are complex semiconductor devices that have three terminals: a base, a collector, and an emitter. There are many, many ways to use transistors. However, in this book, transistors will work as switches. By altering the voltage on the base, you can make the emitter and collector appear to be an open-circuit or a short-circuit (for practical purposes). You'll read more about transistors in Chapter 3. Although transistors can work as switches, there are some restrictions. For example, transistors don't do a good job switching AC current. Also, some high-power applications may require expensive, large transistors.

- **Relays** — For cases where transistors won't work or they are not convenient, you can use a relay. A relay is just a coil of wire that forms an electromagnet. When current flows through the coil, it generates a magnetic field. This magnetic field manipulates a switch. This allows you to have a switch that you can turn on or off by changing the voltage on the coil. However, coils have electrical properties of their own (inductance) that require some special techniques if you don't want to blow up other parts of your circuit as you'll see in Chapter 3.

There are other components you'll use in this book. Some you'll be familiar with already (like batteries, speakers, and switches). Others, you'll read about when you get ready to use them.

Digital Systems in an Analog World: A Few Laws

The Stamp, like most microprocessors, is a digital device. However, the real world is a decidedly analog place. The Stamp communicates via eight or 16 pins that you can connect to things. These pins are digital — they take on values of 0V for a 0 or 5V for a 1. If you are connecting to another digital device, that's probably all you really need. But most of the time, you'll be connecting to something else.

For example, suppose you want to make an LED turn on. This should be simple. But, be careful; an LED is not really a digital device in the strictest sense of that word. If you haven't used an LED before, it behaves like a diode, but it lights up when current flows through it. Current flows through the diode when the anode is more positive than the cathode by a certain amount. You can see a schematic diagram of a diode and a battery in Figure 1.7. The triangular-looking device marked D1 is the LED. B1 is the battery and S1 is a switch. When you close S1, the LED will light. However, if you reversed the + and − leads of the battery, the LED would not light up.

Figure 1.7   An impractical LED circuit.

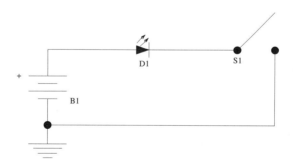

The only problem with the circuit in Figure 1.7 is that won't really work. When you press the switch, current flows from the battery and through the LED. However there is nothing to limit the current flow, so either the battery will drain, or (more likely) the LED will burn out! You basically are short-circuiting the battery with this circuit.

A practical circuit appears in Figure 1.8. This circuit uses a resistor (R1) to limit the current flowing from the "battery." In this case, the battery is really an output pin on the Stamp. You can breadboard this circuit with any kind of Stamp you are using. You can also simulate the circuit using the emulator software because it is set up with LEDs on all outputs anyway.

Figure 1.8   Driving an LED with a Stamp.

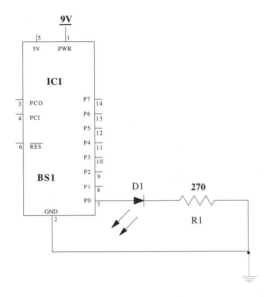

If you build the circuit, run the following software to make it work:

```
top:
    TOGGLE 0
    PAUSE 500
    GOTO top
```

This simple Stamp program is easy to understand. The first line ends with a colon. This indicates that it is a *label*. A label is simply someplace we want to leave a book-mark in our program for later use. We can use nearly any word that isn't already reserved for some other purpose for the label. I might have picked BEGIN or LINE0 or GETGOING. It is a good idea to pick something descriptive, of course. This program only has one label, but many programs will have lots of labels.

The second line, TOGGLE, causes pin 0 to become an output (if it isn't already) and flips the current state of the pin. So if the pin was generating a 0, it will now generate a 1. When the Stamp starts, all pins are inputs and if you switch them to outputs, the output will be 0 until you tell it otherwise. The only reason this command is working with pin 0 is because of the 0 I put after the keyword TOGGLE. You could toggle any pin in this manner.

The third line tells the Stamp to take a break for 500 milliseconds (half a second). The next line tells the program to go back to the label top (our bookmark on the first line) and start again. If you think about it for a minute, you'll see that pin 0 will swing from 0V to 5V and then back to 0V again, pausing a half second between each transition.

Because the LED is connected to ground, it lights when the pin has 5V on it. When the pin has 0V on it, the LED has no voltage across it, and therefore goes dark. Of course, you could as easily reverse the LED and connect the free end to 5V. Then the Stamp would bring the pin to a 0 state (often known as the *low state*) to light the LED. Bringing the pin high (that is, to a 1 state) would extinguish the LED.

The resistor's purpose is to prevent the LED from simply shorting the pin to ground. As such, it really doesn't matter if you connect the resistor between the Stamp and the LED, or the LED and ground. Either way, it serves its purpose.

5V LEDs

As a convenience, you can get LEDs that have an integral resistor built into them (I mentioned these earlier). Then you can connect the LED directly between the Stamp and the power supply, but only because the resistor is built-in. These LEDs may be a bit more expensive, but they are very handy, especially when working with a solderless breadboard.

Often people use a small resistor with an LED that they know from experience will work. However, it isn't hard to calculate the right value if you understand Ohm's law. Ohm's law is the fundamental calculation that will help you understand most electronic circuits, so you ought to know it anyway.

When two or more components are in series (that is, connected end to end), that means that power flows through one component to the next component, and so on. This is the same arrangement our LED circuit uses. Current flows from the battery's + terminal (the Stamp, in this case) to the resistor, to the LED, and then to ground (the – terminal). If you study physics, you know that current really flows the opposite direction (that is, – to +). However, it is customary to think of it as + to –, and for practical circuits, it doesn't matter. In a series circuit, the current through each component is the same. However, each component may have a different amount of voltage across it.

If the battery supplies a particular voltage (5V, in this case), then the circuit elements (the LED and the resistor) must be consuming (or, more commonly, dropping)

5V. This is one of Kirchoff's laws. We don't know exactly how much voltage is across each element, but we know that if we add the voltages, they will equal 5V. The other thing that we know about a series circuit is that the current through each element is the same.

LEDs require enough voltage to light and sufficient current as well. A typical red LED needs, perhaps 15mA (0.015 amperes) at 1.2V. You can find the exact specifications from the manufacturer's data sheets or the catalog or store where you bought them. The specifications you need are the V_f (forward voltage) and the I_f (current).

To light the LED, you want V_f across the LED when the current is equal to the I_f. Because there are only two components in series, the supply voltage minus the voltage across the LED must equal the voltage across the resistor. So the voltage we want across the resistor is $5 - 1.2 = 3.8$. Because the current is the same through each element of the circuit, we know the resistor's current will be the same as the LED's (15mA).

This is where Ohm's law comes into play. Ohm's law states that the voltage in a linear circuit (like a resistor) will be equal to the current times the resistance. In other words:

$$E = I \times R$$

In the equation above, E is voltage (E stands for electromotive force — an uncommon word for voltage), I is current, and R is resistance. Simple algebra will allow you rearrange the equation to solve for any variable. If your algebra is rusty, you might like the diagram in Figure 1.9. To solve for a variable, put your finger over it. What's left is the formula you need. For example, if you put your finger over the I, you'll see the formula for I is E/R. Notice that this equation does not hold true for non-linear devices (like diodes, light-emitting, or otherwise).

Using Ohm's law, we can find the value of the resistor by dividing the voltage across the resistor by the current through the resistor.

$$3.8 / 0.015 = 253.3\Omega$$

Of course, you can't get a 253Ω resistor, so you'll pick the closest value (270Ω). This will decrease the current a bit, but not enough that anyone will notice. Besides, the resistors are usually no better than 5% tolerance, so the actual value could be anywhere from 256Ω to 284Ω.

Ohm's law will come into play quite often in a variety of situations. You can use it to analyze everything from voltage dividers and wheatstone bridges, to op amp feedback networks. However, for our explorations into microcontrollers, this is all the Ohm's law you'll probably need.

Figure 1.9 The Ohm's law triangle.

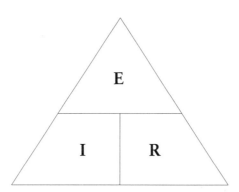

Pull-up and Pull-down Resistors

Speaking of resistors, another common use for resistors is as pull-up or pull-down resistors. These resistors are useful when you want to guarantee a default state for an input pin.

Consider the circuit in Figure 1.10 (page 24). The switch, when pressed, connects the Stamp's pin to ground. What happens when the switch is not pressed? The Stamp sees a 1 because the resistor pulls the input line to 5V. If the resistor was absent, the Stamp would see random noise on the input, which might be a 1 or might be a 0 — you'd never know for sure. The resistor to the 5V supply is a pull-up resistor. You can also put a resistor to ground to ensure a solid 0 input. This is a pull-down resistor.

Selecting the value of a pull-up (or pull-down) resistor isn't very hard. You have to make sure there is enough current for the Stamp's input to register (which isn't very much at all), but not so much current that the device that will drive the line (the switch, in this case) can't pull the pin to the opposite state.

Of course the switch — because it just shorts the pin to ground — could handle any pull-up resistor, no matter how small. However, be sure your power supply can handle it (or your battery). A 10Ω pull-up for example, would have a half-amp (500mA) running through it when the switch pulls the pin down! Not only would this drain your battery (or blow the regulator on your Stamp), the resistor would need to dissipate 2.5 watts of power (power is E^2R) — way too much for this simple job. In practice, you'll probably settle on a 10K, 22K, or 47K resistor for a pull-up. As long as the device driving the line can sink enough current, you'll be fine.

Figure 1.10 Adding a switch and a pull-up resistor.

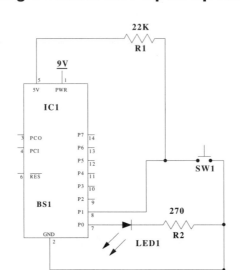

About the listings in this book

Most of the small code examples in this book will work with little or no changes on any Stamp. However, because of this, they are not always presented in the way you'd probably write them for a single type of Stamp.

For example, suppose I want to light an LED that is connected to pin 0 and ground through a resistor. The generic code will look like this:

```
HIGH 0
```

However, this isn't a very good practice because it hard codes the number 0 in the program. If you make 10 references to this pin in the program and then decide to change the pin, you'll have a lot of work to fix the program. Also, the number 0 doesn't really describe the function of the pin. For the Stamp I, you'd be more likely to write:

```
SYMBOL workingLED = 0
HIGH workingLED
```

On the Stamp II, however, you can't use SYMBOL, so you'd write:

```
workingLED con 0
HIGH workingLED
```

The same problem arises with variable names. Many of the short programs in this book use variable names directly (for example, W0 or B2) because these are the same regardless of the type of Stamp. However, for the same reasons mentioned for I/O pins, you'd be better off supplying variables with symbolic names. On the Stamp I:

```
SYMBOL loopctr = W1
```

Or on the Stamp II:

```
loopctr VAR WORD
```

You'll learn more about SYMBOL and VAR in Chapter 2.

The most recent versions of the Basic Stamp editor requires you to have a special comment (a directive) at the start of each file to indicate which Stamp you are using. Since many of the programs in this book are not dependent on the type of Stamp, I've omitted these comments. You'll need to add the appropriate comment by hand, or use the Directive command in the Stamp editor. For example, to select the Basic Stamp II, you'd put this comment at the start of a listing:

```
'{$STAMP BS2}
```

Putting it All Together: Your Next Program

The schematic with the switch (Figure 1.10) also incorporates the same LED circuit from the previous example. Here's a program to try:

```
top:
    IF in1=1 THEN top
    TOGGLE 0
    PAUSE 500
    GOTO top
```

This is similar to the previous program, except that the LED only toggles when you press the button for a moment. If you hold the button for more than half a second, the LED will blink. The line that begins with IF tests the line connected to the switch. If the state is 1 (indicating the button is not pressed), the program doesn't do anything. When you press the button, the program executes as before.

You might wonder why PAUSE is still necessary. Switches are mechanical devices, so when you press them they will actually connect and disconnect several times before making a solid connection. This is known as *bounce*. Of course, if you are using the simulator, you won't see bounce because the simulator has perfect electronic switches.

There are better ways to combat bounce, but for now, the program just waits for a half a second. Any switch that is bouncing for that long is a poor switch indeed. Take out the PAUSE statement, if you like, and see what happens.

As an exercise, consider this: could you wire the switch to the 5V line and use a pull-down resistor? If so, what would you change in the program?

Summary

This chapter covered a lot of ground if you are new to electronics. You've learned what kind of Stamps are available and the ways you can prototype circuits with them. In addition, you saw several small programs and learned about labels, IF, GOTO, DEBUG, TOGGLE, and PAUSE.

This book will concentrate on the Stamp's hardware and go into much greater detail about writing software for the Stamp. If you followed the schematics and the electronics theory in this chapter, you'll have little trouble with most of the projects in this book. However, if you find you need more work on electronics theory, check out Chapter 11 for some places to look for more information.

Exercises

1. Convert the following numbers to decimal:
   %10110001
   %11110000
   $F1
   $AA

2. Convert the following numbers to hex:
   %11111010
   %00011001
   100
   64

3. Convert the following numbers to binary:
   133
   99
   $FA
   55

4. Normal LEDs require a dropping resistor when using a 5V supply to operate them. Why?

5. Suppose you want to light two LEDs in series using the same output pin of a microprocessor (5V or 0V). Each LED drops 1.2V, and you want to use 20mA through the LEDs. Assuming you want to use only one resistor, find a value for the resistor.

6. Contrast the operation of a pull-up resistor and a pull-down resistor.

For answers to the exercises, see the Answer Key, page 425.

Chapter 2

The Nitty Gritty —
A Stamp Reference

The famous comedian Steve Martin used to do a bit about being a millionaire and never paying taxes. He would talk like a late-night TV ad announcer and tell people that they could become millionaires and never pay taxes. When asked how, he'd reply, "First, get a million dollars. Then..."

Well, his exact plan for not paying taxes was to tell the IRS that you simply forgot about it. But that's not really what struck me as funny. The funny part, to me, was the idea that to become a millionaire, you simply get a million dollars. Of course! As the old saying goes, "the devil is in the details."

So, how do you learn to build Stamp projects? First, learn all about the Stamp. Then... there's those pesky details again. That's the purpose of this chapter. First, it will acquaint you with the basic software commands and language details you'll need to work with the Stamp. Second, it will serve as a reference as you build your own programs.

I should mention that the Parallax manuals are available on the Web (at www.parallaxinc.com) and on the accompanying CD in Adobe Acrobat format. However, I've always found these manuals somewhat less than satisfying. First, many people don't have them in printed form. I'm a big fan of the computer, but I do a lot of reading, umm... well... let's just say, not in front of the computer. Also, the manuals treat each Stamp separately and the commands in alphabetical order. That's great for looking them up if you know their names, but not so great if you are looking for information on how to do something.

In this chapter, I'll show you the Stamp commands (often known as PBASIC or Parallax Basic) grouped logically. If you need to look them up alphabetically, you can refer to Table 2.1. I'll also show you how each Stamp does the same chore, all in one place. First, you'll need to find out about each Stamp's memory resources and expression handling, because this differs between the Stamp families. If you've ever programmed in Basic, you'll find the commands familiar. However, there are important differences due to the Stamp's limitations and special features that you'll need to master.

The Stamp D and the Stamp I are identical from a software standpoint. The Stamp II and the Stamp IISX are almost identical. However, the Stamp IISX has a few more commands. The Stamp IIE is exactly the same as the Stamp IISX (software-wise, at least). The Stamp IIP has even more new commands. Also, because newer stamps tend to be faster, some of the commands that depend on timing operate a bit differently than on an ordinary Stamp II. You'll find all of these details in this chapter.

Table 2.1 Stamp commands in alphabetical order.

Command	Stamp	Category	Description	See:
&, |, ^	I, II, IISX, IIE, IIP	Logic	AND, OR, and XOR	page 161
&/, |/, ^/	I	Logic	Inverted logic	page 162
**	I, II, IISX, IIE, IIP	Math	High multiply	page 151
*/	II, IISX, IIE, IIP	Math	Fraction multiply	page 152
//	I, II, IISX, IIE, IIP	Math	Remainder (modulus)	page 153
+,-,*,/	I, II, IISX, IIE, IIP	Math	Standard math operators	page 150
>>, <<	II, IISX, IIE, IIP	Math	Shift left or right	page 154
ABS	II, IISX, IIE, IIP	Math	Compute absolute value	page 156
AUXIO	IIP	Specialized I/O	Switch to auxilliary I/O	page 136
BRANCH	I, II, IISX, IIE, IIP	Flow Control	Computed GOTO	page 84
BSAVE	I	Data	Save object code to file	page 64
BUTTON	I, II, IISX, IIE, IIP	Digital I/O	Read a button	page 106
CON	II, IISX, IIE, IIP	Data	Define constant	page 60
COS	II, IISX, IIE, IIP	Math	Compute cosine	page 158

Table 2.1　Stamp commands in alphabetical order. (Continued)

Command	Stamp	Category	Description	See:
COUNT	II, IISX, IIE, IIP	Digital I/O	Count pulses	page 105
DATA	II, IISX, IIE, IIP	Data	Define EEPROM data	page 65
DCD	II, IISX, IIE, IIP	Logic	Set a specified bit	page 164
DEBUG	I, II, IISX, IIE, IIP	Data	Debugging output	page 56
DIG	II, IISX, IIE, IIP	Math	Select decimal digit	page 159
DTMFOUT	II, IISX, IIE, IIP	Analog I/O	Make touch tones	page 119
EEPROM	I	Data	Define EEPROM data	page 63
END	I, II, IISX, IIE, IIP	Flow Control	End program	page 76
FOR	I, II, IISX, IIE, IIP	Flow Control	Loop	page 91
FREQOUT	II, IISX, IIE, IIP	Analog I/O	Make tones	page 117
GET	IISX, IIE, IIP	Data	Read from scratch pad	page 72
GOSUB	I, II, IISX, IIE, IIP	Flow Control	Subroutine call	page 86
GOTO	I, II, IISX, IIE, IIP	Flow Control	Transfer control	page 80
HIGH	I, II, IISX, IIE, IIP	Digital I/O	Set pin to logical 1	page 98
I2CIN	IIP	Specialized I/O	Input from I2C device	page 137
I2COUT	IIP	Specialized I/O	Output to I2C device	page 137
IF	I, II, IISX, IIE, IIP	Flow Control	Conditional test	page 81
INPUT	I, II, IISX, IIE, IIP	Digital I/O	Make pin an input	page 96
IOTERM	IIP	Specialized I/O	Switch to main or auxilliary I/O	page 138
LCDCMD	IIP	Specialized I/O	Send commands to a parallel LCD	page 139
LCDIN	IIP	Specialized I/O	Read from a parallel LCD device	page 139
LCDOUT	IIP	Specialized I/O	Write to a parallel LCD	page 139
LET	I	Data	Assignment (optional)	page 62
LOOKDOWN	I, II, IISX, IIE, IIP	Tables	Find a value in a table	page 134

Table 2.1   Stamp commands in alphabetical order. (Continued)

Command	Stamp	Category	Description	See:
LOOKUP	I, II, IISX, IIE, IIP	Tables	Index into a table	page 133
LOW	I, II, IISX, IIE, IIP	Digital I/O	Set pin to logical 0	page 99
MAINIO	IIP	Specialized I/O	Switch to main I/O	page 136
MAX	I, II, IISX, IIE, IIP	Math	Select maximum value	page 155
MIN	I, II, IISX, IIE, IIP	Math	Select minimum value	page 155
NAP	I, II, IISX, IIE, IIP	Flow Control	Low-power pause	page 78
NCD	II, IISX, IIE, IIP	Logic	Select set bit	page 165
NEXT	I, II, IISX, IIE, IIP	Flow Control	End of loop	page 93
OUTPUT	I, II, IISX, IIE, IIP	Digital I/O	Make pin an output	page 97
OWIN	IIP	Specialized I/O	Read from a 1-Wire device	page 141
OWOUT	IIP	Specialized I/O	Write to a 1-Wire device	page 141
PAUSE	I, II, IISX, IIE, IIP	Flow Control	Pause	page 77
POLLIN	IIP	Event Handling	Specify pins to watch for events	page 143
POLLMODE	IIP	Event Handling	Sets mode for event polling	page 144
POLLOUT	IIP	Event Handling	Specify output pins that react to polled events	page 145
POLLRUN	IIP	Event Handling	Specifies a program to run when event occurs	page 146
POLLWAIT	IIP	Event Handling	Wait for event to occur	page 147
POT	I	Analog I/O	Read a potentiometer	page 113
PULSIN	I, II, IISX, IIE, IIP	Digital I/O	Input a pulse	page 103
PULSOUT	I, II, IISX, IIE, IIP	Digital I/O	Output a pulse	page 102
PUT	IISX, IIE, IIP	Data	Write to scratch pad	page 70
PWM	I, II, IISX, IIE, IIP	Analog I/O	Pulse-width modulation	page 111
RANDOM	I, II, IISX, IIE, IIP	Data	Get random number	page 73

Table 2.1 Stamp commands in alphabetical order. (Continued)

Command	Stamp	Category	Description	See:
RCTIME	II, IISX, IIE, IIP	Analog I/O	Measure resistance	page 114
READ	I, II, IISX, IIE, IIP	Data	Read EEPROM data	page 67
RETURN	I, II, IISX, IIE, IIP	Flow Control	Return from subroutine	page 90
REV	II, IISX, IIE, IIP	Logic	Reverse bits	page 163
REVERSE	I, II, IISX, IIE, IIP	Digital I/O	Switch pin direction	page 101
RUN	IISX, IIE, IIP	Flow Control	Run new program	page 94
SERIN	I, II, IISX, IIE, IIP	Serial I/O	RS232 input	page 121
SEROUT	I, II, IISX, IIE, IIP	Serial I/O	RS232 output	page 128
SHIFTIN	II, IISX, IIE, IIP	Serial I/O	Synchronous input	page 130
SHIFTOUT	II, IISX, IIE, IIP	Serial I/O	Synchronous output	page 131
SIN	II, IISX, IIE, IIP	Math	Compute sine	page 158
SLEEP	I, II, IISX, IIE, IIP	Flow Control	Low-power pause	page 79
SOUND	I	Analog I/O	Make a tone	page 116
SQR	II, IISX, IIE, IIP	Math	Square root	page 157
SYMBOL	I	Data	Define symbol	page 59
TOGGLE	I, II, IISX, IIE, IIP	Digital I/O	Invert pin	page 100
VAR	II, IISX, IIE, IIP	Data	Define variable	page 61
WRITE	I, II, IISX, IIE, IIP	Data	Write EEPROM data	page 68
XOUT	II, IISX, IIE, IIP	Digital I/O	Issue X10 commands	page 108

General Program Formatting and Labels

Regardless of which Stamp you use, there are a few conventions that are the same. First, programs are not case sensitive. These three lines are the same:

```
RANDOM W1
random w1
RaNdOm W1
```

Of course, the third line is a bad idea because it is hard to read and looks like a ransom note.

You can place labels in your programs to identify a particular spot that you'll want to refer to later. For example, you can use the GOTO command to cause execution to continue at a label. Here's a program that prints increasing numbers on the debug terminal:

```
top:
    W1=W1+1
    DEBUG ?W1
    GOTO top
```

The label is just a word followed by a colon. When you refer to the label (like in the GOTO statement) you don't use a colon. You can't create a label that is otherwise in use. For example, you can't have a label named GOTO.

One other formatting nuance is the inclusion of comments in your code. A comment is just an apostrophe followed by any text you want to describe your code. The comment continues to the end of the line. So here's the counting program with some comments:

```
' Small counting program sample
' By Al Williams
top:
W1=W1+1  ' current count
' print number
DEBUG ?W1
GOTO top    ' do it again
```

Comments are usually not essential, but they do make it easier for others to read and understand your code. It also helps you when you haven't looked at a piece of code for a long time and you need to understand it. Better to have too many comments than too few.

There is one place where you should use a comment if you are using the Windows Stamp editor: at the beginning of your program. The editor can read the Stamp type from a special comment on the first line of your program and will adjust its operation accordingly. Without this comment, you'll have to remember to force the editor to use the proper type of Stamp.

For example, if you are using a Stamp II, you could write:

```
'{ $STAMP BS2}'
```

You can also use BS2e, BS2sx, or BS2p as the Stamp type. In this book, I rarely include this comment since many of the programs will work on different Stamps and I don't know which one you are using. However, if you write a program for one type of Stamp, this directive can save you a lot of problems.

Another use of the $STAMP directive is to set up a single download to load multiple program slots. Of course, only the BSIIE, SX, and P have multiple slots. Suppose you have five files, one each for the first five program slots on a BSIIP. You name the first file `PROG1.BAS` and the last file `PROG5.BAS`. Obviously, the second file is `PROG2.BAS` and so on. You could start `PROG1.BAS` with this comment:

```
'{$STAMP BS2p, PROG2.BAS, PROG3.BAS, PROG4.BAS,PROG5.BAS}
```

When you download PROG1.BAS, it will automatically load the other programs in the appropriate slots. The file names do not have to have the same base name, nor do they have to contain a number. The editor decides which slot to use by the file's position in the list. So you could as well write:

```
'{$STAMP BS2p,dog.bas, cat.bas, rabbit.bas, tools.bas}
```

Many programs require you to use constant numbers. When you write a normal number in your Stamp program, it is a decimal number. However, you can precede hex numbers with a dollar sign ($) and binary numbers with a per cent sign (%). You can enclose ASCII characters in double quotes ("). *ASCII* is a standard way to encode letters as numbers. So you might write:

```
B1=100
B2=$64     ' 64 hex is 100 decimal
B3=%01100100' binary 100
B4="A"     ' ASCII A (64 decimal)
```

As you'll see shortly, you can name a constant with the Stamp I `SYMBOL` command, or use `CON` with the other Stamps.

The Stamp I Memory Map and I/O

The Stamp I (and, of course, the Stamp D) has a small amount of read-write memory (known as *Random Access Memory*, or *RAM*) that you can use in your programs. Sometimes, memory locations are known as *registers*, although they don't really resemble the registers you find in assembly language programming. There are 14 bytes of memory you can use to store variables that your program needs to manipulate.

Stamp I Memory Access

These 14 bytes are accessible as individual bytes or as seven 16-bit words. Also, you can manipulate one of the 16-bit words as a set of bits. You may think that 14 bytes is not much memory, but you'll be surprised what you can do with them. Remember, your program resides in EEPROM memory, not RAM, so your program doesn't use up this space. It is possible to store data in EEPROM, but it is slower, and the EEPROM eventually will wear out (see the section "READ I, II, IISX, IIE, IIP" on page 67 and "WRITE I, II, IISX, IIE, IIP" on page 68 commands for more about this).

Of course, the Stamp's variables can only hold integer numbers, i.e., numbers without decimal points. A byte can store a number from 0 to 255 and a word can store from 0 to 65,535. There are ways to deal with floating point (decimal) and even negative numbers, that you'll see later in this chapter.

To access the Stamp's variable memory you'll use special designators beginning with "W" for word-sized access, or "B" for byte-sized accesses. For example W0 is the first 16-bit register. As you can see in Figure 2.1, the first 16-bit register is also B0 and B1, the first two 8-bit registers. For example, consider this code fragment (dollar signs represent hex numbers):

```
B0=$AA
B1=$55
```

W0 now equals $AA55, just as if you had written:

```
W0=$AA55
```

Figure 2.1 Stamp I memory map.

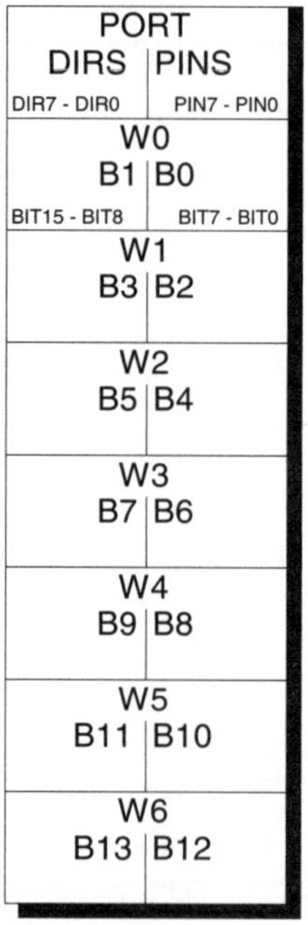

PORT	
DIRS	PINS
DIR7 - DIR0	PIN7 - PIN0
W0	
B1	B0
BIT15 - BIT8	BIT7 - BIT0
W1	
B3	B2
W2	
B5	B4
W3	
B7	B6
W4	
B9	B8
W5	
B11	B10
W6	
B13	B12

Unlike the other registers, W0, B0, and B1 also share space with the 16 bit-sized registers BIT15 to BIT0. This can be handy when you want to split words apart into bits. For example, in the above sample, $AA55 is (in binary) %1010101001010101 (the percent sign signifies a binary number in PBASIC). So reading BIT0 would result in a 1. Reading BIT1 would provide a 0.

Don't use these variables!

You should be aware that if you use GOSUB (covered later in this chapter) to call subroutines, it uses W6, and you won't be able to use it yourself. As a result, you should avoid using W6 just in case you want to use GOSUB.

The same advice applies to W0 (and, of course, B0 and B1 that make up W0). Because variables like W0 are the only ones that allow you to operate on bits, you should reserve it for those times that you need its special abilities.

Of course, both of these rules are really guidelines. If you are out of variables, but you could use W0, then go ahead. For W6, you can use it as long as you aren't using subroutines (see "GOSUB I, II, IISX, IIE, IIP" on page 86 for more information).

I/O Registers

In addition to the data registers, there are several registers you use to read and write the eight I/O pins and control their function. The first of these is the DIRS register. Each bit in this register corresponds to one of the eight I/O pins on the Stamp. If the DIRS register bit is 0, then the pin is an input. If the DIRS register bit is 1, then the pin is an output. You can also use names for each individual pin (DIR0, DIR1, DIR2, and so on). At first that seems handy, but it takes up a lot of space in your limited 256 bytes of program memory. So instead of writing:

```
DIR0=1
DIR2=1
DIR7=1
```

You'd be better off writing:

```
DIRS=$85    ' or %10000101
```

The second statement does the same thing, but consumes less program space. The same is true for the INPUT and OUTPUT statements, which simply manipulate the DIRS register's bits (see the "COMMAND REFERENCE" beginning on page 54 of this chapter).

Another 8-bit register of importance to I/O is the PINS register. Reading from the PINS register reads the state of the input ports. Writing to PINS sets the state of the output pins. This can be handy when you want to output a byte of data at once. Usually, you'll find it easier to manipulate the PINS register a bit at a time using PIN0,

PIN1, and so on. You can also use the HIGH and LOW commands you'll read about later in this chapter.

You can also treat the DIRS and PINS register as a single 16-bit word named PORT. For example, you could write:

```
DIRS=%11110000
PINS=%10100000
```

Or, use this line to conserve program space:

```
PORT=%1111000010100000
```

Of course, values you set when writing to inputs have no immediate effect. However, the Stamp does remember what you write to the pins and if you later change the pin to an output, the Stamp uses the last value you wrote to the PINS variable. This isn't often useful behavior, but you should understand how it works nonetheless.

Using Meaningful Names

Although you can use the predefined names for registers and I/O pins, doing so makes your program hard to read. The Stamp I allows you to define new names for these symbols using the SYMBOL command.

You'll read more about the SYMBOL command in the reference portion of this chapter. However, a simple example will quickly convince you of the value of SYMBOL. Suppose you examined the following code:

```
W1=W1+1
B3=B3*2
PIN3=W1 & 1
```

This is a bit confusing. But consider this snippet:

```
SYMBOL count=W1
SYMBOL mask=B3
SYMBOL statebit=PIN3

count=count+1
mask=mask*2
statebit=count & 1
```

That is much easier to read. Besides, you can easily change the I/O pins or variables you use if necessary by making a single change to the correct SYMBOL line. You can also set constants using this method. For example:

```
SYMBOL delay=100
```

Stamp I Expressions

The Stamp I has a limited capacity to evaluate mathematical expressions. Limited, because the Stamp only recognizes expressions in a LET (an assignment) statement. So, consider these statements:

```
W2=W1*100+6
IF W0*2 > 30 THEN TRY
```

The first statement is legal because it is a LET statement (the LET is implied; see "LET I" on page 62). However, the second line is not legal because the Stamp doesn't handle expressions except on the right of an assignment statement. To make the test, you'd need to use an intermediate variable:

```
W5=W0*2
IF W5>30 THEN TRY
```

The Stamp recognizes the operators in Table 2.2 (see the "COMMAND REFERENCE" beginning on page 54 for more details). However, be sure you understand that the Stamp evaluates expressions from left to right. This is different from the normal way you learned to do math. For example, any high school algebra student can tell you that:

$$5 + 3 \times 2 = 11$$

That's because in the real-world, we understand that multiplication has higher precedence than addition. Therefore, you (or your calculator) perform the multiplication before the addition. However, the Stamp I interprets this from left to right, so on the Stamp, this is actually 16. In many computer languages you could use parentheses to force some operations to occur first, but not with the Stamp I. You simply have to be careful when you write your expressions that you get the result you expect.

Table 2.2   Stamp I operators.

Operator	Name	Notes
+	Add	
-	Subtract	
*	Multiply	Returns low 16 bits of result
**	Multiply-high	Returns high 16 bits of result
/	Divide	
//	Modulo	Returns remainder from division
MIN	Minimum	Returns minimum value
MAX	Maximum	Returns maximum value

Table 2.2   Stamp I operators. (Continued)

Operator	Name	Notes
&	And	Logical AND
|	Or	Logical OR
^	Xor	Exclusive OR (use ^$FFFF to get NOT)
&/	And Not	
|/	Or Not	
^/	Xor Not	

Another thing to watch for with Stamp (and other microprocessor) math is that the numbers are integer-only. So if you ask the Stamp to calculate:

3 / 2

You'll get the answer 1. Of course, you can also use the // operator to learn the remainder of this operation. So:

```
x=3//2    ' x is equal to 1
```

The // operator (known as the *modulo operator*) will help you deal with fractions and decimals. You'll read more about solving this problem later in the chapter.

The Stamp II Memory Map and I/O

The Stamp II's memory map is quite similar to that of Stamp I. However, the Stamp II has access to both more memory and more I/O pins. You can find the register layout in Figure 2.2. The I/O registers are similar, but with a few differences. In addition, the Stamp II can access the variables in many different ways.

You can modify a variable by using a period and a modifier (see Table 2.3). This allows you to operate on a byte, a bit, or a nibble (four bits) from any variable. If you want to set the low bit of variable W1, for example, you might write:

```
W1.LOWBIT = 1
```

Figure 2.2   Stamp II memory map.

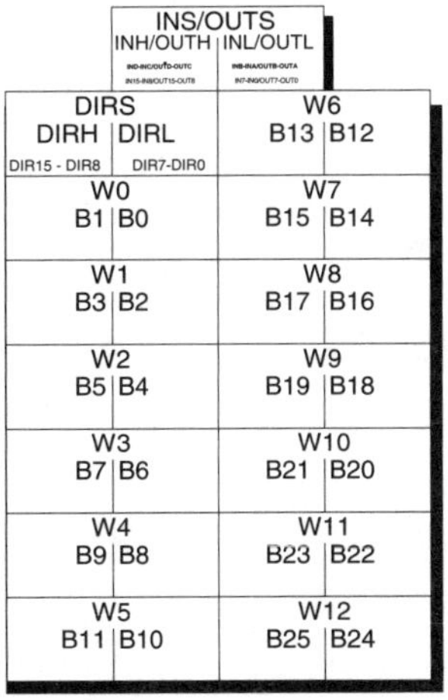

Table 2.3   Variable modifiers for the Stamp II.

Modifier	Definition
LOWBYTE	Low byte of a word
HIGHBYTE	High byte of a word
BYTE0	Byte 0 (low byte) of a word
BYTE1	Byte 1 (high byte) of a word
LOWNIB	Low nibble of a word or byte
HIGHNIB	High nibble of a word or byte
NIB0	Nibble 0 of a word or byte
NIB1	Nibble 1 of a word or byte
NIB2	Nibble 2 of a word
NIB3	Nibble 3 of a word
LOWBIT	Low bit of a word, byte, or nibble
HIGHBIT	High bit of a word, byte, or nibble
BIT0	Bit 0 of a word, byte, or nibble
BIT1	Bit 1 of a word, byte, or nibble
BIT2	Bit 2 of a word, byte, or nibble
BIT3	Bit 3 of a word, byte, or nibble
BIT4	Bit 4 of a word or byte

Table 2.3   Variable modifiers for the Stamp II. (Continued)

Modifier	Definition
BIT5	Bit 5 of a word or byte
BIT6	Bit 6 of a word or byte
BIT7	Bit 7 of a word or byte
BIT8	Bit 8 of a word
BIT9	Bit 9 of a word
BIT10	Bit 10 of a word
BIT11	Bit 11 of a word
BIT12	Bit 12 of a word
BIT13	Bit13 of a word
BIT14	Bit14 of a word
BIT15	Bit15 of a word

Another exciting feature of the Stamp II software is that it will automatically assign variables for you, if you like. You can still select exactly what variables you want to use, but you don't have to. Instead, you can just ask the Stamp software to pick variables for you. However, you probably won't want to mix methods — either manually pick the variables you want to use, or let the Stamp software pick them for you.

To ask the Stamp to allocate a variable, you use the VAR command. You also have to specify the size of the variable. You might write:

```
counter   VAR   BYTE
```

This makes the Stamp assign one of the byte-sized variables to the variable named counter. Which one? It doesn't matter. You can select WORD, BYTE, NIB (a 4-bit nibble), or BIT as the size of a variable.

Of course, you can run out of variables if you try to reserve too many. Then you might try using the normal variables (like W1 or B5). This may help because you can determine when you no longer need a variable and reuse it for another purpose. The Stamp software is not that smart. Once it reserves a variable, it will not use it again. However, see the Pong game in Chapter 9 for some ideas about overlaying variables.

Another thing you can do with the VAR command is to create an alias for a variable. For example, you might want to know if counter is odd or even. When a number is odd, the least-significant bit in that number will be 1. So you could write:

```
countodd   VAR   counter.LOWBIT
```

Array Variables

You can also allocate an array using VAR. An *array* is when you have multiple items of the same type. For example, you might want a list of three bytes, so you could create an array, like this:

```
narray    var    byte(3)
```

Then you could write (for example):

```
narray(0) = 1
narray(1) = 10
narray(2) = 100
```

Notice that the numbers you use to access the array variable range from 0 to one less than the size of the array (three in this case). However, if you use numbers that are too large, the Stamp will not report an error, and will instead access memory that belongs to another variable. When you use an array's name with no subscript (the number in parenthesis), you refer to the first element of the array (that is, element 0).

Input/Output

Like the Stamp I, the Stamp II provides a DIRS register to set the direction of each I/O pin. A 1 in this register indicates an output; a 0 stands for an input. You can also ask for a particular bit of the DIRS register by using a number (just like the Stamp I, except the number can be up to 15). So you can work with DIR0 or DIR10, for example. You can also use DIRH (or DIRL) to access the top eight bits (or the bottom eight bits) of the DIRS register. Finally, you can use DIRA, DIRB, DIRC, and DIRD to work with DIRS four bits (a nibble) at a time. DIRA is the least-significant four bits and DIRD is the most-significant bits.

To work with the actual I/O pins, things are a bit different than the Stamp I. The Stamp II provides separate registers for input (INS) and output (OUTS). You can also use numbers to specify a particular bit (IN0, or OUT4, for example). Like the DIRS register, you can also use the H, L, A, B, C, and D suffixes to work with the port as a byte or nibble.

When you write to the OUTS register, the register remembers what you wrote, even if some bits are not outputs at this time. If you switch the bits to outputs (using DIRS), the output pins will use the value that exists in the OUTS register.

Stamp II Expressions

Stamp II expressions are a bit more capable than Stamp I expressions. First, you can use math expressions nearly any place that an ordinary number can appear. So for Stamp II programs, it is legal to say:

```
B1=10
INPUT B1+1  ' make pin 11 an input
```

The Stamp II, like the Stamp I, evaluates math expressions from left to right. However, you can use parentheses to force a particular order. In the Basic Stamp I section, you saw this example:

```
5+3 * 2
```

Using normal math, the answer is 11 because you perform multiplication before addition. However, using the Stamp, the result is 16. The Stamp handles things left to right. However, you can force the correct ordering with parentheses:

```
5+ (3 * 2)
```

You can use up to eight levels of parentheses. It is always a good idea to use parentheses if there is any doubt about how you mean for the expression to evaluate.

Operators

The Stamp II has unary (one argument) and binary (two argument) operators. In other words, a unary operator works on one value and a binary operator works with two arguments. You'll see a list of operators in Table 2.4. (see the "COMMAND REFERENCE" beginning on page 54 for more details).

Table 2.4   Basic Stamp II operators.

Operator	Type	Description
ABS	Unary	Absolute Value
SQR	Unary	Square Root
DCD	Unary	Calculate 2^n
NCD	Unary	Finds position of most-significant bit
SIN	Unary	Sine of angle (expressed in brads)
COS	Unary	Cosine of angle (expressed in brads)
+	Binary	Add
-	Binary	Subtract

Table 2.4   Basic Stamp II operators. (Continued)

Operator	Type	Description
*	Binary	Multiply (low 16-bits)
**	Binary	Multiply (high 16-bits)
/	Binary	Divide
//	Binary	Remainder from division
*/	Binary	Fractional multiply
MIN	Binary	Minimum value
MAX	Binary	Maximum value
DIG	Binary	Returns decimal digit
<<	Binary	Shifts left
>>	Binary	Shifts right
REV	Binary	Reverses bits
&	Binary	Logical AND
|	Binary	Logical OR
^	Binary	Logical exclusive or, XOR

Constants

The Stamp II allows you to specify named constants with the CON keyword. You might write:

```
maxdelay con 1000
```

Now everywhere you use maxdelay in your program, the Stamp will treat it as 1,000.

The Stamp software can also precalculate expressions that only contain constants. For example, suppose you write:

```
W1=maxdelay * 2
```

The Stamp software will automatically convert this to the equivalent:

```
W1=2000
```

This works for expressions that contain the +, -, *, /, <<, >>, &, |, and ^ operators. All other operators force the Stamp to calculate the result at run time, even if the numbers involved are all constants.

TIP

Initial values
When either Stamp resets, it clears all of its registers. This includes the DIRS I/O direction register. That means that all variables initially contain 0 and all I/O pins are initially inputs. That means you can save a bit of program space by not initializing pins as inputs. Of course, to save the most space, you'll use the DIRS register to set all the pins at once, anyway.

Handling Large, Negative, and Floating Point Expressions

One challenge with Stamp programming is the fact that all math on the Stamp uses positive integer numbers. This is not uncommon in the microcontroller world because handling floating point numbers requires a lot of extra hardware. Another limitation is the size of the variables. A bit can hold either a 1 or a 0. Nibbles can hold numbers from 0 to 15. Bytes and words can handle 0 to 255 or 0 to 65,535, respectively.

Does this mean that you can't use the Stamp unless you are only dealing with small positive integer numbers? Not at all. It does mean you'll have to be a little crafty to get around these problems.

Negative Numbers

It is possible to work with negative numbers (in many cases) using a technique known as *two's compliment arithmetic*. This works for addition, subtraction, and multiplication. However, it isn't effective for division. It also cuts the range of numbers you can handle in half. So a byte can either store 0 to 255 or –128 to 127.

Here's how it works. To form a negative number, write out the positive representation of the number in binary form. Then invert all the bits (that is, make 1s into 0s and vice versa). Finally, add 1 to get the result. So here's how you'd find the two's compliment value for –33 (working with a byte):

```
(positive number)    33 = %00100001
(invert bits)        %11011110
(add 1)              %11011111   (or $DF)
```

How does this work? The key is to realize that when the Stamp performing byte-sized math calculates a value greater than 255, it just chops off the extra bits on the left to form a single byte. The same applies when working with words, except the value there can't exceed $FFFF or 65,535. So if you add 100 and −33 (which is $64 and $FFDF in hexadecimal) using word-sized arithmetic you'll find:

```
$64 + $FFDF = $10043
```

However, the Stamp will chop the top bits off, leaving $0043, which is 67 decimal. This is the correct answer. You'll notice that for a negative number, the topmost bit (bit 7, in this case) will be 1. Positive numbers will always lead with a 0 bit. Consider this example:

```
$0010 + $FFDF = $FFEF   (in decimal, this is 16 + -33)
```

Because the top bit is 1, $FFEF is a negative number. To find out what value it has, you can reverse the above steps to decode the two's compliment number:

```
(subtract 1)    $FFEE
(invert bits)   $0011  (or 17)
```

So the result is −17, the correct answer. Of course, if you are getting ready to use the value again, you don't need to convert it anyway. You only need to convert it when you want to display the answer. The Stamp II provides the SDEC modifier for use with DEBUG and SEROUT that will convert the answer for you (but only for a word-sized value). The Stamp I doesn't do any conversion for you, so you'd have to do it yourself. For example, here's some code to print a signed number in W1 on the Stamp I:

```
' This code destroys W2
' and leaves the absolute value of W1 in W1
W2 = W1 & $8000  ' test top bit
IF W2<>$8000 THEN pos
DEBUG "-"
W1=W1 - 1 'SUBTRACT'
W1=W1 ^ $FFFF   ' invert bits
pos:
DEBUG #W1
```

Division poses a similar problem. You need to decide if the topmost bits of both numbers are the same. If they are (that is, both numbers are positive, or both numbers are negative), the result will be positive. If they are not, the result will be negative. Here's some example Basic Stamp II code:

```
' Try changing these values
W1=99
W2=-33

B9=(W1>>15) ^ (W2>>15)  ' See text
```

```
' Convert W1 and W2 to positive
W1=ABS w1
W2=ABS w2
' Do division
W3=w1/w2
' Make answer negative if necessary
if B9=0 then pos
W3=-W3
pos:
debug sdec w3    ' print out
```

The B9 variable acts as a flag (and could be a bit) that indicates if the answer should be positive or negative. By shifting W1 and W2 to the left 15 places, you wind up with a 1 or a 0 depending on the topmost bit. The exclusive or, will then set B9 to 0 only if both bits are the same. This is a more compact way to determine the flag. There are other ways, of course. For example:

```
B9=0
IF W1 & $8000 = 0 THEN P1
B9=B9+1
P1:
IF W2 & $8000 = 0 THEN P2
B9=B9+1
P2:
IF B9<>2 THEN proceed
B9=0
proceed:
```

This is probably easier to read, but is much more code to write. Don't forget the Stamp only has a little space for programs, so every bit you can save is worthwhile.

Large Numbers

It is possible to work with numbers larger than normally allowed, but you have to resort to a bit of trickery to do so. Many microprocessors have a carry bit that tells you when an addition overflows (or a subtraction underflows). However, the Stamp doesn't support a flag like this. Therefore, you have to simulate it with software.

The maximum number you can store in a given number of bits, n is:

$2^n - 1$

For 16 bits, this works out to 65,535. Suppose, however, that you want to add two 16-bit numbers. The maximum possible result is:

```
$FFFF + $FFFF = $1FFFE
```

Notice that the most you can need is 17 bits. Let's say that we want to add some numbers together, but we need more range. You can do this by concatenating several registers together (in your mind, at least).

Listing 2.1 shows the code that adds two 32-bit numbers. The first number is in W1 and W2. The second number is in W3 and W4. It is a simple matter to add the low bits, and check to see if there was an overflow. If there was an overflow, the result will be less than the original value. In that case, the code adjusts the high bits. Then it adds the high bits. W5 servers as temporary storage. You can perform the same trick with subtraction too (see Listing 2.2). Just remember that an underflow during subtraction will result in a number larger than the original, not less than the original.

Listing 2.1 Adding a 32-bit number.

```
W1=$2
W2=$FFFF
W3=0
W4=1

Incr:
' Add W1:W2 + W3:W4

W5=W2
W2=W2+W4
IF W2>=W5 THEN nocy ' if w2 < its old value then carry!
W1=W1+1
nocy:
W1=W1+W3

Debug HEX4 W1, HEX4 W2, cr
Goto Incr
```

Listing 2.2 Subtracting 32-bit numbers.

```
W1=$3
W2=$0000
W3=0
W4=1

Decr:
' Sub W1:W2 - W3:W4

W5=W2
W2=W2-W4
IF W2<=W5 THEN nobor  ' if W2>W5 then borrow
W1=W1-1
nobor:
W1=W1-W3
Debug HEX4 W1, HEX4 W2, cr
Goto Decr
```

Multiplying is a bit more difficult. Why? Because multiplying two 16-bit numbers may require a 32-bit result! After all, $FFFF × $FFFF is $FFFE0001, and that's too big to put in the Stamp's variables. Luckily, both types of Stamp takes this into account. The trick is to realize that the * operator only returns the bottom 16 bits of the result. However, the ** operator returns the top 16 bits. For example, this program will calculate the 32-bit result of $FFFF × $FFFF:

```
W1=$FFFF
W2=$FFFF
W3=W1*W2
W4=W1**W2
Debug HEX4 W4, HEX4 W3
```

Multiplying larger numbers is relatively difficult. You can decompose any multiplication to a series of additions, but that isn't very efficient. You could also code the multiplication using any of the more efficient schemes (like Booth's algorithm) for doing multiplication, but this is even uglier than the multiword addition code. Luckily, multiplying to 32 bits is usually enough for most purposes.

Dividing provides a similar challenge. You can, of course, decompose any division problem into a repeating subtraction. More sophisticated algorithms are available, but difficult to code. Note that dividing two 16-bit numbers will never result in more than 16 bits of result, because $FFFF / $0001 = $FFFF.

Non-Integer Numbers

In many Stamp applications, handling numbers that are not integers is of great importance. You can deal with this problem in several ways, depending on your exact needs.

For a simple case, consider converting centigrade temperature (or Celsius, if you are younger than I am) to Fahrenheit. The traditional formula for this is:

```
F = 9/5 * C + 32
```

Of course, $9/5$ is 1.8, but the Stamp can't handle that very well. In this simple case, a little algebra will get you out of trouble. You can rewrite this formula as:

```
F = 9 * C / 5 + 32
```

The Stamp can do that! Another possibility would be to scale 1.8 to 18 so the result would be in units of $1/10$ of a degree. So:

```
F10 = 18 * C + 320
```

Notice that you must scale the 32° offset to 320. It is easy to get your units confused.

Another way you could write this expression (but only on the Basic Stamp II) is:

```
F = C */ $01CD + 32
```

The */ operator treats its second argument ($01CD, in this case) as two 8-bit numbers. The top eight bits ($01, in this case) is the whole number portion to multiply by. The second eight bits ($CD or 205) represents the fractional part of the number in $1/256$ units. The ratio $205/256$ is almost 0.8, so the above code effectively multiplies 1.8 times C. Because the second argument is really two 8-bit numbers, it is often clearer to write it in hex. Using 461 (the decimal equivalent of $01CD) is not nearly as clear.

To calculate constants for use with the */ instruction, put the whole number portion in the upper byte, then multiply the fractional part by 256 and put that in the lower byte. For instance, consider π (about 3.14159). The upper-byte would be $03 (the whole number), and the lower would be 0.14159 * 256 = 36 ($24). So the constant for use with */ would be $0324. Of course, this isn't exactly the value of π, but what is? The error is quite small, and well within acceptable limits for most cases.

Even on the Stamp I you can often pull a similar trick. Consider π again. Archimedes found that it lies between $223/71$ and $22/7$. Although you might have learned $22/7$ in high school, $223/71$ is a slightly closer approximation (0.02% off versus 0.04%). Another good approximation is $355/113$, but the larger the numerator, the more it limits the range of numbers that you can handle. So if you need to calculate the circumference of a circle and the diameter is in W1, you might try this:

```
W2=223 * W1 / 71
```

This would work on either Stamp, of course. With a little ingenuity, you can handle practically any formula (with some limitations). Consider the formula for the reactance of a capacitor:

$$Xc = \frac{1}{2\pi FC}$$

Where Xc is the reactance in ohms, F is the frequency (usually in Hertz), and C is the capacitance (usually in Farads). This formula poses several problems. First, real capacitors usually have values that are a fraction of a Farad. The reciprocal (dividing 1 by a number) also poses a problem.

The first problem has an easy solution. Although capacitors usually have very small values, the frequencies you use tend to be large. For example, if you express the frequency in MHz (millions of Hertz), you can express the capacitance in microfarads. This allows you to specify relatively small numbers. So if F is 2MHz, and C is 2µF, you can easily see that:

```
2000000 x .000002 = 4
2 x 2 = 4
```

Using 223/71 for π, you can rewrite the reactance formula as:

$$Xc = \frac{1}{2\dfrac{223}{71}FC}$$

Using some basic algebra, you can rewrite this as:

$$Xc = \frac{1}{\dfrac{446FC}{71}} = \frac{71}{446FC}$$

This appears to be suitable for use with the Stamp, but there is still one problem. Remember that F and C must be integers. This will make the denominator larger than 71 (actually, greater than or equal to 446). Because the Stamp does integer division, the answer will always be zero! Not very useful.

The trick here is to represent the answer in a larger scale, perhaps in hundredths of an ohm. On a calculator, it would be easy to multiply the answer by 100, but for the Stamp, multiplying 0 by 100 will still give you 0. But, if you do a little simplifying algebra first, you could make 7,100 the numerator of the formula. This puts everything in the range of calculation, and leaves the results in units of 0.01Ω. Look at this Stamp code that uses a frequency of 2MHz and capacitance of 2μF:

```
W1 = 2
W2 = 2
W3 = 7100 / (446 * W1 * W2)
DEBUG ? W3    ' Answer is 3
```

Of course, this isn't completely accurate. The real answer is 0.0397, but that's the price of integer math. Usually the things you want to do with a Stamp don't require much precision anyway. You could change the factor in the denominator to 4,460 to gain another digit of accuracy (the answer then is 39 and is in units of $^1/_{1,000}\Omega$).

The thing to watch for is overflowing the 65,535 maximum number. For example, you might be tempted to change 7,100 to get more accuracy. The problem is, multiplying 7,100 by 10 give you 71,000, too large for the Stamp. The same problem occurs with the denominator. If you use the 446 factor, the product of W1 and W2 must be less than 147. If you use the 4,460 factor, the product must always be 14 or less.

If this seems like a big restriction, don't despair. You can usually come up with some way to get the results you want. Another possibility is to send raw data to a PC and convert it to engineering units there where math is not a big problem. You'll see more about that in Chapter 6.

COMMAND REFERENCE

The remainder of this chapter is a task-oriented reference to each Stamp keyword and operator. If you want to look up a particular command, see Table 2.1. Table 2.5 shows the major tasks you'll find in this section along with the starting page number.

Table 2.5   Task sections.

Task:	See:
Data Commands	page 55
Flow Control	page 75
Digital I/O	page 95
Analog I/O	page 110
Serial I/O	page 120
Tables	page 132
Specialized I/O	page 135
Event Handling	page 142
Math Operators	page 149
Logic Operators	page 160

If you are looking for an alphabetical listing, check out Table 2.1 on page 30 (or the index in the back of the book).

Each section has a brief description of the contents of the section. Each page in the section has a title that indicates the command name and which Stamps support it. The pages use a conventional notation to designate the syntax of each command. Items in curly braces are optional. Ellipses (three periods) indicate that items can repeat.

Section I — Data Commands

The lifeblood of any computer program is data. The Stamp has a variety of methods to manipulate data in memory. The SYMBOL, VAR, and CON keywords help you use symbolic names instead of direct register names. Most of the code in this chapter, however, uses register names to ensure compatibility with both Stamp families.

The assignment statement, otherwise known as the LET statement, is particularly important for the Stamp I because it is the only place you can perform math operations. The Stamp II is more liberal, allowing arithmetic expressions in any reasonable location.

Another important family of data commands allow you to store and retrieve data from the Stamp's EEPROM. This is the same EEPROM that stores program code, but you can use any left over memory for nonvolatile storage. Just be careful. The Stamp's EEPROM may wear out after 10,000,000 cycles or so.

There are a few oddball commands that don't really fit anywhere in this section, including RANDOM and DEBUG. The RANDOM command lets you generate random numbers (great for games), and the DEBUG command displays data on the debugging window of the Stamp programming software to help you visualize what's going on inside your program.

DEBUG **I, II, IISX, IIE, IIP**

Syntax

```
DEBUG output clause, { output clause, ...}
```

Description

The DEBUG command lets you print values to the debugging terminal managed by the Stamp programming software. This allows you to view variables or track the flow of execution through your program.

Stamp I

The output clause can consist of strings or variables. The format of the clause depends on which Stamp you are using. For the Stamp I, naming a variable causes a debugging display to appear that shows the variable name and its decimal value.

You can also use one of the characters in Table 2.6 in front of a variable to modify how the Stamp displays it. You can combine the # character with any of the other characters in Table 2.6 to suppress the variable name display. In other words, $ displays the variable name and the hex value, but #$ just displays the hex value. You can also use the special clause CLS to clear the debugging screen or CR to start a new line.

Table 2.6   Stamp I DEBUG modifiers.

Character	Meaning
#	Display only value (no variable name)
$	Display only hex value
%	Display only binary value
@	Display ASCII character

Stamp II

When you just specify a variable, the Stamp interprets it as an ASCII character, which can be confusing. For example:

```
B2=65
DEBUG B2
```

This piece of code will mysteriously print an "A" on the debug terminal screen. That's because 65 is the ASCII code for an uppercase A. Sometimes this is what you want, but more often you want to see the numeric value.

You can precede the variable with a question mark, and it will use the Stamp I format. That is, it will display the variable name, an equal sign, and the decimal value. You can also use one of the modifiers in Table 2.7 to control the formatting.

Many of the modifiers take an optional field width that you may supply immediately after the modifier. Consider these lines:

```
B2=15
DEBUG HEX B2      ' outputs F
DEBUG HEX2 B2     ' outputs 0F
```

You'll find another peculiarity in the STR modifier. Normally, this modifier prints a string from an array until it reaches a byte that contains zero. However, you can use a special syntax to display a particular length string, if you prefer. For example, to display three characters at the array UID, you could write:

```
DEBUG STR UID\3
```

The REP modifier uses the same scheme to determine how many times to repeat a character. This is useful when formatting a debugging display:

```
DEBUG REP "*"\10
```

Speaking of formatting, the Stamp II's debugging terminal recognizes several special characters. You can find these characters (and their symbolic names) in Table 2.8. These characters are useful when you want to display your results in an easy-to-read format.

Table 2.7   Stamp II DEBUG modifiers.

Modifier	Field width	Effect	Example
ASC?	N/A	Prints character with variable identification	B2 = 'X'
DEC	1–5	Decimal	100
SDEC	1–5	Signed decimal number (use with 16-bit numbers)	–33
HEX	1–4	Hexadecimal format	F121
SHEX	1–4	Signed hex (use with 16-bit number)	–F0
IHEX	1–4	Hex with preceding $	$F121
ISHEX	1–4	Signed hex with preceding $	$-22
BIN	1–16	Binary	101001

DEBUG I, II, IISX, IIE, IIP

DEBUG I, II, IISX, IIE, IIP

Table 2.7   Stamp II DEBUG modifiers. (Continued)

Modifier	Field width	Effect	Example
SBIN	1–16	Signed binary	-1010
IBIN	1–16	Binary with preceding %	%101011
ISBIN	1–16	Signed binary with preceding %	%-1101
STR	N/A	Displays ASCII string from byte array until zero byte	Hello
REP	N/A	Repeats a byte (see text)	****

Table 2.8   Stamp II DEBUG characters.

Name	Value	Description
CLS	0	Clear the screen
HOME	1	Move cursor to the top left of the screen
BELL	7	Ring the bell
BKSP	8	Backspace
TAB	9	Tab to next tab stop (multiples of 8)
CR	13	New line

Compatibility Notes

There are only slight differences between the Stamp I and Stamp II debug commands. It is unusual to use this command for part of the actual function of a program. Normally, you'll only use it to view variables while debugging. That means that code that uses DEBUG usually isn't critical and you can easily change it if you are porting your code from one Stamp to another.

```
W1=10+20*3
DEBUG ? W1    ' is it 90 or 70?
```

SYMBOL **I**

Syntax

```
SYMBOL id = value
```

Description

Causes the Stamp I software to replace one symbol with another symbol or a constant. This can make your code much more readable. The ID portion must be a valid identifier name (a letter or underscore followed by any alphanumeric characters or an underscore). The value can be a constant, or another symbol.

Compatibility Notes

Not present on the Stamp II. Instead, use VAR to define variables and CON to define constants.

Sample Program

```
SYMBOL maxcount = 100
SYMBOL counter = b1    ' Use register B1 for counter

FOR counter = 0 to maxcount
  DEBUG ? counter
NEXT
```

CON **II, IISX, IIE, IIP**

Syntax

```
id CON value
```

Description

Causes the Stamp II software to define a constant to make your code more readable. The ID portion must be a valid identifier name (a letter or underscore followed by any alphanumeric characters or an underscore). The value can be any constant.

Compatibility Notes

Not present on the Stamp I. See "SYMBOL I" on page 59.

Sample Program

```
maxcount CON 100
FOR B1=0 to maxcount
    DEBUG ? B1
NEXT
```

VAR **II, IISX, IIE, IIP**

Syntax

```
id VAR size{(array_size)}
id VAR alias
```

Description

The VAR keyword causes the Stamp II programming software to reserve a register of the appropriate size. You can also use this keyword to create arrays. The ID portion must be a valid identifier name (a letter or underscore followed by any alphanumeric characters or an underscore). The size may be any of the following: BIT, NIB (four bits), BYTE, or WORD (16 bits).

When defining arrays, you place the number of elements you wish to create in parentheses after the size designator. The first element of the array will be zero, so the maximum array index will be one less than the size. That is, if you define an array of five bytes, the indices you can use will range from 0 to 4.

You can also use the VAR keyword to define one variable as an alias for another. This is especially useful when you want complete control of register allocation, or when you want to make an alias for a portion of another variable (see the following sample program).

Compatibility Notes

Not available on the Stamp I. See "SYMBOL I" on page 59.

Sample Program

```
maxcount CON 100
ct VAR BYTE      ' a variable
FOR ct=0 to 100
  DEBUG ? ct
NEXT ct

aword VAR WORD
hbyte VAR aword.highbyte    ' byte-sized aliases for aword
lbyte VAR aword.lowbyte

samples VAR byte(10)
samples(0)=0
samples(9)=100
```

LET **I**

Syntax

```
{LET} variable = expression
```

Description

The LET keyword is optional (and rarely used) on the Stamp I. The Stamp II doesn't support using the keyword LET, so you must omit it in Stamp II programs. The effect of this keyword is to assign the expression's value to the variable. In the Stamp I, this is about the only place you can perform math and logic operations (like addition and subtraction). In other words, for the Stamp I, you can't say,

```
FOR b1 = 1 to b2*10+3  ' wrong
```

Instead, you'd need to use a temporary variable like this:

```
LET b3=b2*10+3
FOR b1=1 to b3
```

By using the special registers that correspond to the I/O registers, you can perform I/O and set direction registers using LET. For example:

```
B1 = IN1
OUT4 = 1
```

This is especially handy when you want to deal with a group of I/O pins as a single binary number. You can also use the INPUT, OUTPUT, REVERSE, HIGH, LOW, and TOGGLE commands to do I/O on a bit-by-bit basis.

Compatibility Notes

The Stamp II doesn't use LET. You simply omit it and write the assignment statement without using the LET keyword.

Sample Program

```
LET B1=100   ' not legal on Stamp 2
B1=100       ' same thing but legal on both Stamps
LET W1=B2*100+7
W1=B2*100+7     ' same thing
```

EEPROM I

Syntax

```
EEPROM address, ( data_list)
```

Description

This command places literal data into the Stamp I's EEPROM. This is the same EEPROM that the Stamp uses to store its program. You can then read the data at run time with the READ command. This is useful for storing messages, constant tables, or any other data you want to read from the EEPROM. Of course, at run time, you can write over these values using the WRITE command.

The data list can consist of byte-sized constants or a quoted string. It is important to realize that the EEPROM command stores the data as the program downloads from the PC. Some of the Stamp manuals indicate that you can use variables in the data list, but this is not correct because the Stamp software can't know the value of variables as it is downloading to the chip.

How do you know what address to use when storing data? The Stamp's program starts at the top of EEPROM memory and works down. That leaves locations starting at address 0 free for your data (unless the Stamp is completely full). You can determine at run time the lowest address your program is using by reading location 255. This always returns the lowest address in use.

Compatibility Notes

The Stamp II uses the DATA command for a similar purpose.

Sample Program

```
' Print message to serial device on pin 7
EEPROM 0, 14     ' size of message
EEPROM 1,"Madam I'm Adam"
READ 0,B1
FOR B0 = 1 to B1
  READ B0,B3              ' get characters in B3
  SEROUT 7,N2400,(B3) ' write to serial port
NEXT
```

BSAVE **I**

Syntax

BSAVE

Description

This command, which may appear anywhere in your program, causes the Stamp programming software to store a 256-byte file named CODE.OBJ that contains the data that the program will download to the Stamp.

You can use this file, along with the BSLOAD program to program a Stamp without the full software. You can also use the file with the Stamp simulator that comes with this book.

Compatibility Notes

Not available for the Stamp II. With the Windows-based software, you can save the program tokens using the menu instead.

DATA **II, IISX, IIE, IIP**

Syntax

```
label DATA data_list
```

Description

The DATA statement stores bytes into the Stamp II's EEPROM at compile time. By default the data begins at location zero, and moves upwards in EEPROM. The Stamp's program begins at the top of the EEPROM and works downward.

You'll usually precede the DATA statement with a label so you can refer to the address later in your program. The list is a series of byte-sized constants, or quoted strings all separated by commas. You can also store a 16-bit value by preceding the data with the special keyword WORD. Of course, the READ command only reads bytes, so you won't be able to directly read it back as a word.

It is possible to skip locations in two different ways. First, you can use the @ sign to specify an absolute address to start at. The second method is to use a number in parentheses to skip over a specified number of bytes. If you precede the parentheses with a byte, that byte will fill the skipped memory locations. You'll find examples of these different uses of DATA in the example program.

Compatibility Notes

Not available on Stamp I. See "EEPROM I" on page 63.

```
PauseX    DATA     word 4000    ' 4000 milliseconds
Msg1      DATA     "Power On",$0d,$0a,0
Blanks    DATA     " "(80)       ' 80 blanks
Loc200    DATA     @200,$FF,$FF  ' sets locations 200 and 201


' Print the message
printit:
B1=Msg1
loop:
   READ B1,B2
   IF B2=0 THEN ENDMSG
   B1=B1+1
   SEROUT 16,84,[B2]
   GOTO loop
```

```
ENDMSG:
 READ PauseX,B0      ' read 16-bits in two steps
 READ PauseX+1,B1
 PAUSE W0                      ' W0 = B1 and B0
GOTO printit
```

READ **I, II, IISX, IIE, IIP**

Syntax

READ address, variable

Description

READ accesses the Stamp's internal EEPROM. It allows you to read bytes from EEPROM into a Stamp variable. For the Stamp I, the address must be a constant or variable from 0 to 255. The Stamp II variation allows any expression that generates a result between 0 to 2,047. In either case, the second argument must be the name of a variable. Regardless of the size of the variable, the READ command only retrieves a byte.

Both Stamps place program code in the EEPROM starting at the top of memory. This leaves the low locations free for you to use for data storage. Of course, data stored in EEPROM is nonvolatile. That is, it persists even when the Stamp loses power.

To learn how much space is available for data, you can read byte 255 on the Stamp I. This location always contains the lowest address in use. For the Stamp II, you can examine the memory map using the Stamp programming software to determine the lowest address.

For the Stamp IISX and IIE, this command always operates on the current EEPROM bank. However, the Stamp IIP allows you to select with the STORE command.

Compatibility Notes

The Stamp II has more EEPROM than the Stamp I, so the address parameter is different between the two. On the Stamp I, the maximum address is 255. On the Stamp II, the top address is 2,047. Of course, many of the higher addresses will contain your program, so the actual top address that is available will depend on your program (see the description above).

Sample Program

See DATA, EEPROM, and WRITE for sample programs.

WRITE **I, II, IISX, IIE, IIP**

Syntax

WRITE address, data

Description

Use the WRITE command to store data in EEPROM at run time. This differs from the DATA and EEPROM keywords, which store data in EEPROM during downloading.

WRITE always works with bytes. You can retrieve the bytes with the READ command. You should be aware that there is a limit to the number of times you can write to the EEPROM before it may fail. This limit is high (about 10,000,000 cycles), but it isn't infinite. Suppose you want to read a temperature and store it to EEPROM every second. It would take around 116 days to wear out the EEPROM.

Also, writing to EEPROM takes more time than reading it or writing to an ordinary variable. It can take several milliseconds to write data to the EEPROM.

For the Stamp IISX and IIE, this command always operates on the current EEPROM bank. However, the Stamp IIP allows you to select with the STORE command.

Compatibility Notes

The Stamp II has more EEPROM than the Stamp I, so the address parameter is different between the two. On the Stamp I, the maximum address if 255. On the Stamp II, the top address is 2,047. Of course, many of the higher addresses will contain your program, so the actual top address that is available will depend on your program (see the description for "READ I, II, IISX, IIE, IIP" on page 67).

```
' For Stamp I use this line:
'EEPROM 0,0
' For Stamp II use this line:
loopct:    DATA 0          ' this is address 0

toploop:
     ' Do some work
     PAUSE 1000      ' simulated work
' for Stamp II, could use READ loopct,B1
     READ 0,B1        ' get count
```

```
      B1=B1+1
' for Stamp II, could use WRITE loopct,B1
      WRITE 0,B1      ' write count
       GOTO toploop
```

PUT **IISX, IIE, IIP**

Syntax

```
PUT address, byte
```

Description

The PUT keyword allows you to store data in the Stamp's scratchpad RAM (which is not available on the normal Stamp II nor is it present on the Stamp I). This extra RAM retains its value when you switch to another program. However, it is RAM, so it does not retain values when the Stamp powers down. When the Stamp resets from a power failure or a reset input, it sets all scratchpad RAM locations to 0.

The Stamp IISX has 64 bytes of scratchpad RAM, so the address must range from 0 to 63 on that processor (or the Stamp IIE). However, the top byte (address 63) contains the current program number (see the "RUN IISX, IIE, IIP" command on page 94 for more details). This leaves locations 0 through 62 available for data storage.

The Stamp IIP has 128 bytes of scratchpad, so the address can range from 0 to 127. The top byte stores the current program (in the lower four bits) and the current EEPROM bank for READ and WRITE commands (in the upper bits). You should not change this location.

Compatibility Notes

Only the Stamp IISX, IIE, and IIP have scratchpad RAM.

Sample Program

Here is a program that calls program #1 to convert a Celsius temperature to Fahrenheit. Because the conversion program is separate, it must use the scratchpad for storage.

```
' Program #0
' In this program, program 1 contains code to perform a calculation
C  CON  1   ' location 0 for prog #1's argument
F  CON 2    ' location 1 for prog
GET 0,B0
IF B0<>0 THEN convertdone
PUT C,10
PUT 0,0  ' Set our "return address"
RUN 1
convertdone:
```

```
GET F,B1
DEBUG "10C=", DEC B1, "F",CR
END
' Program #1
' Convert Celsius to F
C CON 1
F CON 2
GET C,B1
B2=(9*B1)/5+32
PUT F,B2
GET O,B1    ' Get original program
RUN B1      ' return to it
```

GET **IISX, IIE, IIP**

Syntax

GET address, variable

Description

The GET keyword allows you to read data from the Stamp IISX's scratchpad RAM. This extra RAM retains its value when you switch to another program. However, it is RAM so it does not retain values when the Stamp powers down. When the Stamp resets from a power failure or a reset input, it sets all scratchpad RAM locations to 0.

The Stamp IISX and IIE have 64 bytes of scratchpad RAM, so the address must range from 0 to 63. However, the top byte (address 63) contains the current program number (see the "RUN IISX, IIE, IIP" command on page 94 for more details). This leaves locations 0 through 62 available for data storage. The Stamp IIP has 128 bytes (although it also reserves the top location) so on that processor you can use addresses from 0 to 127 (with 0–126 being the practical range).

Compatibility Notes

Only the Stamp IISX, IIE, and IIP have scratchpad RAM.

Sample Program

See "PUT IISX, IIE, IIP" on page 70 for a sample program.

RANDOM **I, II, IISX, IIE, IIP**

Syntax

```
RANDOM variable
```

Description

For many computer games and simulations it is useful to have a number that appears to occur at random. The RANDOM keyword takes an input byte or word and scrambles its bits in a random way. You can repeatedly call RANDOM to generate a sequence of numbers.

Because the RANDOM command only scrambles the input's bits, it generates the same result for a given input. That means you must have some way to get an unpredictable starting point. A common technique is to increment a variable while waiting for user input. Because the user will take an unpredictable amount of time to respond, this can serve as an initial value for the random number generator (see the following sample program).

The number the Stamp generates will be between 0 and 255 (for byte-sized variables) or between 0 and 65,535 for word variables. If you want a different number, you'll need to calculate it yourself. The mod operator (//) is handy for this because it returns the remainder from integer division. If you want, for example, a number between 0 and 5, you could mod the random number with 6. If you wanted a number between 1 and 6, just add 1 to the previous result.

However, if you reduce the range of the number, don't use the reduced number the next time you call RANDOM. Instead, use the full return from the last call. This ensures the maximum random distribution of numbers. By the same token, you will get better results using a full word instead of a byte because there are more numbers to choose from in a word.

Compatibility Notes

Available on all Stamps.

Sample Program

For this program, connect a switch between pin 11 and ground. Also place a 10K pull-up resistor between pin 11 and the 5V supply. The result appears on the debug terminal. You could change it to work with the Stamp I by changing the DEC keywords in the DEBUG statements to # and using a lower I/O pin.

```
' Simulated electronic die
' Press active low switch on pin 11 to start
' Random number
W5=0
wloop:  ' wait for user
W5=W5+1
IF in11=1 then wloop
RANDOM W5
B2=W5//6+1  ' 1-6
DEBUG "Die 1: ", DEC B2, CR
RANDOM W5      ' Note: use W5 here not B2
B3=W5//6+1
DEBUG "Die 2: ", DEC B3, CR
DEBUG "Total: ", DEC B2+B3, CR
PAUSE 1000
GOTO wloop
```

Section II — Flow Control

Moving data around in a program is important. It is also important to be able to control the path your program takes through your instructions. That's the purpose of flow control.

Some flow control statements make decisions and redirect your program based on those decisions. Others allow you to execute the same set of commands repeatedly forming a loop. Many Stamp programs control something and therefore spend most of their time in one big loop. Many Stamp programs you'll see in the real world will look something like this:

```
Top:
    ' Read some inputs
    ' Calculate values based on inputs
    ' Write outputs based on calculations
    ' Optional pause
    GOTO Top
```

The Stamp has familiar flow control primitives like IF and GOTO. It also has some odd ones, like BRANCH and NAP. Besides that, some of the familiar words (notable GOSUB and IF) have some odd twists when compared to real Basic programming.

END **I, II, IISX, IIE, IIP**

Syntax

END

Description

This command simply stops your program putting the Stamp in a low-power consumption mode. The Stamp programming software always puts an END command after your program, so if you run past the end of your code, the Stamp executes an END. All outputs stay in the last state your program put them in.

When the Stamp is in low-power mode, the Stamp actually resets every few seconds (2.3 seconds to be exact). During this time, the I/O pins all become inputs for a brief period (about 18mS) before the Stamp recovers and puts the I/O pins back in their programmed state. If you can't tolerate this, simply put the Stamp in an endless loop when you want to stop. Of course, this doesn't engage the low power mode, but it also doesn't cause the outputs to hiccup every 2.3 seconds.

Compatibility Notes

Available on all Stamps.

Sample Program

If you want to see the results of the 2.3 second hiccup, connect an LED and a resistor between pin 0 and ground and try this program:

```
HIGH 0
END
```

PAUSE **I, II, IISX, IIE, IIP**

Syntax

```
PAUSE delay
```

Description

This command makes the Stamp delay execution for the specified number of milliseconds. On the Stamp I, this delay must be a constant or a variable name. On the Stamp II, it can be a constant, a variable name, or an expression.

Because the delay is a 16-bit word, the most you can delay is 65,535mS (just over 65.5 seconds, because there are 1,000mS in one second). If you need to delay more than this, you can use a loop to delay more than once.

The Stamp processors use a ceramic resonator to generate an internal clock. This resonator sets the basic accuracy of any timing the Stamp performs (about ±1%). Also, it takes the Stamp I about 1mS to fetch the PAUSE command from EEPROM and the next command, so for critical applications you might consider subtracting 1mS from the total you wish to delay because there is 1mS of "hidden" delay just from fetching instructions. The Stamp II and its variants take less time to fetch instructions, so this is less of a problem on those chips. For the Stamp II, count on about 0.6mS of overhead. The Stamp IISX has even less fetching overhead (around 0.25mS).

Compatibility Notes

Available on all Stamps.

Sample Program

```
' Delay for 10 minutes
FOR B1=1 to 10
PAUSE 60000     ' pause 1 minute
NEXT            ' but pause 10 times!
```

NAP **I, II, IISX, IIE, IIP**

Syntax

```
NAP period
```

Description

The NAP command causes the Stamp to enter low-power mode for a time determined by the period argument. The period may be off by quite a bit (up to 100% error), depending on the supply voltage, the temperature, and other factors. Nominally, the period factor (which ranges from 0 to 7) causes the Stamp to nap for a particular number of milliseconds according to the following formula:

$$nap = 2^{period} \times 18ms$$

So, a period of 0 naps for 18mS, and a period of 7 naps for about 2.3 seconds. Remember, this time is not exact. The NAP command is similar to the END command in that all outputs will momentarily become inputs for about 18mS when the nap completes.

Compatibility Notes

Available on all Stamps.

Sample Program

```
top:
TOGGLE 0      ' turn on/off LED on pin 0
NAP 7         ' low-power for 2.3 seconds
GOTO top
```

SLEEP **I, II, IISX, IIE, IIP**

Syntax

SLEEP period

Description

This command puts the Stamp in low-power mode for the specified number of seconds. This command is similar to NAP, but the interval is both much longer and more accurate (within 1%). Because the period may be a 16-bit constant or variable, you can sleep for up to 65,535 seconds (about 18 hours).

Like all the low power instructions, the Stamp will reset every 2.3 seconds and for a brief period (about 18mS) all outputs will temporarily become inputs.

Compatibility Notes

Available on all Stamps.

Sample Program

```
top:
TOGGLE 0     ' turn on/off LED on pin 0
SLEEP 10     ' sleep for 10 seconds
GOTO top
```

GOTO **I, II, IISX, IIE, IIP**

Syntax

```
GOTO label
```

Description

Using GOTO causes your program to jump to the specified label and continue execution at that label. In some modern programming languages, it is considered bad form to use GOTO statements, but with the Stamp, it is practically a necessity.

To specify a target line for the GOTO, you must create a label. Labels are like variable names, but they appear first on a line and have a colon at the end of them.

Compatibility Notes

Available on all Stamps.

Sample Program

```
top:          ' a label!
TOGGLE 0      ' Blink LED
PAUSE 500
GOTO top      ' resume at top
INPUT 0       ' This line never executes!
```

IF **I, II, IISX, IIE, IIP**

Syntax

```
IF { NOT } condition { conjunction { NOT } condition . . . } THEN label
```

Description

The IF statement allows your program to make decisions. The Stamp evaluates the portion between the IF and the THEN by testing each condition. A condition might look like this:

```
x=0      ' x is zero
y<10     ' y less than 10
z<>30    ' not equal to
```

If the NOT keyword appears before a condition, it reverses the sense of the test. So these two conditions are the same:

```
NOT x=0
x<>0
```

You can join two conditions together with a conjunction (either AND or OR). If you use AND, then both conditions must be true for the joined condition to be true. If you use OR, then it is sufficient if either of the conditions are true. You can join more than two conditions together. Then the Stamp evaluates them left to right.

After evaluating the entire set of conditions, the Stamp chooses one of two options. If the condition is true, the Stamp executes a GOTO to the label you specify. If the condition is false, then execution continues with the next line in sequence.

As usual, the Stamp I can only accept variables and constants for the parts of the condition. In fact, the first part of a condition must be a variable, and the second part can be a variable or a constant. The Stamp II can handle any expression. You can use = (equal), <> (not equal), < (less than), > (greater than), <= (less than or equal to), or >= (greater than or equal to) as conditions.

Compatibility Notes

This command exists on all Stamps.

Sample Program

Here is a simple craps game that uses the dice code from the RANDOM example. You could change it to work with the Stamp I by changing the DEC keywords in the DEBUG statements to #. For this program, connect a switch between pin 11 and ground. Also place a 10K pull-up resistor between pin 11 and the 5V supply.

```
' Craps game for Basic Stamp II
' Press active low switch on pin 11 to start
' Random number
W5=0
newgame:
B6=0   ' # of turns
B4=0   ' point to make
wloop:    ' wait for user
W5=W5+1
IF in11=1 then wloop
RANDOM W5
B2=W5//6+1   ' 1-6
DEBUG "Die 1: ", DEC B2, CR
RANDOM W5      ' Note: use W5 here not B2
B3=W5//6+1
DEBUG "Die 2: ", DEC B3, CR
B5=B2+B3
DEBUG "Total: ", DEC B5, CR
B6=B6+1
IF B6=1 THEN first     ' goto first if first roll
' not the first roll
IF B4=B5 THEN pointmade     ' make the point?
IF B5=7 OR B5=11 THEN craps ' crapped out?
PAUSE 500
GOTO wloop
' First roll, check for win or set point
first:
IF B5=7 OR B5=11 THEN pointmade
B4=B5  ' Set point
DEBUG "Point is ", DEC B4, CR
PAUSE 500
GOTO wloop
craps:
DEBUG "Loser!",CR
PAUSE 1000
```

```
GOTO newgame
pointmade:
DEBUG "Winner!", CR
PAUSE 1000
GOTO newgame
```

BRANCH **I, II, IISX, IIE, IIP**

Syntax

Stamp I
```
BRANCH value,(label1 {, label2 ...})
```

Stamp II
```
BRANCH value,[label1 {, label2 ...}]
```

Description

This command provides a shorthand way to jump to a different label depending on a value. On the Stamp II, consider this line:

```
BRANCH B1,[cmd0, cmd1, cmd2]
```

This line has the same effect as these lines:

```
IF B1=0 THEN cmd0
IF B1=1 THEN cmd1
IF B1=2 THEN cmd2
```

In other words, the Stamp uses the value to select one of the labels from the list and jumps to that label. In the above example, if B1 is greater than 2, the Stamp continues executing the line following the BRANCH.

Compatibility Notes

This command is available on all Stamps. The Stamp I encloses the labels in parentheses while the Stamp II uses square brackets.

Sample Program

Here is some code that you could use to convert a random die roll to a pattern of LEDs.

```
DIRS=$7F      ' LEDs on Pin 0 to Pin 7
top:
' Code to wait for button omitted
RANDOM W1
B0=W1//6    ' 0 to 5
BRANCH B0,[one,two,three,four,five,six]
' Should never get here
```

```
one:
  OUTL=$40   ' pattern for 1
  GOTO top
two:
  OUTL=$22 ' pattern for 2
  GOTO top
' other labels omitted
```

GOSUB **I, II, IISX, IIE, IIP**

Syntax

GOSUB label

Description

The GOSUB keyword is similar to a GOTO with one major exception: the code that appears at the label can return to the original program by using the RETURN statement. This allows you to define subroutines that your program can call repeatedly to perform a task. For example, suppose your program needed to double the B1 register, and if the result was more than 100, it would reset B1 to 0. Of course, you could write:

```
top:
' Some program
B1=B1*2
IF B1<=100 THEN cont0
B1=0
cont0:
' more stuff here
B1=B1*2
IF B1<=100 THEN cont1
B1=0
cont1:
' even more stuff here
GOTO top
```

However, it would be easier to write this using GOSUB, as in the following sample program. This way you could call the subroutine as many times as you wanted, making your code more compact and more readable.

You must be careful where you place subroutines in your program. The Stamp doesn't provide any special protection for subroutines. So if you place your subroutines before your main program, the first subroutine will run, not the main program. Likewise, if your main program can fall into a subroutine, it will execute just like any other program code. Consider this:

```
GOSUB secretnumber
DEBUG "The secret number is ", DEC W1,CR
```

```
secretnumber:
DEBUG "Finding secret number",CR
W1=42    ' The meaning of life
RETURN
```

In this simple program, you will see the "Finding secret number" message twice. Once as a result of the GOSUB statement, then again when execution just continues into the secretnumber routine. Then the RETURN statement will cause unexpected behavior because there is no correct place to return. The solution, of course, is to place an END before the subroutine.

The Stamp I only allows 16 GOSUBs per program. In addition, the Stamp I can only handle four nested subroutines. That means that if you call S1, and S1 calls S2, and S2 calls S3, and S3 calls S4, then S4 can't call any more subroutines! If it does, the Stamp will not behave properly.

Another subtle point for the Stamp I is that the Stamp uses W6 to keep track of GOSUBs in progress. Therefore, you can't use W6 if you are using subroutines. If you use it in your main program, using GOSUB will destroy its contents. If you use it from inside a subroutine, the RETURN statement will misbehave.

For a little insight on why these limitations exist, consider how the Stamp I handles GOSUBs. When you write a GOSUB statement, the Stamp software on the PC assigns the GOSUB a number from 0 to 15 (a 4-bit number). When a GOSUB is in effect, the Stamp stores the number of the GOSUB in part of the W6 register. Because W6 holds 16 bits, the Stamp can track four 4-bit numbers.

The Stamp II series processors allow up to 255 GOSUBs per program. However, you still can't nest subroutines more than four deep. Unlike the Stamp I, the Stamp II doesn't use any registers that you can access to track the GOSUBs.

GOSUB I, II, IISX, IIE, IIP

Hidden returns

You can often save a few bytes of code (at the expense of some readability) by using hidden returns. Suppose you have two subroutines: S1 and S2. If your code looks like:

```
GOSUB S1
' More things here
END
S1:
    ' Do some work
    GOSUB S2
    RETURN
S2:    ' Do whatever
    RETURN
```

You can shorten into this:

```
GOSUB S1
' More things here
END
S1:
    ' Do some work
    GOTO S2
' More code here
S2:    ' Do whatever
    RETURN
```

By changing the GOSUB/RETURN to a single GOTO, you save code space and help avoid the limit on nesting subroutines.

Compatibility Notes

The Stamp I allows 16 GOSUBs per program. With the Stamp II. you may use 255 GOSUBs per program. Each Stamp IISX, IIE, or IIP program allows 255 GOSUBs independent of the other programs loaded.

Sample Program

```
top:
' Some program (take 2)
GOSUB doubleb1
' more stuff here
GOSUB doubleb1
' even more stuff here
GOTO top
doubleb1:
   B1=B1+1
   IF B1<=100 THEN doubleb_ret
   B1=0
doubleb_ret:
   RETURN
```

GOSUB I, II, IISX, IIE, IIP

RETURN I, II, IISX, IIE, IIP

Syntax

RETURN

Description

You'll use the RETURN statement to force a subroutine to end, returning control to the program that used GOSUB to call the routine. See the "GOSUB I, II, IISX, IIE, IIP" entry on page 86 for more details.

Compatibility Notes

The Stamp I allows 16 GOSUBs per program. With the Stamp II, you may use 255 GOSUBs per program. Each Stamp IISX, IIE, or IIP program allows 255 GOSUBs independent of the other programs loaded.

Sample Program

See the sample program for GOSUB.

FOR **I, II, IISX, IIE, IIP**

Syntax

```
FOR variable = start TO end {STEP stepvalue }
```

Description

This powerful looping construct allows you to execute a piece of code repeatedly. When you don't include the step value, the variable you use will take each value from the start value to the end value. So when you write:

```
FOR B1=1 TO 10
DEBUG ?B1
NEXT
```

The B1 variable will take on values ranging 1–10 in sequence, and the DEBUG statement will execute 10 times. You can use the step value to determine how much is added to the variable each time through the loop. Using a step value of 1 is the same as not using STEP at all. If you used a step value of 5 in the above example, the loop would only execute twice, once with B1 set to 1 and again with it set to 6. On the third attempt, the Stamp would set B1 to 11 and exit the loop because 11 is greater than 10.

If you want to count backwards, you can use a negative step value (including –1). Of course, any of the values (start, end, and step) may be variables or constants (or, on the Stamp II, expressions). You can even modify the end and step values during the loop itself.

Be sure to remember that the Stamp uses 16-bit arithmetic. This can lead to a subtle bug if you are approaching 65,535 with your count variable. For example:

```
FOR W1=65000 to 65500 STEP 1000
' Do something
NEXT
```

This code will loop more than once! The first pass through the loop sets W1 to 65,000. When the Stamp adds 65,000 and 1,000, it overflows 16-bit arithmetic, setting W1 to 464. Because 464 is less than 65,500, the loop continues — not exactly what you would expect.

Compatibility Notes

This command is available on all Stamps.

Sample Program

```
' Print Odd numbers between 1 and 99 in reverse order, 10 times.
W1=1   ' Start value
W2=100 ' End Value ' must be odd

FOR W3=1 to 10   ' Make 10 copies
' Change DEC to # for Stamp 1
DEBUG "Odd numbers (copy ", DEC W3, ")",CR
   FOR W4=W2 to W1 STEP -2
      DEBUG DEC W4,CR
   NEXT
NEXT
```

NEXT **I, II, IISX, IIE, IIP**

Syntax

Stamp I
```
NEXT { variable }
```

Stamp II
```
NEXT
```

Description

Use this statement with the FOR loop keyword. See the "FOR I, II, IISX, IIE, IIP" section on page 91 for more details.

Compatibility Notes

The Stamp II does not allow you to place the variable name after the NEXT statement. On the Stamp I the variable name is optional.

Sample Program

See the section on "FOR I, II, IISX, IIE, IIP" on page 91.

NEXT I, II, IISX, IIE, IIP

RUN **IISX, IIE, IIP**

Syntax

RUN program

Description

Although the Basic Stamp IISX (and the IIE and IIP) has 16K of program memory, you can't write a single program that exceeds 2K (the same as a regular Basic Stamp II). However, you can store eight different programs on the chip at one time! You use the RUN command to transfer control from one program to another.

When the Stamp first powers up or resets, it runs program 0. However, program 0 can use the RUN command to switch to another program. The new program may later execute another RUN to switch to yet another program. The program number may be a constant or a variable and ranges between 0 and 7.

When the RUN command executes, the Stamp's registers (including the I/O registers) and scratch pad RAM stay intact. Scratch pad location 63 has the number of the currently executing program on a Stamp IISX or IIE. The Stamp IIP stores the same information in the low four bits of scratch pad location 127 (the top bits are the current value of the STORE command).

Compatibility Notes

Only available on the Stamp IISX, IIE, and IIP.

Sample Program

See "PUT IISX, IIE, IIP" on page 70.

Section III — Digital I/O

Because the Stamp is a digital device, it makes sense that it has many commands that handle digital I/O. Of course, because the I/O pins have pseudo-variables, you can use ordinary assignment statements to perform I/O instead of special commands. This is especially useful when you want to use more than one bit of the port simultaneously.

Nearly all of the digital I/O instructions require a pin number. This can be a constant or a variable (or, on the Basic Stamp II, an expression). If the pin number is a variable or expression, the Stamp uses the value you'd expect. However, this leads to a common programming error. Suppose you are programming a Stamp I and you want to make pin 3 an input. It is very natural to write:

```
INPUT pin3
```

This is incorrect. In reality, you will read pin 3 (which will have a 1 or a 0 in it) and then make that pin an input. So the effect is that you've just made pin 0 or pin 1 an input. The correct statement, of course, is:

```
INPUT 3
```

Some of the digital I/O commands are quite complex. The BUTTON command provides sophisticated logic for debouncing pushbuttons and providing extras like key repeats. The XOUT command can send signals to X10 power controllers used to wirelessly control lamps and appliances.

INPUT I, II, IISX, IIE, IIP

Syntax

```
INPUT pin
```

Description

This command places the specified pin into input mode. You can also accomplish the same task by setting the DIRS register. This is especially useful when you want to set several pins at once. For example, if you wanted to set all eight I/O lines on the Stamp I to inputs, you could write eight separate INPUT statements or simply write:

```
DIRS=0
```

Usually, the pin number you specify is a constant. However, if it is a variable or an expression (on the Basic Stamp II), the number the variable contains specifies the pin. This leads to a common programming mistake. Suppose you are programming a Stamp I and you want to make pin 3 an input. It is very natural to write:

```
INPUT pin3
```

This is incorrect. In reality, you will read pin 3 (which will have a 1 or a 0 in it) and then make that pin an input. So the effect is that you've just made pin 0 or pin 1 an input. The correct statement, of course, is:

```
INPUT 3
```

Compatibility Notes

Available on all Stamps. Note that the Stamp I and Stamp II regard any voltage higher than 1.4V as a logic 1. The Stamp IISX, IIE, and IIP, however, regard anything over 2.5V as a logic 1. For normal logic (0V and 5V) this is no problem. However, marginal circuits (or those circuits that exploit the threshold voltage) may be sensitive to this threshold difference.

Sample Program

```
INPUT 0
wait0:
' For Stamp II use IF in0=1 THEN ?
IF pin0=1 THEN wait0
Debug "Button pushed", CR
End
```

OUTPUT **I, II, IISX, IIE, IIP**

Syntax

```
OUTPUT pin
```

Description

This command places the specified pin into output mode. You can also accomplish the same task by setting the DIRS register. This is especially useful when you want to set several pins at once. For example, if you wanted to set all eight I/O lines on the Stamp I to outputs, you could write eight separate OUTPUT statements or simply write:

```
DIRS=$FF
```

The pin number can be a constant or a variable (or an expression on the Basic Stamp II). See the introduction to this section beginning on page 95 for details about a common programming mistake you may make when specifying pin numbers.

Compatibility Notes

Available on all Stamps.

Sample Program

```
OUTPUT 0
' Generate a pulse
pin0=1  ' use out0 for Stamp II
PAUSE 500
pin0=0
END
```

HIGH I, II, IISX, IIE, IIP

Syntax

HIGH pin

Description

This command forces the pin to be an output and sets the output bit to a high state (logic 1). You can also set a bit to a logic 1 by writing to the pin or in registers, but this doesn't automatically force the pin to an output.

The pin can be a constant or a variable (or an expression on the Stamp II). See the introduction to this section beginning on page 95 for details about a common programming mistake you may make when specifying pin numbers.

Compatibility Notes

Available on all Stamps.

Sample Program

```
loop:
HIGH 0   ' make a fast square wave
LOW 0
GOTO loop
```

LOW **I, II, IISX, IIE, IIP**

Syntax

LOW pin

Description

This command forces the pin to be an output and sets the output bit to a low state (logic 0). You can also set a bit to a logic 0 by writing to the pin or in registers, but this doesn't automatically force the pin to an output.

The pin number can be a constant or a variable (or an expression on the Stamp II). See the introduction to this section beginning on page 95 for details about a common programming mistake you may make when specifying pin numbers.

Compatibility Notes

Available on all Stamps.

Sample Program

See the program for "HIGH I, II, IISX, IIE, IIP" on page 98.

LOW I, II, IISX, IIE, IIP

TOGGLE I, II, IISX, IIE, IIP

Syntax

```
TOGGLE pin
```

Description

Use the TOGGLE command to force a pin to be an output and invert its previous state. That is, if you were outputting a 0 on this pin, TOGGLE will output a 1 and vice versa. This is very useful for making LEDs blink, or otherwise generating square waves.

The pin number can be a constant or a variable (or an expression on the Stamp II). See the introduction to this section beginning on page 95 for details about a common programming mistake you may make when specifying pin numbers.

Compatibility Notes

Available on all Stamps.

Sample Program

```
loop:
TOGGLE 0    ' Blink LED
PAUSE 500
GOTO loop
```

REVERSE **I, II, IISX, IIE, IIP**

Syntax

REVERSE pin

Description

REVERSE makes input pins outputs and output pins inputs.

The pin number can be a constant or a variable (or an expression on the Stamp II). See the introduction to this section beginning on page 95 for details about a common programming mistake you may make when specifying pin numbers.

Compatibility Notes

Available on all Stamps.

Sample Program

```
' Generate pulse
HIGH 0    ' forces pin 0 to output
PAUSE 10
LOW 0
' Listen for echo
REVERSE 0
Debug DEC pin0    ' use in0 on Stamp II
```

PULSOUT **I, II, IISX, IIE, IIP**

Syntax

```
PULSOUT pin, time
```

Description

The PULSOUT command forces the specified pin to be an output, toggles the pin for the specified time, and then toggles the pin again. For the Stamp I, the time measurement is in 10µS units. The Stamp II and IIE uses 2µS units, and the Stamp IISX is 0.8µS per unit. The Stamp IIP uses a 1.18µS interval. Consider a Stamp I program that contains the line:

```
PULSOUT 0,10
```

If you wanted to convert this program for the Stamp II, you'd use 50 as the time. For the Stamp IISX, you'd have to use 125.

The pin and time can be constants or variables (or expressions on the Basic Stamp II). However, the largest time you can use is 65,535. That means that there is an upper limit to how long PULSOUT can operate. On the Stamp I, the maximum is about 655mS. The Stamp II's limit is about 131mS and the Stamp IISX reaches its limit in just over 52mS. The Stamp IIP is somewhere inbetween at 55.5mS.

Compatibility Notes

Available on all Stamps. Note that the time units differ, however.

Sample Program

```
' Generate Pulse
' 1ms for Stamp 1, 200us for Stamp II or IIE, 80uS (IISX), 118uS (IIP)
PULSOUT 0, 100
```

PULSIN **I, II, IISX, IIE, IIP**

Syntax

PULSIN pin, state, result

Description

Use PULSIN to measure input pulses. The pin argument specifies which pin will monitor the pulse (this pin is changed to an input if it isn't already one). It can be a constant, a variable, or (on the Stamp II) an expression. The state argument specifies what state (1 or 0) will start the measured pulse. The result argument specifies a variable that receives the result.

The Stamp I measures the pulse in 10µS units. The Stamp II and IIE use 2µS and the Stamp IISX measures using a 0.8µS count. The Stamp IIP uses 1.8µS as the interval.

The Stamp only registers a pulse when it senses a change in the pin's state that brings it to the same value as the state variable. In other words, consider this line:

```
PULSIN 0, 1, W1
```

When this line executes, suppose that pin 0 is at a high level (logic 1). The command will not begin counting. The pin's level will have to go to 0, and then return to the 1 state to begin the count. Because the maximum result is 65,535, there is a limit to how long the pulse can be. For the Stamp I, this limit is about 655mS. The Stamp II and Stamp IISX can record about 131mS and 52mS, respectively. The Stamp IIE's limit is the same as an ordinary Stamp II, while the Stamp IIP can time up to around 55.5mS. This time also represents the maximum amount of time the Stamp will wait for the pulse to begin. If the pulse is too long, or fails to start within the maximum time period, the result will be 0.

If you store the result in a byte, make sure the pulse won't be very long. This command always uses a 16-bit count. If you use a byte variable, the Stamp simply returns the low byte of the counter (which will be misleading if the pulse is wider than 255 time periods).

Compatibility Notes

Available on all Stamps. Note that the time units differ, however.

Sample Program

```
PULSIN 0,1,w1
w2=w1*10    ' use 2 for Stamp II
' For Stamp I:
DEBUG #W2, "uS",CR
' For Stamp II:
'DEBUG DEC W2, "uS', CR
```

COUNT **II, IISX, IIE, IIP**

Syntax

```
COUNT pin, time, variable
```

Description

COUNT monitors the specified pin for a given amount of time. The Stamp counts the number of state changes that appear on the pin and stores the count in the variable that you specify. The Stamp II and IIE allows you to specify time in milliseconds. The Stamp IISX uses a 0.4mS time. The Stamp IIP uses a .287mS interval.

The Stamp II and IIE can detect pulses as short as 4µS in length. The Stamp IISX can detect 1.6µS transitions. The Stamp IIP monitors pulses wider than 1.2µS.

If you try to monitor signals that rise slowly (an audio waveform, for example), you may get false readings. If you suspect this will be a problem, you should square the signal to logic levels using a schmitt trigger or a comparator.

Compatibility Notes

Available on Stamp II series. There are timing differences between the different variations, however.

Sample Program

```
COUNT 0,1000,W1
DEBUG DEC W1, "Hz"   ' Assume Stamp 2
```

BUTTON **I, II, IISX, IIE, IIP**

Syntax

BUTTON pin, dnstate, rptdelay, rptrate, work, targetstate, label

Description

The BUTTON command is used inside a loop to handle common processing required for monitoring buttons. Mechanical buttons "bounce." That is, they do not make clean connections, but instead bounce between the on and off state rapidly for a few milliseconds before making a solid contact. Your program may falsely respond to these false transitions. For example, suppose you have a pullup resistor tied to pin 0 and a switch between pin 0 and ground. When you push the switch, you expect to see the pin change from a 1 to a 0. Consider this program:

```
    INPUT 0
    W1=0
wloop:
    IF in0=1 THEN wloop
    W1=W1+1
    IF W1=10 THEN done
ploop:    ' wait for it to go up
    IF in0=0 THEN ploop
    GOTO wloop
done:
    DEBUG DEC W1
    END
```

You'd expect to get a debug display after pushing the button 10 times. However, depending on the design of the switch, you may get several counts on each button push and therefore need fewer than 10 switch closures.

The BUTTON command handles the mechanical bouncing. It also allows for key repeat, if you want to use that feature.

The important thing to realize about this command is that you must use it in a loop to get the proper results. The pin argument specifies the I/O pin that monitors the button. The dnstate argument is a value that indicates if the button registers a 0 or a 1 when pressed.

The rptdelay and rptrate specify the time it takes for the key to begin repeating, and then how often it repeats. Unlike other Stamp commands, these two arguments don't have any specific units. Instead, they correspond to the number of loop executions. That means that the actual time depends on how often your loop repeats, and on the Stamp type (because each Stamp executes code at a different speed).

If the rptdelay argument is 0, the button command performs no debouncing or autorepeat functions. If you use 255, the button command debounces the switch, but doesn't perform autorepeat. Any other value determines how many loop cycles the switch must be on for autorepeat to occur.

The workspace variable is a byte that you must reserve for the BUTTON command's use. Make sure it is 0 before you start or you may get erratic results.

The final two arguments determine when and where the command jumps to another portion of code. If the targetstate argument is 0, then the command jumps when the button is not pressed (as determined by the downstate argument). When targetstate is 1, the command jumps when the button is pressed. The label argument determines where the command jumps when the specified state is present.

Compatibility Notes

Available on all Stamps. Because the timing parameters deal with loop counts, the repeat delay and repeat rate will differ between slower and faster Stamps.

Sample Program

```
INPUT 10
work var BYTE
work=0
top:
BUTTON 10, 0, 1000, 100, work, 1, pb
goto top


pb:
  Debug "Push!",CR
goto top
```

XOUT **II, IISX, IIE, IIP**

Syntax

XOUT dpin, cpin, [house\keycmd{\cycles}{, house\keycmd{\cycles}...}]

Description

X10 is a standard protocol (developed by BSR) that allows a controller to send signals over the existing AC power lines to turn lights and appliances on and off. Several companies make compatible modules, and you can buy them at many hardware stores as well as Radio Shack.

The Basic Stamp II and Stamp IISX can generate signals suitable for controlling X10 devices. The signals still require a power line modem that you can purchase from companies that sell the X10 modules. The PL-513 and TW-532 are common power line modems that interface with a standard phone cable (RJ11 connector). The PL-513 only allows transmitting, which is sufficient because the Stamp has no provisions for receiving X10 signals (although you could probably roll your own solution).

The connection to the modem requires two pins: a data pin and a zero-crossing detector pin. These are the first two arguments to XOUT. After that, you can place any number of commands (separated by commas) in the square brackets. Each command consists of a house code, a key or command, and an optional number of cycles (the default is 2).

The X10 protocol specifies 16 keys. Using a key value of 0 to 15 corresponds to X10 keys 1 to 16. You can also use one of the codes in Table 2.9 to control various devices.

Table 2.9   X10 control commands.

Command	Value	Description
unitOn	%10010	Turn specified unit on
unitOff	%11010	Turn off specified unit
unitsOff	%11100	Turn all units off
lightsOn	%10100	Turn on all lights
dim	%11110	Reduce brightness of light
bright	%10110	Increase brightness of light

Programming X10 is a very specialized procedure, but there is an application note from Parallax on the CD-ROM that has a complete example.

Compatibility Notes

Only available on the Stamp II and Stamp IISX.

Sample Program

See Parallax's Stamp II Application Note #1 for a complete sample.

Section IV — Analog I/O

Although the Stamp is essentially a digital device, it has a surprising amount of analog capabilities. Of course, you can always add additional hardware to do analog input and output, but even without anything extra, the Stamp comports itself well.

Of course, sometimes you'll have no choice but to resort to external hardware of some sort. There are a variety of devices that communicate with processors like the Stamp via a serial protocol, saving scarce pins for other purposes. You'll learn more about these devices, and analog I/O in general, in Chapter 4.

PWM **I, II, IISX, IIE, IIP**

Syntax

PWM pin, dutycycle, duration

Description

This command sets the pin to an output and generates a train of pulses with an average duty cycle that you specify. It continues to do so for the specified duration. The duration value's units depends on the Stamp you are using. For the Stamp I, each duration unit is about 5mS. For the Stamp II and IIE, the duration is in milliseconds. The Stamp IISX uses units of 450µS (0.45mS), while the IIP uses 652µS units. Of course, while the Stamp is delivering pulses, program execution halts until the duration expires.

The main use for PWM is to generate analog voltages. If you charge a capacitor through a resistor using PWM you'll generate a voltage across the capacitor proportional to the dutycycle argument. A dutycycle of 0 will result in 0V. When dutycycle is 255, the capacitor will charge to 5V. In particular, you can calculate the voltage by multiplying 5 by dutycycle and dividing by 256. That means that adding 1 to the dutycycle argument will increase the output voltage by about 3.9mV (.0039V).

Of course, if you draw any current from the capacitor, it will discharge, especially after the PWM command stops. The larger the capacitor, the better it will retain the voltage. However, larger capacitors take more time to charge to the correct voltage. In other words, smaller capacitors can supply less current, but also require smaller duration arguments to charge.

No matter how large your capacitor is, you'll quickly discharge it with any significant load. This isn't much of a problem if the voltage will drive a high-impedance input (like an op amp or a comparator input, for example). If you need to drive more current, consider using an op amp to buffer the output voltage. The op amp presents practically no load to the capacitor, but can itself source a great deal of output current. You'll find an example of this in Chapter 4.

PWM is useful for other things besides analog voltage output. For example, it is possible to control motor speeds or LED brightness using PWM.

You should notice that the output duty cycle is an average, and is probably not what you expect. For example, if you use a duty cycle of 128 for 1mS, you might expect to see the PWM pin turn on and off at 500µS intervals. That's not how it works. Instead, the Stamp will emit a series of pulses that average to 50% duty cycle. For the Stamp II, the minimum pulse size is 4µS, so a 50% duty cycle will result in the pin going high for 4µS and then low for 4µS. If you select a duty cycle of 1, however, you'll see a 4µS pulse followed by 1.02mS with no activity.

Compatibility Notes

Available on all Stamps. Timing differs between Stamps, however.

Sample Program

```
' Variable brightness LED
' Place an active low switch on input 10
' and an LED on pin 8
' Hold down the button to make the LED get brighter
' Eventually the duty cycle will overflow and the LED
' will get dimmer
top:
PWM 8,B1,1000
IF in10=1 THEN top   ' Stamp I: use pin10
B1=B1+5
GOTO top
```

POT **I**

Syntax

```
POT pin, scale, variable
```

Description

This command charges a capacitor through a resistor connected to the pin. When the capacitor charges to a logic 1, the Stamp places the elapsed time into the variable you specify after scaling it to a range of 0 to 255.

The primary purpose of this command is to read a variable resistor (a *potentiometer*, or *pot*). However, you can use it to read any resistive or capacitive device. For example, you might use this command to read a thermistor or a photocell to measure temperature or light intensity, respectively.

The scale parameter allows you to get full-scale resolution for the device in question. You should set it to a value that provides nearly 0 at the minimum value of the measured quantity and nearly 255 at the maximum value of the measured quantity. If you use the DOS-based Stamp I editor, you can press Alt+P to download a simple program that will help you decide what values to use.

Compatibility Notes

Only available on the Stamp I. For Stamp II programs, use RCTIME.

Sample Program

```
POT 0,100,b1
DEBUG ?b1
```

RCTIME **II, IISX, IIE, IIP**

Syntax

```
RCTIME pin, state, variable
```

Description

The RCTIME command measures a time interval it takes for the input pin to reach the state you specify. This is usually used to measure a variable resistance or capacitance. If you connect a capacitor between the 5V supply and the stamp pin and a resistor between the pin and ground, you can use this command to measure the time it takes for the circuit to charge. The time will be proportional to the resistance and capacitance used. This is useful for measuring the position of a potentiometer, the resistance of a thermistor (a temperature-sensitive resistor), or other resistive or capacitive sensors.

Of course, the RCTIME command can also measure pulses from any source. The Stamp II (and IIE) measures the time for this command in 2µS units. The Stamp IISX uses 0.8µS intervals while the Stamp IIP uses a .9µS timebase. If the time exceeds 65,535 time units, the command returns 0.

When you use the RCTIME command with a variable resistor or capacitor (an RC circuit), you'll want to charge or discharge the circuit first (use HIGH or LOW followed by a PAUSE). Then you'll use this command to wait for the discharge (or charge, as the case may be).

Always allow at least 4RC seconds to set the initial state of the RC circuit. The returned time will be proportional to the RC time constant. On the Stamp II, you can figure that the value in the variable will equal about 600 times the resistance in KΩ times the capacitance in microfarads. On the Stamp IISX, IIE, and IIP, the threshold voltage is 2.5V instead of 1.5V so, the value will be about 693 times the resistance in kilo-ohms (KΩ) times the capacitance in microfarads (µF).

Compatibility Notes

Only available on the Stamp II series. There are slight differences in timing between the two devices.

Sample Program

```
result var word
top:
high 0 ' Discharge the cap
```

```
pause 1 ' for 1 ms.
RCTIME 0,1,result ' Measure RC charge time.
debug dec result
goto top
```

SOUND I

Syntax

```
SOUND pin, (note, duration {, note, duration ...})
```

Description

This command generates a square wave with a specified frequency and duration. You can connect the pin to a piezoelectric speaker and hear tones when using this command. You can also use a 32Ω–40Ω speaker (or an 8Ω speaker with a 32Ω resistor in series) and a 10μF capacitor between the pin and the speaker. To get any appreciable volume, however, you'll need to drive an external amplifier of some kind to bring the audio volume to an acceptable level.

The note values can be 0 for silence, 1–127 for tones, and 128–256 for white noise of ascending frequencies. The formulae for converting note values into frequency (F) and vice versa are:

$$Note = 127 - \frac{\frac{1}{F} - 0.000095}{0.000083}$$

$$F = \frac{1}{0.000095 + 0.000083(127 - Note)}$$

The duration values are in units of 12mS.

Compatibility Notes

Only available on the Stamp I. See "FREQOUT II, IISX, IIE, IIP" on page 117 for Stamp II programs.

Sample Program

```
SOUND 0, (100,15,100,15,125,5)
```

FREQOUT **II, IISX, IIE, IIP**

Syntax

```
FREQOUT pin, duration, freq1 {, freq2 }
```

Description

You can use FREQOUT to generate one or two tones from a speaker. Unlike the Stamp I's SOUND command, FREQOUT uses PWM to generate the tones, so you'll want to use some filtering to remove any residual high-frequency noise. You can connect the pin to a piezoelectric speaker or use a 32Ω–40Ω speaker (or an 8Ω speaker with a 32Ω resistor in series) and a 10μF capacitor between the pin and the speaker. A 10μF capacitor between the speaker and ground will filter out the high-frequency components. To get any substantial volume, you'll need to drive an external amplifier.

The duration is in milliseconds for the Stamp II and IIE, and in 0.4mS units for the Stamp IISX. The Stamp IIP uses 0.265mS as its time base. The frequency is in Hertz for the Stamp II and IIE, and may range from 0 to 32,767 (0 is silence). For the Stamp IISX, the units are 2.5Hz and the IIP uses 3.77Hz units. When you specify two tones, the tones mix together. If you want to generate touch tones (a common reason to generate two tones), see the "DTMFOUT II, IISX, IIE, IIP" command on page 119.

Compatibility Notes

Available on the Stamp II series. The various members of the family use different timing units for this command. See "SOUND I" on page 116 for single tone generation in Stamp I programs.

```
i var byte ' Counter for position in tune.
fq var word ' Frequency of note for Freqout.
A con 440 ' A note
B con 500 ' B note?
C con 523 ' C note.
D con 587 ' D note
E con 659 ' E note
F con 740 ' F note?
G con 784 ' G note
Z con 0 ' Silent pause (rest).
i = 0
```

FREQOUT II, IISX, IIE, IIP

```
loop:
' happy birthday
'lookup i,[G,G,A,G,C,B,Z,G,G,A,G,D,C,-1],fq
' twinkle twinkle
lookup i,[C,C,G,G,A,A,G,Z,F,F,E,E,D,D,C,-1],fq
IF fq=-1 THEN nomore
i=i+1
FREQOUT 9,350,fq
GOTO loop
nomore:
END
```

DTMFOUT **II, IISX, IIE, IIP**

Syntax

DTMFOUT pin, { ontime, offtime, } [digit {, digit ...}]

Description

This command generates touch tone signals suitable for dialing a telephone. You can connect the pin to a speaker (see the "FREQOUT II, IISX, IIE, IIP" command on page 117 for more details), or connect the pin to the phone line with appropriate hardware (see Figure 4.4 in Chapter 4).

The optional ontime and offtime parameters allow you to control the length of the tones and the pause between digits in milliseconds for the Stamp II (and IIE), 0.4mS units for the Stamp IISX, and 0.265mS units for the Stamp IIP. The default timing is 200 units on and 50 units off.

When specifying the digits, you may use 0–9 for the normal telephone keys, 10 for the star character, 11 for the *octothorpe* (commonly called the *pound sign*), and 12–15 for the special A, B, C, and D keys which do not normally appear on phones.

Compatibility Notes

Available only on the Stamp II series. The different variations of the Stamp use a different time unit for the ontime and offtime delays.

```
DTMFOUT 9,[3,3,4,4,3,4,1]
```

Section V — Serial I/O

Because I/O pins on the Stamp are at a premium, serial communications are especially important. The Stamp can use standard RS232 I/O (useful for talking to PCs and other devices). The Stamp also has special commands to interface to serial shift register devices (many periphial devices use a shift register protocol).

SERIN **I, II, IISX, IIE, IIP**

Syntax

Stamp I
```
SERIN pin, mode {, (qual,?) }, { {#} variable ...}
```

Stamp II
```
SERIN pin{\handshake}, mode, {parity_label, } {timeout, timeout_label,}[input]
```

Description

The SERIN command sets the specified pin to an input and receives RS232 data via that pin. Although all Stamps have this command, the syntax and capabilities are quite different between the Stamp I and Stamp II families.

For the Stamp I, the mode argument is a number from 0 to 7 (or you can use a predefined constant). This selects a baud rate between 300 and 2,400 baud (see Table 2.10). It also selects the polarity of the serial data. The other serial parameters are fixed at eight data bits, one stop bit, and no parity.

If you are using an inverting buffer (such as a MAX232 or most line receivers), you'll want to use the true modes from Table 2.10. If you are using TTL-level signals, you'll use the inverted modes. It is also possible to use the inverted mode with a single resistor in series with the pin. This allows the static protection diodes on the Stamp's input to safely absorb the excess voltage supplied by RS232 voltages (+ and –12V).

With the Stamp I, you may place qualifiers in parentheses. You can use constants, variables, or quoted strings for the qualifier. You can also choose not to use any qualifiers. The Stamp will not proceed until the input stream exactly matches the qualifier data you supply.

After matching any qualifiers, the Stamp reads bytes of data into the variables you specify. If you precede a variable name with #, the Stamp will convert ASCII values into numbers for you. So suppose you use this statement:

```
SERIN 0,T2400, #B1
```

Also, suppose you connect pin 0 to a serial terminal and type "1" and "0" on the terminal. The result is that B1 will contain the number 10.

The Stamp II (and Stamp IISX) has many more capabilities. The first of these has to do with specifying the input pin. You can follow the pin number with a backslash and another pin number (the handshake pin). This pin will become an output and drops to a false while the Stamp is reading data. When the Stamp is no longer accepting data, the handshake pin becomes true. Exactly which logic level appears depends on the mode you specify (see Table 2.10). If you specify an inverted mode, then false is a logic 1. If you specify an non-inverted mode, the a false is a zero.

Table 2.10 Serial mode constants.

Parameters (baud/bits/parity)	Inverting driver?	Open collector?	Stamp I Name	Value	Stamp II/IIE	Stamp IISX/IIP
300/8/N	Yes	No	T300	3	3313	N/A
300/8/N	No	No	N300	7	19697	N/A
300/8/N	Yes	Yes	OT300	11	36081	N/A
300/8/N	No	Yes	ON300	15	52465	N/A
300/7/E	Yes	No	N/A	N/A	11505	N/A
300/7/E	No	No	N/A	N/A	27889	N/A
300/7/E	Yes	Yes	N/A	N/A	44273	N/A
300/7/E	No	Yes	N/A	N/A	60657	N/A
600/8/N	Yes	No	T600	2	1646	4146
600/8/N	No	No	N600	6	18030	20530
600/8/N	Yes	Yes	OT600	10	34414	36914
600/8/N	No	Yes	ON600	14	50798	53298
600/7/E	Yes	No	N/A	N/A	9838	12338
600/7/E	No	No	N/A	N/A	26222	28722
600/7/E	Yes	Yes	N/A	N/A	42606	45106
600/7/E	No	Yes	N/A	N/A	58990	61490
1200/8/N	Yes	No	T1200	1	813	2063
1200/8/N	No	No	N1200	5	17197	18447
1200/8/N	Yes	Yes	OT1200	9	33581	34831
1200/8/N	No	Yes	ON1200	13	49965	51215
1200/7/E	Yes	No	N/A	N/A	9005	10255
1200/7/E	No	No	N/A	N/A	25389	26639
1200/7/E	Yes	Yes	N/A	N/A	41773	43023
1200/7/E	No	Yes	N/A	N/A	58157	59407
2400/8/N	Yes	No	T2400	0	396	1021
2400/8/N	No	No	N2400	4	16780	17405

Table 2.10 Serial mode constants. (Continued)

Parameters (baud/bits/parity)	Inverting driver?	Open collector?	Stamp I Name	Value	Stamp II/IIE	Stamp IISX/IIP
2400/8/N	Yes	Yes	OT2400	8	33164	33789
2400/8/N	No	Yes	ON2400	12	49548	50173
2400/7/E	Yes	No	N/A	N/A	8588	9213
2400/7/E	No	No	N/A	N/A	24972	25597
2400/7/E	Yes	Yes	N/A	N/A	41356	41981
2400/7/E	No	Yes	N/A	N/A	57740	58365
4800/8/N	Yes	No	N/A	N/A	188	500
4800/8/N	No	No	N/A	N/A	16572	16884
4800/8/N	Yes	Yes	N/A	N/A	32956	33268
4800/8/N	No	Yes	N/A	N/A	49340	49652
4800/7/E	Yes	No	N/A	N/A	8380	8692
4800/7/E	No	No	N/A	N/A	24764	25076
4800/7/E	Yes	Yes	N/A	N/A	41148	41460
4800/7/E	No	Yes	N/A	N/A	57532	57844
9600/8/N	Yes	No	N/A	N/A	84	240
9600/8/N	No	No	N/A	N/A	16468	16624
9600/8/N	Yes	Yes	N/A	N/A	32852	33008
9600/8/N	No	Yes	N/A	N/A	49236	49392
9600/7/E	Yes	No	N/A	N/A	8276	8432
9600/7/E	No	No	N/A	N/A	24660	24816
9600/7/E	Yes	Yes	N/A	N/A	41044	41200
9600/7/E	No	Yes	N/A	N/A	57428	57584
19200/8/N	Yes	No	N/A	N/A	32	110
19200/8/N	No	No	N/A	N/A	16416	16494
19200/8/N	Yes	Yes	N/A	N/A	32800	32878
19200/8/N	No	Yes	N/A	N/A	49183	49262
19200/7/E	Yes	No	N/A	N/A	8224	8302
19200/7/E	No	No	N/A	N/A	24608	24686
19200/7/E	Yes	Yes	N/A	N/A	40992	41070
19200/7/E	No	Yes	N/A	N/A	57376	57454
38400/8/N	Yes	No	N/A	N/A	6	45

SERIN I, II, IISX, IIE, IIP

Table 2.10 Serial mode constants. (Continued)

Parameters (baud/bits/parity)	Inverting driver?	Open collector?	Stamp I		Stamp II/IIE	Stamp IISX/IIP
			Name	Value		
38400/8/N	No	No	N/A	N/A	16390	16429
38400/8/N	Yes	Yes	N/A	N/A	32774	32813
38400/8/N	No	Yes	N/A	N/A	49158	49197
38400/7/E	Yes	No	N/A	N/A	8198	8237
38400/7/E	No	No	N/A	N/A	24582	24621
38400/7/E	Yes	Yes	N/A	N/A	40966	41005
38400/7/E	No	Yes	N/A	N/A	57350	57398

Open collector modes only valid for SEROUT. Stamp I program can use the name or the value.

You don't have to specify a handshaking pin, but you can. Notice that the Stamp has no buffer for serial I/O. The sender must immediately stop sending when the handshake pin goes high. Many PC programs assume they have some leeway when it comes to handshaking.

Another point about the pin number. Although the Stamp II family only has I/O pins 0 to 15, you may specify 16 as the pin number if you wish. This is convenient because it uses the Stamp's programming port (which is a proper RS232 port) for communications.

Automatic echo

Be aware that the Stamp internally connects the programming port's input to its output, so using port 16 always echoes everything back to the sender. You'll need to take this into account when writing software that both talks and listens to pin 16.

The mode you specify for the Stamp II allows you to set the baud rate between 300 and 38,400 baud (see Table 2.10). You can also select the inverted or non-inverted modes, and it is possible to pick between eight bits and no parity, or seven bits and even parity. In any case, you'll always use one stop bit. Notice that the Stamp IISX and IIP use different mode parameters than the Stamp II.

If you select even parity (and seven bits) you are allowed to include the parity_label argument. The Stamp will jump to this label if a parity error occurs. You can also specify a timeout in milliseconds. If the Stamp doesn't get any input for the specified number of milliseconds, it will jump to the timeout_label. Notice that it doesn't matter if the input is what the Stamp expects. Any input will restart the timeout.

The input data list may be one or more byte variables separated by commas. In this case, the Stamp fills in each variable with an input character. However, many more complicated expressions are possible. You can use any of the modifiers in Table 2.11. These are similar to the DEBUG commands, with a few exceptions.

Execution speed
In most cases, the Stamp is not fast enough to receive data, do any appreciable processing on that data, and then read more data if the sender is transmitting at full speed. You'll have to design your programs around this limitation. Custom software is one alternative. Another is to try to read fixed-size blocks of data and ensure a pause between blocks.

Table 2.11 SERIN **modifiers.**

Modifier	Field width	Effect	Example
DEC	1–5	Decimal	DEC W1, DEC3 W2
SDEC	1–5	Signed decimal number (use with 16-bit numbers)	SDEC W1, SDEC3 W2
HEX	1–4	Hexadecimal format	HEX W1, HEX4 W2
SHEX	1–4	Signed hex (use with 16-bit number)	SHEX W1, SHEX4 W2
IHEX	1–4	Hex with preceding $	IHEX W1, IHEX4 W2
ISHEX	1–4	Signed hex with preceding $	ISHEX W1, ISHEX4 W2
BIN	1–16	Binary	BIN W1, BIN8 B5
SBIN	1–16	Signed binary	SBIN W1, SBIN8 B5
IBIN	1–16	Binary with preceding %	IBIN W1, IBIN4 B5
ISBIN	1–16	Signed binary with preceding %	ISBIN W1, ISBIN4 B5
STR	N/A	Reads ASCII string into byte array for count bytes; use second argument to specify end character (i.e., 13 is carriage return)	STR anary\5 STR anary\5\13

SERIN I, II, IISX, IIE, IIP

Table 2.11 SERIN **modifiers. (Continued)**

Modifier	Field width	Effect	Example
WAIT	N/A	Waits for bytes or string (up to six characters)	WAIT (13,10,B1) WAIT("ready")
WAITSTR	N/A	Waits for text in a byte array	WAITSTR anary
SKIP	numeric	Skips the specified number of bytes	SKIP 22
SPSTR	numeric	Reads the specified number of bytes into scratch pad RAM (starting at location 0); BS2P only	SPSTR 64

Compatibility Notes

Available on all Stamps; however, there are significant differences between the Stamp I and Stamp II families. Also, baud rate modes differ depending on which Stamp you use.

```
' Stamp I
' Read input in the form of x+y and print answer
top:
SERIN 1,T2400,(#W1, B9, #W2)
IF B9<>"+" THEN errm
W3=W1+W2
SEROUT 1,T2400,(#W3,CR)
GOTO top

errm:
SEROUT 1,T2400,("Unknown input",13)
GOTO top
' Stamp II
' Same program, but do subtraction too
A1 var Word
A2 var Word
op var Byte
baud con 84
sport con 16
TOP:
SEROUT sport,baud,["? "]
```

```
SERIN sport,baud,[SDEC A1, op, SDEC A2]
IF op="+" THEN ADDIT
IF op="-" THEN SUBIT
SEROUT sport,baud,["Bad input",13]
GOTO TOP
ADDIT:
  SEROUT sport,baud,[SDEC A1+A2,13]
  GOTO TOP
SUBIT:
  SEROUT sport,baud,[SDEC A1-A2,13]
  GOTO TOP
```

SEROUT **I, II, IISX, IIE, IIP**

Syntax

Stamp I
```
SEROUT pin, baudmode, ( {#}data {, ...} )
```

Stamp II
```
SEROUT pin, baudmode, {pace,}[output]
SEROUT pin\handshake, baudmode, {timeout, timeout_label,}[output]
```

Description

The SEROUT command outputs data suitable for transmission to RS232 devices via the specified pin. Of course, the Stamp's pins do not use the + and −12V that most RS232 devices use: therefore you'll often use driver circuitry to interface the Stamp pins to true RS232 levels. However, it is possible to interface some serial devices directly to the Stamp pin. Doing so violates the RS232 standard, but often works anyway.

The Stamp I's capabilities are quite simple. Each piece of data represents a byte to write to the serial device unless you precede it with the octothorpe (#). If you use the # prefix, the Stamp writes the number as a string of ASCII digits.

The Stamp II, as usual, has many more capabilities. You can specify a handshaking pin or use the pace argument to pause in-between bytes (the pace argument is in milliseconds). If you are using handshaking, you can select a timeout and specify a label that the Stamp will jump to if it does not get permission to send data in the time you allot. The baud rate and other parameters depend on the baudmode setting (see Table 2.10).

On the Stamp II family you can specify pin 16 to use the programming port instead of a general-purpose I/O pin. This is convenient since the programming port uses legal RS232 voltage levels.

The output data can be constants or variable and can include the modifiers you'll find in Table 2.12. These are similar to the modifiers you can use for the DEBUG command.

Table 2.12 SEROUT **modifiers.**

Modifier	Field width	Effect	Example
ASC?	N/A	ASCII value and character	ASC? B2
DEC	1–5	Decimal	DEC W1, DEC3 W2
SDEC	1–5	Signed decimal number (use with 16-bit numbers)	SDEC W1, SDEC3 W2
HEX	1–4	Hexadecimal format	HEX W1, HEX4 W2
SHEX	1–4	Signed hex (use with 16-bit number)	SHEX W1, SHEX4 W2
IHEX	1–4	Hex with preceding $	IHEX W1, IHEX4 W2
ISHEX	1–4	Signed hex with preceding $	ISHEX W1, ISHEX4 W2
BIN	1–16	Binary	BIN W1, BIN8 B5
SBIN	1–16	Signed binary	SBIN W1, SBIN8 B5
IBIN	1–16	Binary with preceding %	IBIN W1, IBIN4 B5
ISBIN	1–16	Signed binary with preceding %	ISBIN W1, ISBIN4 B5

One thing that both Stamp families have in common is that they can use an open collector RS232 mode (except when using pin 16 on the Stamp II). What this means is that the Stamp pulls the pin low for a 0, but leaves it in input mode for a 1. With the addition of a pull-up resistor, this allows multiple Stamps to connect to the same line. This is useful if you are building a network of Stamps, for example.

Compatibility Notes

Available on all Stamps. However, there are significant differences between the Stamp I and Stamp II series. The baud rate constants differ for each processor type.

Sample Program

See "SERIN I, II, IISX, IIE, IIP" on page 121 for a sample program.

SEROUT I, II, IISX, IIE, IIP

SHIFTIN **II, IISX, IIE, IIP**

Syntax

SHIFTIN datapin, clockpin, mode, [result {\bits}{, ...}]

Description

The SHIFTIN command is very useful for reading data from synchronous serial devices. Because of the popularity of single-chip processors like the Stamp, there are many devices including memory products, analog to digital converters, and digital to analog converters that use serial communications.

In typical use, the Stamp uses one pin (the datapin) to receive data and another pin to clock the data from the device. The SHIFTIN command generates a train of pulses on the clock pin. These pulses are about 16kHz on the Stamp II (and IIE) and 42kHz on the Stamp IISX and IIP. Using the mode argument you can configure the order of the bits and what part of the pulse indicates valid data (see Table 2.13).

Table 2.13 SHIFTIN **modes.**

Name	Value	Description
MSBPRE	0	Most significant bit first; sample before clock
LSBPRE	1	Least significant bit first; sample before clock
MSBPOST	2	Most significant bit first; sample after clock
LSBPOST	3	Least significant bit first; sample after clock

After each variable you wish to read, you can place a backslash and a number of bits (between 1 and 16). If you omit this argument, the Stamp reads eight bits.

Compatibility Notes

Available on the Stamp II series. The Stamp IISX and Stamp IIP use a faster transfer rate.

Sample Program

```
SHIFTIN 0,1,MSBPRE,[B1]
```

SHIFTOUT **II, IISX, IIE, IIP**

Syntax

```
SHIFTOUT datapin, clockpin, mode, [data {\bits}{,...}]
```

Description

Just as SHIFTIN reads data from a synchronous serial device, SHIFTOUT writes data to the same type of device. Everything about this command is practically identical to SHIFTIN, except that the data flows out of the Stamp instead of into the Stamp.

The Stamp holds the data valid on either clock edge, so the only thing you need to set in the mode parameter is the direction of the data bits. Using LSBFIRST causes the least significant bit to appear first, and MSBFIRST reverses the flow.

Compatibility Notes

Available on the Stamp II family only. The Stamp IISX and IIE use a faster transfer rate.

Sample Program

```
SHIFTOUT 0,1,MSBFIRST,[B1]
```

Section VI — Tables

When you are programming, you'll often find it useful to transform one value into another value. For example, you might want to convert a raw number between 0 and 16 into a pressure in pounds per square inch. The Stamp provides two commands, LOOKUP and LOOKDOWN, that let you create tables like this directly into the program, freeing up scarce memory resources for other purposes.

LOOKUP **I, II, IISX, IIE, IIP**

Syntax

Stamp I
```
LOOKUP index,(value0, value1, ...),result
```

Stamp II
```
LOOKUP index,[value0, value1, ...],result
```

Description

LOOKUP selects a value from the list based on the index argument and stores it in the result variable. If the index is 0, the Stamp selects the first value. If the index is 1, it selects the second value, and so on. If the index is greater than the number of items in the list, the Stamp doesn't change the result variable.

Compatibility Notes

Available on all Stamps. The Stamp I uses parentheses for the list while the other Stamps use square brackets.

Sample Program

```
B1=2
' Compute square root*10 of number from 0 to 10 by lookup
LOOKUP B1,[0,10,14,17,20,22,24,26,28,30,32],B2
' Print decimal number
DEBUG DEC B2/10,".",DEC B2//10
```

LOOKDOWN **I, II, IISX, IIE, IIP**

Syntax

Stamp I
```
LOOKDOWN match,(value0, value1, ...),result
```

Stamp II
```
LOOKDOWN match,{operator}[value0, value1, ...],result
```

Description

The LOOKDOWN command scans the list of values looking for a match between the values and the match parameter. If it finds a match, the Stamp stores the index in the list (0 being the first element) in the result variable.

By default, the match parameter must equal the value in the list. With the Stamp II, you can specify any relational operator to set the match criterion. In other words, you can use =, <, >, <>, <=, or >= to specify how the Stamp examines the list. Be careful, though: LOOKDOWN only works with unsigned numbers.

Compatibility Notes

Available on all Stamps. The Stamp I uses parentheses for the list while the other Stamps use square brackets.

Sample Program

```
' Convert a hex character to binary
b1="F"
' The following 2 lines are really 1 line
LOOKDOWN b1,["0","1","2","3","4","5","6","7","8","9",
    "A","B","C","D","E","F"],b2
DEBUG DEC b2, CR
' Same thing
LOOKDOWN b1,["0123456789ABCDEF"], B2
```

Section VII — Specialized I/O

The BSIIP has much greater I/O capabilities than its older siblings. In addition, one version of the BSIIP can have twice the I/O pins available on a regular Stamp. The BSIIP can handle the following special devices:

- **I2C** — A serial bus used by many microprocessor peripherals and memory devices.
- **LCD** — Parallel LCD displays that use a Hitachi (or Hitachi-style) controller.
- **1-Wire** — The Dallas Semiconductor 1-Wire bus.

The BSIIP is available in a 28-pin package that is compabile with an ordinary BSII. However, you can also find the device in a 40-pin package that offers twice the I/O pins. The trick is that the 32 pins are in two 16-bit groups. This allows all the commands to work with pin numbers between 0 and 15. You simply select which bank of I/O you want to use. That bank remains in force until you change the bank again.

Consider this command:

```
TOGGLE 4
```

On a 40-pin BSIIP you can't tell exactly what this will do without examining the code above it. It might toggle the main pin 4 or the auxiliary pin 4. Of course, when the program starts running the main bank is active, so if the previous code line were the entire program, there would be no ambiguity.

AUXIO, MAINIO **IIP**

Syntax

```
AUXIO
MAINIO
```

Description

The Stamp IIP uses two banks of I/O pins, each with 16 pins. Parallax labels the main port as P0-15 and the auxiliary port as X0-X15. After issuing an AUXIO command, further I/O command (like HIGH, TOGGLE, or PWM, for example) will refer to the corresponding auxiliary pins instead of the main port pins. MAINIO makes the commands operate on P0-15 again.

Compatibility Notes

Available on the Stamp IIP. Only useful on the 40-pin device.

Sample Program

```
AUXIO
HIGH 5      ' AUX 5 HIGH
MAINIO
LOW 5       ' MAIN 5 LOW
```

AUXIO, MAINIO IIP

I2CIN, I2COUT **BSIIP**

Syntax

```
I2CIN Pin, SlaveID, Address {\LowAddress}, [InputData]
I2COUT Pin, SlaveID, Address {\LowAddress}, [OutputData]
```

Description

The I^{2}C (or IIC) protocol allows memory and other devices to connect to a microcontroller via a two-wire bus. Each device has a unique slave ID that identifies it. In addition, memory devices have an address. These commands allow you to read or write from a specified address in a particular slave device.

The Pin argument can be either 0 or 8. This specifies the first pin used to connect to the I^{2}C bus (The SDA pin). The SCL pin will connect to the next I/O pin (either pin 1 or pin 9). The Address argument may range from 0 to 255. However, some devices require more than eight bits of address data. If this is the case, you'll use the Address argument and the topmost eight bits and the LowAddress argument as the lower eight bits.

The InputData list is similar to the data specified for a SERIN command. The OutputData list resembles data for SEROUT. You can send and receive binary data, or formated strings using modifiers like DEC or HEX.

See Chapter 6 for more on this command.

Compatibility Notes

Available on the BSIIP only.

IOTERM **BSIIP**

Syntax

```
IOTERM value
```

Description

With `IOTERM`, you can switch between the main and auxilliary bank based on a numeric argument or a variable. The `value` argument specifes a 0 to switch to the main I/O bank or a 1 to switch to auxilliary I/O.

Compatibility Notes

Available on the BSIIP only. Only useful on 40-pin devices.

Sample Program

```
banksel VAR bit
  banksel = 1        ' auxillary I/O
  IOTERM banksel
```

LCDCMD, LCDIN, LCDOUT **BSIIP**

Syntax

```
LCDCMD Pin, Command
LCDIN Pin, Command, [InputData]
LCDOUT Pin, Command, [OutputData]
```

Description

These commands operate on a Hitachi-style LCD in 4-bit mode. The `Pin` argument must be either 0, 1, 8, or 9. This determines which pin connects to the LCD's enable (E) pin. The LCD requires six other pins connected as follows:

Pin	When argument is 0 or 1	When argument is 8 or 9
RW -	2	10
RS	3	11
DB4	4	12
DB5	5	13
DB6	6	14
DB7	7	15

Each of the three instructions can send one command to the LCD. In addition, `LCDIN` and `LCDOUT` read or write data to the LCD using a list of data like that for `SERIN` or `SEROUT`.

Note that the LCD must be initialized by your program before you can use it. See the Sample Code section for an example of initializing the LCD.

See Chapter 7 for more on this command.

Compatibility Notes

Available on the BSIIP only.

```
'-----Define LCD constants-----
WakeUp CON %00110000 'Wake-up
FourBitMode CON %00100000 'Set to 4-bit mode
OneLine5x8Font CON %00100000 'Set to 1 display line, 5x8 font
OneLine5x10Font CON %00100100 'Set to 1 display line, 5x10 font
TwoLine5x8Font CON %00101000 'Set to 2 display lines, 5x8 font
TwoLine5x10Font CON %00101100 'Set to 2 display lines, 5x10 font
```

```
DisplayOff CON %00001000 'Turn off display, data is retained
DisplayOn CON %00001100 'Turn on display, no cursor
DisplayOnULCrsr CON %00001110 'Turn on display, with underline cursor
DisplayOnBLCrsr CON %00001101 'Turn on display, with blinking cursor
IncCrsr CON %00000110 'Auto-increment cursor, no display shift
IncCrsrShift CON %00000111 'Auto-increment cursor, shift display left
DecCrsr CON %00000100 'Auto-decrement cursor, no display shift
DecCrsrShift CON %00000101 'Auto-decrement cursor, shift display right
ClearDisplay CON %00000001 'Clear the display
HomeDisplay CON %00000010 'Move cursor and display to home position
ScrollLeft CON %00011000 'Scroll display to the left
ScrollRight CON %00011100 'Scroll display to the right
CrsrLeft CON %00010000 'Move cursor left
CrsrRight CON %00010100 'Move cursor right
MoveCrsr CON %10000000 'Move cursor to position (must add address)
MoveToCGRAM CON %01000000 'Move to CGRAM position (must add address)


main:
PAUSE 1000
GOSUB InitLCD
Start:
LCDOUT 1, ClearDisplay, ["I am a Basic Stamp"]
STOP


InitLCD:
LCDCMD 1, WakeUp 'Send wakeup sequence to LCD
PAUSE 10 'These pauses are necessary to meet the LCD specs
LCDCMD 1, WakeUp
PAUSE 1
LCDCMD 1, WakeUp
PAUSE 1
LCDCMD 1, FourBitMode 'Set buss to 4-bit mode
LCDCMD 1, TwoLine5x8Font 'Set to 2-line mode with 5x8 font
LCDCMD 1, DisplayOff 'Turn display off
LCDCMD 1, DisplayOn 'Turn display on with blinking cursor
LCDCMD 1, IncCrsr 'Set to auto-increment cursor (no display shift)
LCDCMD 1, ClearDisplay 'Clear the display
RETURN
```

OWIN, OWOUT **BSIIP**

Syntax
```
OWIN Pin, Mode, [InputData]
OWOUT Pin, Mode, [OutputData]
```

Description
The Dallas Semiconductor 1-Wire bus allows you to connect multiple devices to a microcontroller with one wire (not counting ground). The Pin argument for this command specifies the pin that corresponds to the 1-Wire bus (this pin should have a 4.7K pull-up resistor connected to it).

The Mode argument determines how the Stamp handles the transaction. This argument can range from 0 to 15 and is really a series of four bits:

Bit 3 — Set to 1 for a high-speed transfer.

Bit 2 — Set to 1 for a bit transfer (otherwise, byte).

Bit 1 — Backend reset (reset after transaction) if 1.

Bit 0 — Frontend reset (reset before transaction) if 1.

Using this command requires knowledge of the 1-Wire protocol and the specific 1-Wire device you are using. See Chapter 6 for more information about 1-Wire.

Compatibility Notes
Available on the BSIIP only.

Section VIII — Event Handling

The BSIIP can almost — almost — handle interrupts. It does this by using a polling event handling scheme. You specify one or more input pins that the Stamp will watch. When one of the pins reaches the state you specified, the Stamp will register that as an event. However, it only checks inbetween other instructions. That means that if you write a PAUSE command to halt execution for 10 seconds, polling will not occur for 10 seconds. (Of course, you could rewrite that PAUSE command to be a loop of 1,000 10mS pauses so the Stamp would poll every 10mS.)

When an event occurs, you can set an output pin to a desired state or you can run a program in a specific program slot. You can even do both. You can also write a program that waits for an event to occur.

Using polling requires several commands. You must define the condition you want to poll for with the POLLIN command. If you want to set up output pins, you'll use POLLOUT for that. POLLRUN selects the program you want to run in response to an event. Finally, POLLMODE orchestrates the interaction of the entire polling system. You can turn polling on or off using POLLMODE and also control what actions actually occur.

POLLIN **BSIIP**

Syntax

`POLLIN pin, state`

Description

This command tells the Stamp to register a polling event when the specified pin reaches the indicated state. Keep in mind that no polling occurs unless you set the `POLLMODE` command to perform polling to begin with.

Compatibility Notes

Available on the BSIIP only.

POLLMODE **BSIIP**

Syntax

POLLMODE mode

Description

This command set the polling mode which controls how the BSIIP handles event polling.

Mode 0	Deactivate polling and reset all POLLIN, POLLOUT, and POLLRUN commands.
Mode 1	Deactivate polling without resetting polling setup.
Mode 2	Activate polling without enabling POLLRUN.
Mode 3	Activate polling only enabling POLLRUN. Switch to mode 1 when event occurs.
Mode 4	Activate polling with all commands active. Switch to mode 2 when event occurs.
Mode 5	Clear POLLIN commands. Don't change polling status.
Mode 6	Clear POLLOUT commands. Don't change polling status.
Mode 7	Clear both POLLIN and POLLOUT commands. Don't change polling status.

In addition, if you add 8 to any of the above modes, the output pin (if any) will latch.

Compatibility Notes

Available on the BSIIP only.

POLLOUT **BSIIP**

Syntax

POLLOUT pin, state

Description

This command tells the Stamp to set the indicated pin to the given state when an event occurs (and the POLLMODE command allows this operation). You can use multiple POLLOUT commands to set up multiple output pins, if you wish.

Compatibility Notes

Available on the BSIIP only.

Sample Code

```
' Poll switches on P8 and P9 until one goes low
' When it does go low, turn on LED on P15
high 15          ' LED OFF
pollin 8,0       ' Watch pin 8
pollin 9,0       ' Watch pin 9
pollout 15,0     ' Set LED pin as poll indicator
pollmode 2       ' Try mode 10 here too
stopp:
' You could do anything you want here (FREQOUT, for example)
' The LED will light when P8 or P9 goes low
' As written, the poll will occur every 100mS. Try
' changing the pause to 2000 and see what happens
 pause 100
 goto stopp
```

POLLRUN **BSIIP**

Syntax

POLLRUN program

Description

This command tells the Stamp to run the program from the indicated program slot (0–7) when an event occurs (and the POLLMODE command allows this operation). Notice that this is like a GOTO and not a GOSUB. There is no way for the new program to return back to the exact point where execution stopped for the old program.

Compatibility Notes

Available on the BSIIP only.

POLLWAIT **BSIIP**

Syntax

```
POLLWAIT period
```

Description

Places the Stamp in a low power mode while waiting for a polled event to occur. The period parameter determines how often the Stamp wakes up to check for events and ranges from 0 to 8. To use this command, POLLMODE must be 2 or 4. The sleep period determines how often the Stamp checks for events. The lower the period, the more responsive the Stamp is, but the more power it consumes. A period of 8 causes the Stamp to respond quickly, but it does not enter the low power state.

Here are the times for the waiting period:

0	18mS
1	36mS
2	72mS
3	144mS
4	288mS
5	576mS
6	1,152mS (1.152 seconds)
7	2,304mS (2.304 seconds)
8	160µS

Compatibility Notes

Available on the BSIIP only.

```
' Poll switches on P8 and P9 until one goes low
' When it does go low, turn on LED on P15
high 15        ' LED OFF
pollin 8,0     ' Watch pin 8
pollin 9,0     ' Watch pin 9
pollout 15,0   ' Set LED pin as poll indicator
pollmode 2     ' Try mode 10 here too
stopp:
```

```
' Enter low power mode
pollwait 4
Debug "Event detected",cr
 goto stopp
```

Section IX — Math Operators

What good is a computer without math? The Basic Stamps handle quite a bit of math, but only integers. You'll find a more detailed description of math tricks you can do with Stamps earlier in this chapter. This section just details each individual operator.

+, -, *, /   I, II, IISX, IIE, IIP

Description

As you'd expect, the Stamp handles the normal four math operations: addition, subtraction, multiplication, and division.

There are several important restrictions you should keep in mind:

1. All math is integer only.
2. All math is, at most, 16-bit; the Stamp will truncate larger numbers.
3. Negative numbers are not supported, although you can work with them using the techniques presented in this chapter.
4. The Stamp processes math expressions from left to right, ignoring standard rules about operator precedence (the Stamp II and Stamp IISX allow you to use parentheses to override the order of evaluation, however).

Compatibility Notes

Available on all Stamps.

** I, II, IISX, IIE, IIP

Description

One of the problems that arises from the Stamp's 16-bit arithmetic limitation is that you can't easily multiply two 16-bit numbers. The reason is that multiplying two 16 bit numbers can generate a 32-bit result ($\$FFFF \times \$FFFF = \$FFFE0001$).

When you use the normal * operator, you only find the bottom 16 bits of the result. So if you write:

```
W1=$FFFF * $FFFF
```

W1 will equal 1 — not exactly the correct answer. However, you can learn what the missing 16 bits are by using the ** operator. If you execute:

```
W2=$FFFF ** $FFFF
```

W2 will equal $\$FFFE$. In this way, you can obtain all 32 bits of the answer.

Compatibility Notes

Available on all Stamps.

*/ II, IISX, IIE, IIP

Description

This odd operator can help you deal with fractions on the Stamp II (and IISX). Through an odd process, the */ operator is similar to multiplication, except it treats its second argument as two 8-bit quantities. The top eight bits represent a whole number, and the lower eight bits specify the numerator of a fraction (the denominator is always 256). Suppose you want to multiply the W1 register by 2.25. You can form the correct number for use with */ by observing that you really need 2 and $^{64}/_{256}$ (which is the same as 2.25). You could then write:

```
W1= W1 */ (2 << 8 + 64)
```

If you prefer hex notation, you could write:

```
W1=W1 */ $0240
```

Compatibility Notes

Available on the Stamp II series only.

// I, II, IISX, IIE, IIP

Description

Because division on the Stamp is an integer-only process, you need a way to find out the remainder (or modulus) of division. You probably remember from grade school (before you learned fractions and decimal numbers) that $^5/_2$ is 2 with a remainder of 1. The // operator returns the remainder from division.

This operator has many practical uses. In particular, computing X//N will produce a result that is sure to be less than N. Look at the code under "RANDOM I, II, IISX, IIE, IIP" on page 73 for a practical application of this.

Compatibility Notes

Available on all Stamps.

>>, << II, IISX, IIE, IIP

Description

These operators (borrowed from the C language) shift a number, bit by bit, to the right (>>) or the left (<<). Each bit you move to the left effectively multiplies by 2, and every bit you move to the right practically divides by 2. These operators may be faster than doing real multiply and divide instructions.

Consider the following code:

```
B1=100
B1=B1>>3
DEBUG DEC B1
```

The result in W1 will be the same as $100/8$ (in other words, 100/2/2/2 or $100/2^3$). Consider the same example, using binary:

```
B1=%01100100
B1=B1>>3
DEBUG IBIN B1    ' Answer = %00011001
```

Compatibility Notes

Available on the Stamp II series only.

MIN, MAX **I, II, IISX, IIE, IIP**

Description

The MIN operator allows you to use a value (the first argument) subject to a minimum value provided by the second argument. This is somewhat confusing since the result of the MIN operator is actually whichever of its arguments is *greater*. The MAX operator returns whichever of its arguments is *smaller*.

So 30 MIN 100 results in a value of 100 and 100 MAX 30 returns 30. If you are used to the way C and other languages handle these operators, you'll find this counterintuitive. The way to think of it is that the MAX operator clamps a value to a maximum, while the MIN operator ensures the value is at a specified minimum value.

Compatibility Notes

Available on all Stamps.

ABS **II, IISX, IIE, IIP**

Description

This operator has no effect on a positive number, but it negates negative numbers. The result is, therefore, always positive. Because the Stamp represents negative numbers in two's compliment form, this operator effectively inverts its argument and adds 1 if the original argument has its top-most bit set to 1.

Compatibility Notes

Available only on the Stamp II series.

SQR **II, IISX, IIE, IIP**

Description

This operator takes the square root of a number. Of course, the result is an integer, so the square root of 9 is 3, and the square root of 10 is 3.

Compatibility Notes

Available on the Stamp II series only.

SIN, COS **II, IISX, IIE, IIP**

Description

These two operators compute the sine and cosine of an angle. The angle is expressed in *brads* (short for binary radians). What this means is that, for the purposes of these operators, a circle has 255 divisions (as opposed to 360° or 2π radians). Also, the calculations are based on a circle of radius 127 so that an integer answer is meaningful. If you need to calculate items using trigonometry, these operators are great. For most programs, you'll never use them.

Compatibility Notes

Available only on the Stamp II series.

DIG **II, IISX, IIE, IIP**

Description

When you need to dissect a number into its component digits, the DIG operator will help. You supply a number and the number of the digit you want. For example, suppose you had an LCD display attached to the Stamp, and you could write an ASCII character to it by placing the character in the char variable and calling wr_LCD. You might write code like this:

```
b VAR byte
b=122  ' number to display
' could use a loop here
char = b DIG 2 + '0'   ' write 3rd digit
GOSUB wr_LCD
char = b DIG 1 + '0'   ' write 2nd digit
GOSUB wr_LCD
char = b DIG 0 + '0'   ' write 1st digit
GOSUB wr_LCD
```

Compatibility Notes

Only available on the Stamp II series.

Section X — Logical Operators

Computers operate on binary numbers no matter how we choose to represent them. The Stamp has several operators aimed at manipulating the bits in a number. You might consider the << and >> logical operators, but I prefer to think of them as math operators because you usually use them to multiply and divide.

If you are accustomed to other programming languages, you might be surprised that the connecting words for IF statements (like AND) are not really logical operators. Instead, these are integral parts of the IF statement.

&, |, ^   I, II, IISX, IIE, IIP

Description

These operators are the normal logical and (&), logical or (|), and logical exclusive–or (^) operators. These examine each bit in the two arguments and apply the indicated logic function to generate the result. Here's a few examples:

```
B1=%11110000
B2=%10101110
B3= B1 & B2     ' B3=%10100000
B3= B1 | B2      ' B3=%11111110
B3=B1 ^ B2       ' B3=%01011110
```

As you can see, the & operator requires that both bits in the arguments be 1 before it will generate a 1 in the result. The | operator sets a 1 if either (or both) bits in the arguments are 1. The ^ operator sets a 1 in the result if either argument has a 1 in that position, but not if both arguments have a 1.

It is possible to flip all the bits in a byte by using the ^ operator with $FF as one of the arguments. To flip a word, use $FFFF. This is often called *logical inversion* or the NOT function.

Compatibility Notes

Available on all Stamps.

&/, |/, ^/ I

Description

These operators perform similar functions to the &, |, and ^ functions, but they also invert the result.

Compatibility Notes

Only available on the Stamp I. You can use combinations of the basic logic functions to achieve the same results on the other Stamps.

REV **II, IISX, IIE, IIP**

Description

This operator extracts the specified number of bits (starting at the right) from the argument and reverses them. Here's an example:

```
debug bin ? %11001011 REV 4 ' result(%1101)
```

Compatibility Notes

Only available on the Stamp II series.

DCD **II, IISX, IIE, IIP**

Description

Use the DCD operator when you want to convert a 4-bit number to one of 16 bits. For example, if you want a word with bit 5 set, you could write:

```
W1=DCD 5   ' W1=%0000000000100000
```

Of course, you could just code this as a constant. The real value to using DCD is when the bit number is not known until run time.

Compatibility Notes

Only available on the Stamp II series.

NCD **II, IISX, IIE, IIP**

Description

The NCD operator is the reverse of the DCD operator. Given a number, NCD returns the highest bit that is set in that number. Here are a few examples:

```
B1=NCD %1100000000000000   ' B1=15
B1=NCD %0000000000000010   ' B1=1
B1=NCD %0000000100000001   ' B1=8
B1=NCD 0 ' B1=0
```

Compatibility Notes

Only available on the Stamp II series.

Exercises

1. What is an alternate way to write this statement?

```
LET x=10
```

2. What is the difference between SEROUT and SHIFTOUT?

3. Compute, using Stamp math the following expressions:

   10 + 3/3

   19//4

   6 − 3 + 2

4. How can you shorten this program?

```
    main:
        gosub bsyled
        gosub action
        gosub notbsy
        gosub ckinput
        gosub process
        goto main


bsyled:   LOW 4
            return


notbsy:   HIGH 4
            return


action:
            . . . .    ' Some processing
            return


process:
          gosub bsyled
            . . . .     ' Some processing
          gosub notbsy
          return
```

```
ckinput:
            . . . .     ' Do something here
        return
```

For answers to the exercises, see the Answer Key, page 426.

3

Chapter 3

Games and Tools: Digital I/O

In Chapter 1, you read about binary (base 2) numbers. I made the observation that people probably used base 10 because they have 10 fingers. Early attempts at building digital computers using base 10 math (like the *Harvard IBM Automatic Sequenced-Controlled Calculator* and the *Eniac*) were extremely complex because they had to handle ten different states for each digit. Electronic hardware is much better at keeping track of two states: on and off.

Someone eventually recognized that binary was better for computers and simplified the design of computers significantly. Some would argue, however, that this complicated the programming of computers for humans. Humans aren't very comfortable with binary. That's too bad. If we learned to count in binary, you could count to 1,024 on your fingers!

Of course, many of the uses for a microcontroller like the Basic Stamp are actually quite suitable for binary representation. For example, to monitor a keypad, you'll need to know if each switch is up or down (on or off). You might monitor a limit switch in a tank of liquid. When it turns on, you might turn off one pump and start another one. All of these are on/off operations and well suited for digital control.

In this chapter, you'll:

- learn about the electrical issues involved in connecting the Stamp to other devices,
- explore how to use the Stamp's I/O commands,
- build several small game projects,
- build a cable tester, and
- build a logic probe.

These projects will show you how to montior and control digital signals. The same techniques will be useful in nearly every project you build — even the most sophisticated device will probably have status indicators or command switches.

Remember: when the Stamp resets, all pins are set to inputs. This is a safety feature as it prevents the Stamp from conflicting with other circuitry and also prevents damage to the Stamp. Imagine if a pin that you connected directly to ground became an output. Your Stamp might melt down trying to drive the short circuit to ground. For practical purposes, a pin in an input state might as well be an open circuit. In reality, the input appears as a very large resistor to ground (perhaps 5M or more) as long as the input voltage stays in the normal 0–5V range.

I/O by Command

The Stamp has several ways you can interact with digital devices. You often have a choice of which method you want to use. Usually, your best choice depends on the exact task at hand.

If you are concerned with turning things on and off, you'll often want to treat each I/O bit as a separate entity using I/O commands. That makes it easy to keep track of what's on and what's off. However, it can waste some program space. The alternative (using I/O registers; see the next section) is very efficient when you want to read or alter a group of I/O pins together.

The easiest way to manipulate I/O bits is to use the specific commands for handling I/O. These include INPUT, OUTPUT, REVERSE, HIGH, LOW, and TOGGLE. With these commands you can change a pin from input to output and make an output pin a 1 or a 0. What you can't do is read the state of a pin. For that you'll need to resort to register-based access, discussed shortly.

You'll often see code that looks like this:

```
OUTPUT 4
HIGH 4    ' Turn on LED
```

There isn't anything wrong with this code *per se*, but it isn't the most efficient code possible. If you read the description of the HIGH command on page 98, you'll see that it forces the pin to become an output. Therefore, the first line in the above code snippet is superfluous. It doesn't hurt anything, but it isn't necessary.

It is easy to think of HIGH as turning something on and LOW as turning something off. However, this isn't always the case — it depends on what you are driving with the pin. Figure 3.1 shows two ways to connect an LED to a Stamp. LED 1 will light when you issue a HIGH 0 command. LED 2 lights with a LOW 1 command.

For the Stamp, the way you wire the LED is up to you. However, some devices will have specific requirements. Also, designers used to working with conventional microprocessors usually use the configuration that turns the load on when the pin is low. That's because many processors (and other logic components) can sink more current than they can source. That is, they can only supply 5V at a low current (and often less than 5V), but they can draw quite a bit of current when they connect the load to ground.

Figure 3.1   Connecting LEDs.

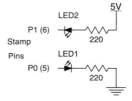

The Stamp I can source 20mA from each pin, or sink 25mA — not much of a difference. However, you must not sink more than 50mA total nor source more than 40mA. In other words, if you are sinking 25mA into one pin, the remaining pins should not be sinking more than 25mA total to avoid damaging the chip. The Stamp II has the same limits, except that the total current restrictions are on each set of eight I/O pins. So the total sink for pins 0 to 7 must be 50mA or less and the total sink for pins 15 to 8 must also be less than 50mA.

The Stamp IISX can sink and source 30mA of current from each pin. Each group of eight pins should not exceed 60mA of current in either direction.

You might wonder how you can calculate these values — consider Figure 3.1. Suppose each LED consumes 20 mA. LED 1 requires that the Stamp source current and the other one has the Stamp sinking current.

Avoid this common bug

The digital I/O instructions require a pin number. This can be a constant or a variable (or, on the Basic Stamp II, an expression) that indicates the pin number to use. A common programming bug often appears when you use these statements. Suppose you are programming a Stamp II and you want to make pin 1 an input. It is very natural to write:

```
INPUT in1
```

This is incorrect. In reality, you will read pin 1 (which will have a 1 or a 0 in it) and then make that pin an input. So the effect is that you've just made pin 0 or pin 1 an input. If you get lucky and pin 1 happens to have 1 on it, the code will work. If you are unlucky, it won't work. If you are really unlucky, it will work sometimes and other times it won't. If you are working with pins other than 0 and 1, it will never work anyway. The correct statement, of course, is:

```
INPUT 1
```

I/O with Registers

Using the pin numbers for I/O is fine when you want to treat each individual bit as a separate entity. However, there are many cases where you want to work with bits as a binary number. For example, you might need to read data from a PC's parallel port (8-bit data). Another common case occurs when you want to drive a seven-segment LED. It would be inconvenient to have to set and reset each segment using HIGH and LOW.

A better idea is to use the I/O registers to treat the ports (and their direction registers) and multi-bit quantities. In the Stamp I, you can use the 16-bit PORT register to refer to the I/O port and direction bits together (the direction bits are in the high byte of the word). If you want to treat the I/O port as a byte, use the PINS register. The direction bits are in the DIRS register. Finally, you can treat each bit individually using the PIN7 to PIN0 and DIR7 to DIR0 registers.

If I/O pin 0 is already set as an output, the following two lines do the same thing:

```
HIGH 0
PIN0=1
```

Of course, the HIGH command forces the pin to be an output, but the assignment statement does not. It is often more compact to set initial conditions using the registers. Consider this startup code:

```
OUTPUT 0
OUTPUT 1
OUTPUT 2
OUTPUT 7
PIN7=1
PIN2=1
PIN1=1
PIN0=1
```

You'd have better code efficiency with this code (which does the same thing):

```
PORT=%1000011110000111
```

Initial values
When the Stamp resets, it clears all of its registers. This includes the DIRS I/O direction register. That means that all variables initially contain 0 and all I/O pins are initially inputs. That means you can save a bit of program space by not initializing pins as inputs. Of course, to save the most space, you'll use the DIRS register to set all the pins at once (as in the previous example) anyway.

The same principles apply to the Stamp II family processors. However, because these chips have 16 I/O bits, the names are a bit different. DIRS, INS, and OUTS refer to the entire 16-bit direction register, inputs, and outputs respectively. You can also replace the S with an H (high-byte), L (low-byte), A, B, C, or D (nibbles from lowest to highest). So to read the high eight bits of inputs, you could refer to INH. To write to the most-significant four bits of the output, use OUTD. You can also refer to each bit individually by replacing the S with a number from 0 to 15 (that is, IN5, DIR0, etc.).

Another technique you can employ with the Stamp II family is to use modifiers with I/O registers. For example, instead of using IN5, you could use INS.BIT5. This is a matter of personal style, and there really isn't any difference as far as the Stamp knows.

An LED Counter

Look at the simple program in Listing 3.1. It counts from 0 to 15 and writes the value out to some LEDs. You can breadboard the circuit you'll find in the schematic (see Figure 3.2) or use the Stamp activity board from Parallax. Notice the LEDs are positioned so they must be low to light. This complicates the code somewhat. Why? To make the LEDs turn on when we count, we have to invert the bit pattern before sending it to the output port. That's the purpose of the exclusive–or operator (^). Taking the exclusive–or of a number and $FF effectively flips all the bits in the number.

Listing 3.1   The LED counter.

```
' Stamp I
' dirs=$FF
' Stamp II
dirs=$F00


top:

for b0=0 to 15
' Stamp I:
'   pins=b0*16^$FF
' Stamp II - per schematic or on Stamp Activity Board
  outc=b0^$FF
  pause 1000
next
goto top
```

Figure 3.2   Circuit for the LED counter.

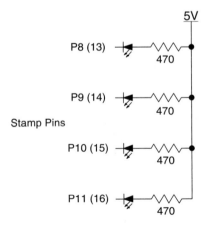

Driving Larger Loads

Lighting LEDs is great fun. However, many real-world devices are not suitable for driving directly from a Stamp pin. A relay is a common example. A relay coil might require 50–100mA to turn on. Incandescent lamps are another example. Even a lamp that doesn't nominally draw more current than an LED can present a problem. The lamp's rated current is usually what it will draw once the filament heats up. Before that, the lamp may draw much more current (known as *inrush current*). This can damage a chip's output circuits, if you don't take it into account. Other large loads include solenoids, annunciators (like buzzers), and valves.

Sometimes these loads don't even require too much current. Sometimes they need more voltage. For example, a 12V light bulb, no matter how small, won't work well with a 5V supply. In either case, voltage or current, you'll need a way to switch the load indirectly.

There are several ways you can switch power to a load indirectly. The simplest way is to use a transistor. It is easy to use ordinary transistors to switch DC current. A transistor has three terminals: the base, the collector, and the emitter. They also come in two flavors: NPN and PNP. In general, you'll want to use NPN transistors to switch between a device and ground. Use PNP transistors to switch between a positive supply and a load.

Without going into too much transistor theory, you want to saturate the transistor. A transistor in saturation acts like a closed switch. To turn things off, you want to cut off the transistor making it look like an open switch. Designing circuits with transistors that operate in the magic region between cut off and saturation is hard. Designing transistor circuits that either saturate or don't is easy.

Consider an NPN transistor first. The base of the transistor is the lead you will use to control the switch. The emitter is the connection to ground. The collector will connect to the ground side of the load (a light bulb in Figure 3.3). For our purposes, the base and emitter of the transistor is a diode (like an LED without the light). This diode will drop about 0.6 or 0.7V (depending on the temperature and other factors). In other words, the base will be about 0.7V higher than the emitter (or, conversely, the emitter will be 0.7V below the base).

Figure 3.3 Driving a light bulb.

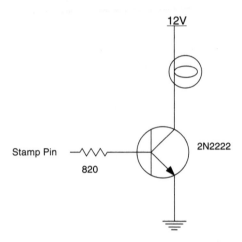

If there is 0V on the base, the diode won't conduct. In fact, when there is less than approximately 0.6V on the base, the diode won't conduct. When the make-believe diode isn't conducting, the transistor is cut off. That means the load won't get any appreciable power (so the light bulb is dark).

If the diode does conduct, however, the transistor will turn on. The collector will sink current (to the emitter). How much current? Well, that depends on several factors. However, to simplify, you can calculate the approximate current by multiplying the base current (the current flowing through the make-believe diode) by the transistor's beta (a value specified by the manufacturer).

If you put enough current into the base, you'll eventually get to the point where the collector current doesn't go up any more. That point is saturation. In theory, the collector voltage at saturation should be the same as the emitter voltage (0V in this case). However, in practice there will be 0.1 or 0.2V on the collector, which isn't a big problem.

How do you feed current into the transistor's base? Just connect it to a Stamp pin through a resistor. The resistor will set the current flowing into the base. You know the emitter is at 0V (it is shorted to ground, after all). Because the diode's drop is about 0.7V, you can see that if the diode is conducting, the base must be at 0.7V. The Stamp's output pin will be at 5V when you turn it on, so the current through the resistor is (5–0.7)/R. This will be the base current.

When you want to use a transistor, you'll need to select one carefully. First, make sure you have the right type (NPN or PNP). Then you need to make sure the transistor's maximum voltage and current specifications exceed your needs. Common transistors for this type of service are 2N2222As and 2N3904s. A 2N2222A's collector current is rated at 800mA and it can handle about 40V on its collector. Of course, for safety, you want to be below these maximums. Also, at high currents, the device may need a heat sink to keep it from melting down.

Determining the amount of current required to saturate the transistor can be a little tricky. Studying the manufacturer's data sheets will usually show a graph of collector current versus base current. Most often this is really a family of curves, with each curve representing a different collector current. Each curve resembles a letter L that curves instead of bends (see Figure 3.4). You want to pick the curve that is nearest your load's current consumption and select a base current that is on the horizontal part of that curve.

Figure 3.4   Collector current curves for a 2N2222A.

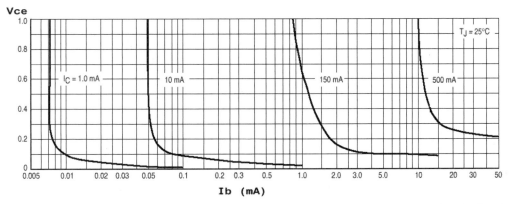

For example, referring to Figure 3.3 and 3.4, suppose the light bulb draws 125mA. The closest curve on the chart is 150mA. Looking at the curve, you can see that anything around 3 or 4mA would do. For safety's sake, pick 5mA.

Recall that the base current will be about (5–0.7)/R. If you want the base current to be 0.005 (5mA), you can solve for R and get the value of 860Ω. Of course, that isn't a standard resistor value, but an 820 will do.

Many people will select the base resistor empirically and that is usually adequate for most noncritical designs. For example, using a 220Ω resistor in the base would certainly slam the transistor into saturation (with nearly 20mA of base current). The tradeoff is, of course, that the more current you draw from the Stamp, the less is available for other purposes. Also, battery-powered systems will want to conserve as much power as possible. So while it is possible to guess at the resistor value, try to strike a reasonable compromise between making sure it works, and making sure it works well.

Driving Relays and Other Inductive Loads

One option for switching a load indirectly is to use a relay. This is especially attractive when you have an AC circuit to switch, or you want complete isolation between the microprocessor and the load. A relay is nothing more than an electromagnet and a switch. When you energize the electromagnet (just a coil of wire, really), it causes the switch to turn on. Like real switches, you can get relays with a wide variety of contact designs.

Some relay coils take quite a bit of current, but others take very little. You might be tempted to try to drive a small coil-style relay directly from a Stamp. Don't do it. Although you might get away with it, it is more likely that you will destroy the Stamp.

Loads that have large coils of wire in them exhibit inductance. Motors, relays, and heating elements can all have significant inductance. Normally you think of inductance as unimportant when working with DC current. Why do you care about inductance when turning on a relay?

The relay's coil (or any coil) conducts DC. But it also creates a magnetic field. This magnetic field also generates electricity in the coil. When you turn the relay on (or off), the change in current causes a reverse current to flow momentarily. This voltage depends on the speed of the voltage change and can be quite high. Your transistor can only stand so much voltage before it fails.

To prevent this problem, you can shunt the relay coil with a diode. The banded end of the diode connects to the positive side of the coil. The other end connects to the grounded end of the coil (that is, the end connected to the transistor's collector). During normal operation, this diode effectively doesn't do anything. However, when the coil generates a reverse voltage, this diode effectively shorts it out. You can see the diode and relay in Figure 3.5).

There are some devices today known as *solid-state* relays. These relays aren't really relays and they won't usually require a reverse diode. There are also many solid-state switching devices (for example, a 4016 CMOS bilateral switch IC) that, of course, have no coils and therefore don't need a diode.

Switching a Relay

Try building the circuit in Figure 3.5. If you don't have a relay, use an LED instead. Measure the voltages at the base and collector when the relay (or LED) is on and when it is off. You can use the code in Listing 3.2 to exercise the circuit. Before you try the circuit, predict if the relay will be turned on or off by the first TOGGLE statement.

Figure 3.5   Driving a relay.

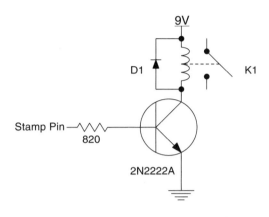

Listing 3.2   Exercising the relay.

```
LOOP:
  TOGGLE 0
  PAUSE 1000
GOTO LOOP
```

Switching Power with PNP Transistors

Most of the time you can arrange your circuit so that you can switch the ground on and off. However, there are a few cases where you need to switch a positive voltage on and off. Consider the case where you want to turn 12V on and off. In this case, you'll need a PNP transistor. Saturating a PNP transistor is nearly the same as operating a NPN transistor, except that the base-emitter diode is reversed. That means that to operate, the base must be 0.7V below the emitter. The most common PNP transistor you'll find is the 2N3906 which has similar characteristics to a 2N3904.

Making the base lower than the emitter is easy to arrange if you connect the voltage (12V in this case) to the emitter. Then you can bring the base to 11.3V (or less) to turn the transistor on. Of course, the Stamp can output 0V which would turn the transistor on, but it can't output the 12V needed to turn the transistor off. However, it is easy enough to use a NPN transistor to switch the ground to the PNP transistor (see Figure 3.6).

Figure 3.6 Switching voltage with a PNP transistor.

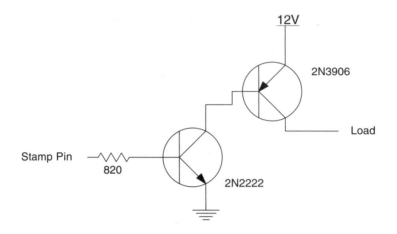

A PNP Driver

Add a PNP transistor to the previous circuit (as in Figure 3.6). Depending on your load, you may also need a small (less than 1K) resistor between the 2N2222's collector and the 2N3906's base. You'll need to ground the relay coil (or LED) and connect the other end to the PNP transistor's collector. Use the same software to toggle the relay. Will the relay be on or off at first? Measure the voltages around each transistor.

Other Switches

There are other transistor styles that you can use. There are a variety of field-effect transistors (FETs) that offer very good switching characteristics. You can also use ordinary or solid-state relays.

For maximum isolation, you can use a variety of *optoisolators*. These are nothing more than an LED and a light-sensitive transistor built together. When you pass current through the LED, it acts like base current to the transistor. This can be useful when you want to make certain that there is practically no connection between the processor and the external load. Relays offer similar isolation, but they are slower, and prone to mechanical failure (not to mention noisy).

For small switching jobs, there are several CMOS bilateral switches available on an IC (for example, the 4066). These chips act like solid-state relays (for DC only).

However, they don't have as much current handling capacity, and for most jobs a transistor will work better.

For nearly all purposes that you'll run into with Stamp programming, a regular transistor will do the job. Just make sure that the transistor's ratings are sufficient for the job at hand. If you will handle more than a few hundred milliamps of collector current, you'll want to consider heat sinking the transistor (a *heat sink* is a metal radiator that fits over the transistor and removes waste heat).

A Word About AC Loads

If you are considering switching AC power, isolation is essential. Relays are doubtlessly the easiest way to switch AC power. There are other devices like triacs and certain optoisolators that can do the job also. However, you need to understand the safety issues involved before using these devices. Don't build AC circuits on solderless breadboards and always use adequately-sized wires. Make sure all connections are insulated.

If you are using relays, they are fairly safe. If you want to use a solid-state solution, you should prototype your switch (but not on a breadboard) before connecting it to the Stamp. You should be able to operate your circuit by connecting it to 5V and 0V through a low-valued resistor. You shouldn't find any high voltages at the resistor if your circuit is working correctly. When you are sure things are working right, then you can connect the Stamp.

Another handy way to control AC devices is with the Stamp II's XOUT command. In conjunction with an X10 powerline modem, this command can transmit codes to X10 controllers. These controllers, in turn, can turn AC devices on or off and dim incandescent lights. The X10 controllers are common and available at many places like Radio Shack and even home improvement stores. The modem you need is a little harder to find. There are several advantages to using X10 instead of controlling AC with a relay or other device. First, you have complete isolation between the device and the Stamp. The X10 modules are very safe and reasonably priced. One X10 modem can control many devices, saving I/O pins. Finally, the Stamp can be physically away from the X10 modules as long as everything is on the same power company transformer.

Simulating Open Collector Outputs

There are many occasions where standard logic-level outputs are not adequate. Consider the case of turning on a 12V lamp. The Stamp (and other logic devices) can't directly switch 12V. As pointed out earlier, you can use an NPN transistor. What if this transistor was built into the chip? That's the idea behind open collector outputs.

A logic circuit that has an open collector output simply uses an NPN transistor and the output is the transistor's collector. That means the output has two states: 0V and (for practical purposes) open circuit. This allows the device to ground a higher voltage load with no problems.

Another use of open collector outputs is to implement a technique known as wired-or. Consider the case where two (or more) devices want to light a single LED. If you connect two normal outputs to the LED, you'll have problems. Suppose the first output is high (5V) and the second output is low (0V). Current will flow between the two pins. At best, you won't be able to predict the output state. At worst, one or both of the output transistors will blow!

Of course, you could use an OR gate, but that's an extra chip. If the outputs are open collector, however, you can safely connect the pins together. If either (or both) outputs are at 0V, the LED will light. If neither output is at 0V, no current flows and the LED remains dark.

What happens if you need a logic level 1 instead of an open circuit? Simply connect a pull-up resistor to the pins. The pull-up resistor can even connect to a different voltage (like +12V or –5V). This is commonly called *wired-or*, but really it is more *wired-nor* because any low output makes the output low.

The Stamp doesn't have any open collector outputs. However, to some extent, you can simulate open collector outputs (especially for wired-or service). The trick is to use the LOW command to output a 0, and the INPUT command to output a 1 (open circuit). Of course, you can do the same thing by manipulating the I/O registers.

Is this really open collector? For many purposes, the answer is yes. This will work fine with 5V wired-or systems. However, you can't use these where the voltage on the pin will go below 0V or exceed 5V. To understand why, you need to know a little about the design of the Stamp's internal microprocessor (a Microchip PIC microprocessor).

To protect the chip, each I/O pin on the PIC has a very hefty diode connected to 5V and another diode connected to ground. This prevents the voltage on the pin from exceeding about 5.7V or dropping below –0.7V. While this is good for protecting the chip, it prevents you from completely simulating an open collector output. As long as the voltage on the pin ranges between 0 and 5V, the diodes aren't important and you usually forget they are there. But if the voltage is out of range, the diodes turn on and you must take them into account.

Working with Pulses

Some digital signals are less concerned with the logic level of the signal, and more concerned with the length of time the signal stays in one state. This is known as a *pulse*. The Stamp is adept at creating pulses, timing pulses, and even counting the number of pulses on a pin.

The Stamp I has two commands related to pulses: PULSOUT and PULSIN. The PULSOUT command inverts the pin you specify for a particular amount of time and then returns the pin to its original output level. You specify the time in 10S units. PULSIN works the same way except you also specify the pin's desired state. The pin must be in the opposite state before PULSIN will begin looking for a transition to the state you specified. When the Stamp detects the leading edge of the pulse, it begins timing (again in 10S units) looking for the trailing edge. If the Stamp doesn't detect the leading edge within 0.65535 seconds, it returns 0.

The Stamp II (and IISX) have the same two commands. On these Stamps, the resolution is greater, but that reduces the length of the pulses you can measure. On the Stamp II, the maximum pulse you can measure is 131mS. The Stamp IISX tops out at 52mS.

The Stamp II family also has the COUNT command. It measures the number of pulses that occur on a pin over an interval you specify in milliseconds (0.4mS interval on the Stamp IISX).

Many practical inputs take the form of pulses. For example, consider a motor or engine rotating a shaft. If you want to know the revolutions per minute (RPM) of the shaft, you have several options:

- Put a white spot (or a black spot if the shaft is light-colored) on the shaft, shine a light on it, and read the reflected light using a phototransistor or other optical sensor.

- Put a magnet on the shaft and watch for the magnet with a reed switch or a hall effect sensor.

- Attach a toothed disk so that the shaft turns it. Pass the teeth through a light source and a light sensor (or a special optical interrupter component designed for this service).

No matter which method you use, you'll get a series of pulses that correspond to the shaft's RPMs. Of course, which method is best depends on your specific application. For example, putting a white dot on the crankshaft of a car is a bad idea, because the car will get dirty, hiding the spot. You may not be able to mount a toothed disk on some equipment. Optical solutions may not work well when ambient light levels are high.

Counting Pulses

Figure 3.7 shows a simple way to connect an LED and a photo transistor to count pulses. Infrared LEDs and detectors work well; try a Radio Shack 276-142 which has a matched detector and LED. The big challenge to making this work is blocking enough ambient light to make the transistor switch off (adjusting the sensitivity would take more components). Try placing electrical tape around the transistor and leaving just a small opening towards the LED. In practice, you'll often mount the detector in a tube to cut down on ambient light, but for this experiment, electrical tape should do the trick. Because the LED emits IR light, you won't be able to easily verify that it is really on. You can measure the voltage across it with a voltmeter, of course.

Figure 3.7   Detecting pulses with infrared light.

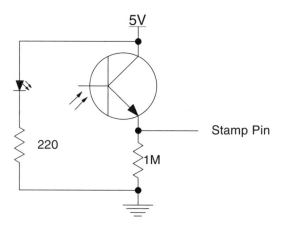

Just to be sure things are working, try reading the Stamp pin input and turning the LED on and off. You should detect the difference. If not, consider measuring the voltage at the Stamp pin. If it changes when you turn the LED on and off, but not enough for the Stamp to read a 1 and a 0, you probably have too much ambient light, or too much space between the LED and the transistor. If the voltage doesn't change, check to make sure you have both the LED and the transistor connected properly.

Once you can sense the light change, cut a disk of cardboard with one protrusion that will interrupt the light beam. Place the disk on a motor shaft, or, if you have no motor, just stick a toothpick through the middle. Load the software in Listing 3.3 and rotate the disk between the light and the sensor. Each time the protrusion breaks the beam, the Stamp will count that as a pulse. If you have one tooth on the disk, you'll find two pulses. One will correspond to the time it takes for the tooth to pass over the sensor. The other will be the time it takes for the tooth to make the rest of the trip and return to the sensor. The total time can tell you the speed of the shaft because you know the circumference of the disk.

Listing 3.3   Counting pulses.

```
LOW 9  ' LED on
top:
pulsin 7,0,w1
debug dec w1,cr
goto top
```

Of course, you can add teeth to decrease the time of each pulse. This will allow for more accurate measurements, especially at slow shaft speeds. Then you'll need to multiply by the number of teeth to get the correct value for the entire disk.

You can also use the same circuit to demonstrate the COUNT command. You could use this to count the number of teeth that pass the sensor in a specified time period. Of course, you could count anything that breaks the light beam, not just teeth on a wheel.

Reading Buttons

How hard can it be to read buttons? Generally you'll connect a button to ground on one side, a Stamp pin on the other, and then use a pull-up resistor on the Stamp pin. That means that if the button is up (open circuit), the Stamp will read a 1 and when someone pushes the button (closes the circuit), the Stamp will read a 0. Simple, right?

There are several problems with this approach. First, real buttons tend to bounce. When you push them, they don't just close the circuit. Instead, they may make and break the contact several times over the space of a few milliseconds. The severity of this bouncing varies depending on the design of the switch.

There are many ways to deal with this problem (including special hardware circuits). The easiest way is to simply not read the switches very fast. For example, suppose you are building a child's organ. Each button makes a tone that lasts 250mS. You can expect that the switch will be through bouncing after 250mS, so you really don't need to debounce because you won't be sampling the switch that often.

Sometimes you don't have this luxury, however. In those cases, you can use the Stamp's built-in BUTTON command. This command is meant to be used inside of a loop that scans a button. You must reserve a byte variable for the command to store temporary data in, and that variable must be 0 the first time through the loop. You can find the details in Chapter 2. The BUTTON command can also handle auto repeat of a button. That is, when the user holds the button down, it acts as though the user is pressing it multiple times.

Experimenting with Button

Listing 3.4 shows a program that you can run on the Basic Stamp activity board (or use the schematic in Figure 3.8). This simple circuit uses two switches to control a voltage. The Stamp uses the PWM command (see Chapters 2 and 4 for more about PWM) to generate voltages. The button connected to P8 is the down button and the button connected to P9 is the up button. Monitor the voltage with a voltmeter at the PWM output (the AOUT connector on the activity board or the top of C1 in the schematic).

When you run the program, the Stamp will output about 2.5V ($^{255}/_{128}$ of 5V to be exact). Pressing the up and down buttons will adjust the voltage until you reach the maximum or minimum possible voltage.

Notice that the repeat delay and the repeat rate are not in any particular time units. Instead, they are in cycles of the loop. So when you specify a rate of 5, that means the button must register in the down state five times to get one repeat.

Try changing the values. You'll notice that if the delay is less than the rate, the behavior seems odd. For example, suppose the up button had a delay of 1 and a repeat of 10. The first press will affect the voltage as you'd expect. Then the repeat fires on the next pass through the loop, moving the voltage up another step. However, the next repeat will take 10 cycles through the loop (as will all the other repeats). This makes it appear that the button repeats twice rapidly and then slows down. Usually, you'll keep the delay and the repeat the same or make the delay larger than the rate.

Listing 3.4 Experimenting with the BUTTON command.

```
vlevel var byte
tmp1 var byte
tmp2 var byte
PWMpin con 12
DNBtn con 8
UpBtn con 9
RPTDelay con 10
RptRate 2

vlevel=128  ' start half way
loop:
  pwm PWMPin,vlevel,10
  button DNBtn,0,RPTDelay,RPTRate,tmp1,0,notdown
  if vlevel=0 then notdown
```

Listing 3.4 Experimenting with the BUTTON command.

```
    vlevel=vlevel-1
notdown:
    button UpBtn,0,RPTDelay,RPTRate,tmp2,0,loop
    if vlevel=255 then loop
    vlevel=vlevel+1
    goto loop
```

Figure 3.8 A circuit for experimenting with the BUTTON command.

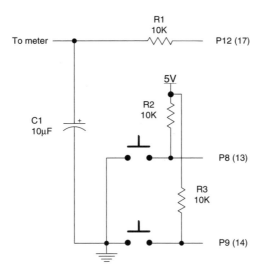

Sharing I/O Pins

Because I/O pins on the Stamp are limited, you often need to consider using tricks to get the most from your resources. One way to do this is to share pins where possible. For example, consider a game that I'll call, "Merlin." When you start the game, Merlin plays a single tone (out of four possible tones) and lights an associated light. You must push the button that corresponds to that tone. Then Merlin plays the same tone followed by a new tone. You must repeat the sequence. This continues until Merlin plays a certain number of tones. If you get the sequence correct, you win. If you miss the sequence at any time, you lose the game.

The hardware for this game will require four LEDs, four switches, and a speaker. That's a total of nine I/O pins. For the Stamp II that isn't a problem, but the Stamp I only has eight pins. Better use a Stamp II, right? Not necessarily.

Consider this: when Merlin plays a tune, you can't press any switches. When you are pressing switches, Merlin doesn't really need to light any lights. You could light the light that corresponds with that note, but it isn't necessary. You certainly don't want to light any other lights.

What if you wired each LED to a Stamp pin so that it lights when the pin goes low? Then you can also connect the corresponding switch to the same Stamp pin and ground. Finish up with a pull-up resistor to the same pin. Now the Stamp can read the switch or light the LED, but not at the same time. As a bonus, when you press the switch, the LED will light up automatically. Now you only need five I/O pins and a Stamp I can do the job.

You can find the circuit for Merlin in Figure 3.9. The Stamp I program appears in Listing 3.5. To conserve memory, the software generates two 16-bit random numbers. The program then treats each two bits of these numbers as a tone from 0 to 3. This would be easier on the Stamp II because the Stamp has arrays, more memory, and shift operations. On the Stamp I, the `geti` routine has to do a bit of math to extract the correct tone.

Figure 3.9   The Merlin game.

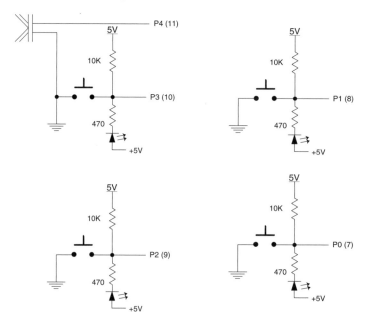

You may notice that the Merlin program doesn't debounce the switch inputs. That's because once you make the switch closure, the game goes off and does something else (like playing a tone) for quite some time and doesn't try to read the switch again. In effect, the program debounces the input by not reading any inputs until enough time has elapsed that the switch won't be bouncing anymore.

Listing 3.5   Merlin for the Stamp I.

```
' Merlin 1.0 - A game like Simon
'(c) 1997 by AWC. All Rights Reserved.
' Uses a Basic Stamp I with 4 switches and LEDs on
' P0-P3 and a speaker on P4.
' Play: Press P0 to start game, Merlin plays a note and
' lights an LED.
' You must press the corresponding switch. Next, Merlin
' adds a note and you must match him until you can play 16
' notes in a row correctly.
' You get a raspberry if you lose and all the lights
' come on if you win.


symbol temp=b0          ' temp storage
symbol maxstep=b1       ' tones in sequence
symbol i=b2             ' loop counter
symbol current=b3       ' current tone #
symbol cstep=b4         ' offset in byte of current tone
symbol ctone=b5         ' current tone (param to Sound)
symbol delay=40         ' general delay
symbol tlen=20          ' length of tone
symbol tone1=80         ' The four frequencies
symbol tone2=90
symbol tone3=100
symbol tone4=110


restart:                ' Wait for start button (1st button)
  w5=w5+1               ' randomize number
  w4=w4+2
  if pin0=1 then restart
restart0:
```

Listing 3.5 Merlin for the Stamp I. (Continued)

```
  if pin0=0 then start  ' wait for release of button
  goto restart
start:
maxstep=0                ' reset stuff
random w4                ' further randomize numbers
random w5

agn:
dirs=%11111              ' set outputs
pause 1500               ' let player "reset"
gosub display            ' display sequence
gosub readsw             ' wait for user input
maxstep=maxstep+1        ' he got it, so bump up and go
if maxstep<16 then agn   ' 16 is a winner
dirs=%11111
pins=0   ' all lamps on
sound 4,(100,delay,0,tlen,100,delay)
pins=15 ' all off
goto restart
' Display current sequence
display:
  for i=0 to maxstep
    pause delay       ' inter tone delay
    gosub geti        ' get current pattern
    lookup current,(14,13,11,7),temp  ' turn on one light
    pins=temp
    sound 4,(ctone,tlen)              ' make tone
    pins=15  ' all lamps off
  next i
  return

' This takes the current value of i and find
' the pattern (current) and the tone (ctone)
' would be easier with arrays
geti:
    cstep=i/4          ' which byte?
```

Listing 3.5   Merlin for the Stamp I. (Continued)

```
    temp=cstep*4      ' which two bits in the byte?
    temp=i-temp
    current=b8   ' load current with correct byte (b8-b11)
    if cstep=0 then getishift
    current=b9
    if cstep=1 then getishift
    current=b10
    if cstep=2 then getishift
    current=b11
getishift:
    if temp=0 then getimask   ' if 1st bits, mask off
    current=current/4              ' otherwise shift right 2 places
    temp=temp-1                    ' bump the count
    goto getishift                 ' and try again
getimask:
    current=current&3              ' chop off last two bits
' convert to tone
    lookup current,(tone1,tone2,tone3,tone4),ctone          return
' Read user's input
readsw:
    dirs=0                 ' change to inputs
    for i=0 to maxstep
      gosub geti ' get pattern
readloop:
    if pin0=0 then hit0    ' wait for a switch
    if pin1=0 then hit1
    if pin2=0 then hit2
    if pin3=0 then hit3
    goto readloop
hit0:
    sound 4,(tone1,tlen)       ' make correct tone
    if current=0 then readswok ' go if correct
    goto readswbad             ' not correct
hit1:
    sound 4,(tone2,tlen)
    if current=1 then readswok
```

Listing 3.5   Merlin for the Stamp I. (Continued)

```
    goto readswbad
hit2:
    sound 4,(tone3,tlen)
    if current=2 then readswok
    goto readswbad
hit3:
    sound 4,(tone4,tlen)
    if current=3 then readswok
readswbad:
    sound 4,(33,1000)    ' lost!
    goto restart
' Success!
readswok:
    if pin0=0 or pin1=0 or pin2=0 or pin3=0  then readswok
' wait for switch to open
    next i  ' keep going
' Got 'em all
    return
```

Expanding I/O

There are other hardware solutions you can use to expand the amount of input and output you can use. In the Merlin game, for example, you could use a demultiplexer IC to change two outputs into one of four lights (because you don't need more than one light on at a time). You could also use a multiplexer to encode the four switches into two bits (again, only one switch on at a time). In this case, this would only add hardware to the circuit and wouldn't save any I/O compared to the first method, but this isn't always the case.

There are many common multiplexer chips including the 74LS153. You can use a 74LS138 to demultiplex three bits into eight lines.

Another way to expand Stamp I/O is with dedicated I/O expanders, I/O coprocessors, or shift registers. Shift registers (like the 74LS299, 74LS595, or 74LS165) can convert serial data to parallel data and vice versa. You can find a simple schematic for an 74LS165 circuit in Figure 3.10. This chip will add eight input lines to the Stamp, while consuming three for a net gain of five pins.

Figure 3.10 Using the 74LS165.

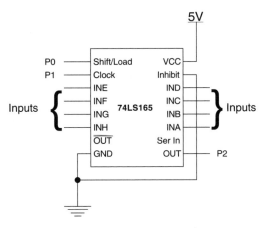

The 74LS165 monitors its inputs (pins 3–6 and 11–14) until the Stamp pulses pin 1 low. This causes the '165 to store a snapshot of its inputs at that time. Once the chip has this snapshot, you can pulse the clock pin (pin 2) and read the data bit from pin 9 (most significant bit first). For the Stamp II, you can use SHIFTIN to handle this. For the Stamp I, you'd need to manually shift the data:

```
' assume pin 0 is LOAD
' pin 1 is CLK
' pin 2 is DATA
PULSOUT 0,5
INPUT 2
FOR B5=1 to 8
  B0=B0 *2
  Bit0 = in2     ' note Bit0 is first bit of B0
  PULSOUT 1,5
NEXT
```

This allows you to read the eight bits connected to the shift register. You can reverse the entire process by using a 74LS595. Then you shift eight bits into the device (using SHIFTOUT, or code comparable to the above) and pulse the LOAD pin to move the new bits to the output.

Dedicated I/O expanders and coprocessors (like the Phillip's PCF8574 and AWC's PAK-III and PAK-IV) use a serial protocol to accept commands from the Stamp. An expander usually adds digital I/O while a coprocessor adds more general purpose I/O (for example, counting, pulse measurement, PWM, etc.).

Polling

The BSIIP has a special feature known as polling that can help with digital I/O. This is similar to — but not exactly — like an interrupt. Polling has several commands, and at first it can seem somewhat intimidating. However, if you approach it logically, it is really quite simple.

Suppose you have a switch on pin 8 that will go low when the user presses it. You'd like to do some action immediately when the user pushes the button. However, you also have "real" work to do. Let's say your program is simple and blinks a LED, sends a count out the serial port, and pauses briefly:

```
LED con 15
B9600 con 240
i var byte
i=0
Loop:
toggle LED
serout 16,B9600,[dec i,cr]
pause 1000
goto Loop
```

If you test the switch at the top of the loop, there will be a delay slightly longer than one second between testing the switch. Actually, one second might be an acceptable delay, but what if the program were more complicated? Testing at the top of the loop might delay the test for many seconds, minutes, or even hours.

You could rewrite your program like this:

```
LED con 15
B9600 con 240
i var byte
i=0
Loop:
if in8=0 then service_user
toggle LED
if in8=0 then service_user
serout 16,B9600,[dec i,cr]
if in8=0 then service_user
pause 1000
if in8=0 then service_user
goto Loop
```

This would work, but it has two drawbacks. First, it eats up your EEPROM rather quickly. Second, it is just a drag to have to type the same line over and over again. These problems would get even worse if you had to monitor more than one input!

Luckily, this is pretty much what polling does. There are a few steps you have to take to set up polling:

1. Tell the BS2P which pin(s) you want to monitor and what state you are watching for (POLLIN).
2. Optionally, tell the BS2P to set outputs to a given state when your poll event is true (POLLOUT).
3. Set the poll mode (POLLMODE).

If you don't want to set an output, you can also wait in a lower mode (POLLWAIT) or run another program (POLLRUN). We won't talk about those in this project.

The downside is that the Stamp only looks for events during the gaps between commands. So suppose you set up a polling event and execute this code:

```
Debug "Press the button now!",cr
PAUSE 10000
Debug "Come on!"
```

If you don't hit the button almost instantly when you see the message, the Stamp will ignore it for 10 seconds. You could push the button several times within that 10-second period, and the Stamp will miss it. Of course, in this case, you could just break the pause into a loop of 20 half-second pauses.

The POLLMODE lets you select if you want to enable or disable polling and how polling behaves. For example, you can set it so the output changes when the event occurs, and returns to its original state with the event is no longer in force. Or, you can cause the output to latch and remain in its active state even if the event is no longer in effect.

You might wonder why setting an output in response to an input is interesting. There are certainly cases where this will be useful, but sometimes you'll just use the output to signal that the Stamp has seen the event. You can then test the output to see if the event occurred at some handy point in your program.

For example, suppose you have instrument that requires configuration in the field. I run into this all the time. You want to be able to get the device's attention and send it some configuration information. As an example, I built a little protoboard with a BS2P, two LEDs (one on pin 15 and one on pin 14 and both with 470Ω resistors, of course), and a switch between ground and pin 8. I also put a 10K pull-up resistor on pin 8. The LEDs turn on when the pin is low and the switch is low when pressed. You can find the schematic in Figure 3.11.

My instrument blinks the LED (on pin 14) at a specific rate for 20 blinks. It is very important (don't ask why) that you get 20 blinks without interruption. The blink rate is in EEPROM and if you push the switch, when the Stamp gets a chance, it will prompt you for a new blink rate (in milliseconds) and use it (storing it in EEPROM for next time).

The default blink time is 250mS. Once you get it working with the code below, enter a blink rate of 5,000 (5 seconds). You can use Windows Hyperterminal to set the parameter. Just select 9,600 baud, eight bits, no stop bits, and — this is important — *no handshaking*. That will let you talk with Hyperterminal through the programming port. Of course, you can't program while Hypertermial is active (use the hang-up button to make the terminal release the COM port — no need to close the programmer or the terminal).

Figure 3.11 Testing Polling on a BS2P.

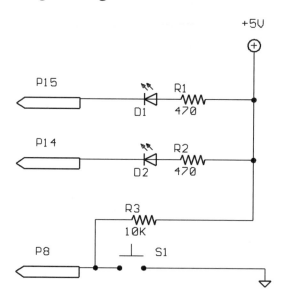

When you have a 5-second delay, you can press the button and notice that the LED on pin 15 doesn't light up right away. If you release the button before the LED turns on, the Stamp won't see the event. Again, a large delay should be split into shorter delays. This is unavoidable with commands that take time to execute like PULSIN, PULSOUT, FREQOUT, etc.

Look at the polling setup excerpted from Listing 3.6:

```
pollin switch,0              ' Wait for the switch input to go low
pollout pollind,0            ' Turn pin 15 to 0 when the event occurs
pollmode 10                  ' Watch for events and latch the output
```

Listing 3.6   Using BSIIP polling.

```
i var byte      ' counter
pamt var word   ' Pause amount
B9600 con 240   ' 9600 baud
lf con 10       ' line feed
switch con 8    ' input switch
pollind con 15
pollinp var in15
LED con 14
' default pause value
pstore data 0,250

read pstore,pamt  ' load defaults
pamt=pamt*256
read pstore+1,i
pamt=pamt+i

' Poll switches on P8 until it goes low
' When it does go low, turn on LED on P15
high pollind  ' LEDs OFF
high LED
pollin switch,0     ' Wait for switch input to go low
pollout pollind,0   ' Turn pin15 to 0 when event occurs
pollmode 10         ' Watch for events and latch output

' This is just a "dummy loop"
reLoop:
i=0
Loop:
toggle LED
pause pamt
i=i+1
if i<>20 then Loop
```

Listing 3.6 Using BSIIP polling. (Continued)

```
if pollinp=1 then reLoop  ' button not pushed?
serout 16,B9600, ["Configure mode, enter delay:",cr,lf]
serin 16,B9600,[dec pamt]
serout 16,B9600,[cr,lf,"Set ",dec pamt,cr,lf]
write pstore,pamt/256
write pstore+1,pamt&$FF
high pollind
pollmode 10
goto reLoop
```

Once these statements execute, pin 15 will go low when the Stamp detects the switch closure. It will stay low, too, until you reset it. The code can execute until it gets to the end of its 20 blinks. Then it examines pin 15 to see if the event occurred. In practice, this means you press the button until LED 15 turns on. Then you can release it. You still may have to wait for the Stamp to prompt you for the blink rate change.

You can find details about the different effects of POLLMODE in Chapter 2. In addition, don't forget that the POLLRUN command can cause the Stamp to run another program when the polled event occurs. However, there is no easy way to make the new program return to the same spot in the original program, so you have to account for this idiosyncracy in your program.

LED Die

All work and no play makes me nervous. This little circuit (Figure 3.12) lets you drive a seven-segment LED (Radio Shack 276-075) and use your Stamp as a really expensive die (half of a pair of dice, you know). For the speaker, use a 32Ω speaker or a piezo transducer. If you use a piezo transducer, you can do away with the two capacitors. If you want a slightly brighter display, try 330Ω resistors in place of the seven 470 Ω resistors.

The program (Listing 3.7) assumes you have pin 0 connected to the LED's "a" segment, pin1 to "b", and so on. Be sure to use a resistor in series. If you wanted to hook up more digits, you could wire the LEDs in parallel and use a Stamp pin to select between the displays. If you do this quickly enough, you can make it appear that both LEDs are on at the same time. There is an example of a similar scheme in the Stamp Manual (Application Note #9 for the Stamp I). Still, you can do a lot with one display. A countdown timer for a model rocket would be a neat idea. You could also use a similar arrangement for a logic probe (1, 0, P for pulse, o for open circuit).

To roll the die, press the button. The LEDs will chase themselves around the display, and the speaker will make a rolling sound. Then release the button to see the result of the throw.

Figure 3.12 The LED die.

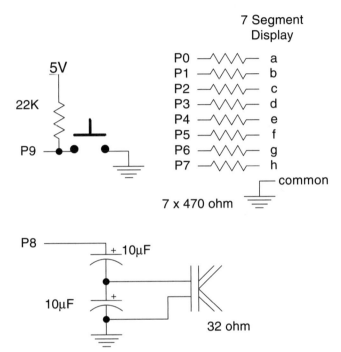

Listing 3.7 The LED die.

```
' Die program for BS2 - Williams
input 8
dirs=$FF
anum var byte
led var byte
out1=$40    ' single dash at the beginning
loop:
anum=anum+1 ' increment anum until switch press
if in8=1 then loop
pause 50 ' debounce  ' wait for switch to quit bouncing (could use button)
loop2:
```

Listing 3.7   The LED die. (Continued)

```
anum=anum+1 ' increment anum until switch release
led=anum//6 ' mask number to be between 0-5 (mod operator)
' The next line makes numbers quickly whiz by when you hold the button
' lookup led,[6,91,79,102,109,125],out1
' This line makes the chasing effect
' either use this line or the one above
out1=1<<(anum//6)
freqout 7,1,250  ' Click...
' Give the user time to admire our "graphics"
pause 45
if in8=0 then loop2
random anum  ' Make up a random # and mask it to 0-5
anum=anum // 6 ' (0-5)
' Generate the number
lookup anum,[6,91,79,102,109,125],out1
' Wait a bit to make sure the button is really up for good
pause 100
goto loop
```

Reaction Game

Here's another Basic Stamp II game, at the request of my youngest son, Patrick. The idea behind the game is to see which of two players has the fastest reaction time. The LED on Stamp pin 0 is the player 1 LED. Pin 1 has player 2's LED. The Stamp lights the player's LED to show who's turn it is. Then, after a random time interval, it lights the LED on pin 7. Push your button (pin 8 for player 1; pin 9 for player 2) as fast as you can. Then the other player takes a turn.

Whichever player wins gets his or her LED to blink for a bit. Then you start over. Both LEDs blink for a tie. If the Stamp sees you have your button pushed right before it lights the LED on pin 7, you get the maximum score (which is bad — you want the minimum score).

The circuitry is simple (see Figure 3.13). However, there are a few interesting points to the code. First, you want a random delay before the starting LED lights. Otherwise, the player might judge when the LED is about to light. But you don't want the delay to be too short, or it isn't fair. The code (see Listing 3.8) starts by pausing for 500mS, and then a random amount. The random amount shouldn't be too long either (65 seconds is too long to wait). So the code masks the number with

$3FF (1,023) to make sure the wait is not too long (you might try different minimum and maximum delays).

Speaking of random numbers, your opponent's reaction time forms the seed for your next delay. This ensures that the number generation is unpredictable. One potential bug: if you wait a really long time and the delay count exceeds $FFFF, the count rolls over, and you could win even if your opponent pressed the switch in a reasonable time. This would be easy to fix by monitoring the count and stopping if it reached $FFFF. Try it!

There are many other possibilities for this circuit. You might make a solitaire version of the game or even modify the program to act as quiz show buttons (see the next project).

Figure 3.13 Reaction timer/quiz show circuit.

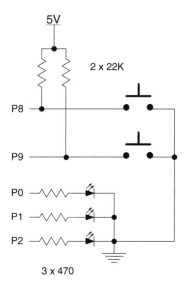

Listing 3.8 Reaction timer.

```
' Reaction time game -- Williams
' Player 1: Wait for LED0 to light, then wait for LED7
' as quick as possible, push SWITCH8
' Player 2: Wait for LED1 then wait for LED7
' as quick as possible, push SWITCH7
' If LED0 begins blinking, player 1 wins!
' If LED1 blinks, player 2 wins.
```

Listing 3.8   Reaction timer. (Continued)

```
t var byte
t0 var bit
t1 var bit
dlya var word
dlyb var word
output 7    ' Go LED
output 0    ' Player 1 LED
output 1    ' Player 2 LED
top:
' player 1
pause 500 ' Give folks a chance to settle
high 0      ' Light player LED
random dlya    ' wait a random amount of time
dlya=dlya&$3FF ' but not too much time
pause 500        ' and not too little either
pause dlya       ' net result: pause from 500-1523 ms
dlya=0           ' Next random seed comes from switch timing
if in8=1 then p1  ' make sure switch is UP
' Player 1 is cheating
' if your switch is already down, your score is FFFF
dlya=$FFFF
goto p1done     p1:
high 7            ' Player didn't jump the gun, so light the GO light
p1loop:
dlya=dlya+1     ' Start counting
if in8=1 then p1loop   ' until the switch goes down
p1done:
low 7' Clear the lights
low 0
dlyb=dlya' P1 score is P2's random seed
' Begin player 2 -- same logic
pause 500
high 1
random dlyb
dlyb=dlyb&$3FF
pause 500
```

Listing 3.8   Reaction timer. (Continued)

```
pause dlyb
dlyb=0
if in9=1 then p2
' Player 2 is cheating
dlyb=$FFFF
goto p2done
p2:
high 7
p2loop:
dlyb=dlyb+1
if in9=1 then p2loop
p2done:
low 7
low 1
' Check for winner
if dlya<dlyb then awin
if dlya=dlyb then tie
for t=0 to 100
' P 2 wins!
'-- ought to make these subroutines,
' but they are so simple...
toggle 1
pause 50
next
low 1
goto goagain
' P 1 wins!
awin:
for t=0 to 100
toggle 0
pause 50
next
low 0
goto goagain
' Tie -- hard to do unless both players were cheating!
tie:
```

Listing 3.8   Reaction timer. (Continued)

```
for t=0 to 100
toggle 0
toggle 1
pause 50
next
low 0
low 1
goagain:
dlya=dlyb ' Player 1's random seed is Player 2's score
goto top
```

Quiz Buttons

With some different software, the circuit in Figure 3.13 can solve what I call the Quiz Show problem. The Stamp signals the person who pushed a button first and locks out the other button. Of course, quiz shows and games aren't the only place this is useful. You might use a similar scheme for determining the winner of a race, for example. This software doesn't use the LED on pin 2, so you can omit it if you like.

There are a few interesting points in the code (Listing 3.9) — first, the switches are active low, so a zero in the corresponding bit means the button is down. The `inc` variable reads four bits from pin 8 to 11. This way the code can sample both switches at the exact same time. Testing each bit separately could cause false readings, especially if you expand the code to handle more than two inputs. The player that buzzes in first gets a 2-second flash from their LED. The program ignores all input until the 2-second interval elapses. To test the individual bits in the input word, I used the logical and function. The input is in B1, so if B1&1 is zero, then player 1 rang in. If B1&2 is zero, player 2's button is down.

In the unlikely event that both buttons are down at the same time, the code generates a random number. If the number is odd, then player 2 wins; otherwise player 1 gets the nod. The code generates the tiebreaker number on each pass through the loop so it is sure to be unpredictable.

You could make lots of fun modifications to this circuit. Adding a speaker would be handy. There could be different tones for player 1 and player 2. You could also give the contestants a certain amount of time (timed in software) before you buzz that they are out of time. It would be simple to add more switches, or change the switches to detect soapbox derby cars, Hot Wheels, or whatever.

Listing 3.9 Quiz show.

```
'Quiz Show -- Williams
input 8
input 9
output 0
output 1
loop:
b1=inc' Read both buttons at once
random b2  ' tie breaker (if necessary)
if b1 & 3 = 0 then tie   ' if both buttons down, its a tie (imagine)
if b1 & 1 = 0 then p1    ' Player 1 gets it
if b1 & 2 = 0 then p2 ' Player 2 gets it
' No buttons pushed
goto loop
tie:
if b2 & 1 then p2
' fall into p1
p1:
high 0
pause 2000
low 0
goto loop
p2:
high 1
pause 2000
low 1
goto loop
```

Logic Probe

I have a pretty well-stocked lab, including several scopes, and a 100Mhz logic analyzer. But sometimes you just want a quick indicator of a logic state. Of course, you can just use an LED and a resistor, but that has several problems. First, it is a high load on the circuit under test. Second, you can't get indications of rapid pulses or open circuit conditions.

This project will show you how to build a simple Stamp-based logic probe that solves all of these problems. For size and cost, you'd probably want to do this with a Stamp I, but I did it with the Stamp II. The code is virtually identical in either case.

The circuit is ridiculously easy to build (see Figure 3.14). Connect the probe tip to port 7 (pin 12) of the Stamp. Place a 100K resistor between port 7 and port 6. Finally, wire three LEDs to ports 8, 9, and 10. Connect the other end of the LEDs to ground (so they light when you set the port high). If you are using a 5V LED, you can just wire it directly to the Stamp pin. If you are using ordinary LEDs, you'll need a dropping resistor in series (say, 470Ω). Be sure to get the polarity correct.

The LED on port 8 shows the state of the probe tip. Off is 0, and on is 1. The LED on port 9 shows an open circuit condition. The LED on port 10 lights when it detects any pulse on the line (since the last time the probe detected an open circuit).

Figure 3.14 Logic probe.

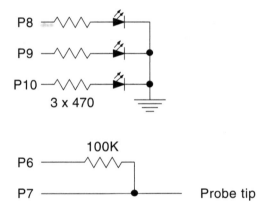

The code (see Listing 3.10) first tries to affect the state of the probe tip through the 100K resistor (this value could be higher if you like — say, 1M). If it is able to drive the state of the pin, the pin must be open circuit (as in an input, or just not touching anything at all). In this case, the code lights the open LED and extinguishes the other two. It also sets laststate to 2, which indicates the probe doesn't know the previous state.

If the code can't manipulate the probe input, there must be a legitimate output attached. The probe reads the value (starting at label notopen) and lights the LED to reflect the state of the pin. Next, the probe determines if the previous state was the opposite of this one. If it is, the pulse LED lights and remains lit until an open circuit is detected.

Although this circuit is simple, it would be easy to add some interesting features to it. For example, if the open circuit indicator is on, you could check a button. If the button is down, you could inject a train of pulses to the circuit under test. You could modify the output to light a seven-segment display instead of individual LEDs (perhaps reading H, L, or O). You might want to reset the pulse LED after a certain time interval.

The Stamp's slow speed makes the probe a bit unresponsive to very fast pulses. However, this would be a great project for a PIC — not hard to code, and a fast PIC would be much more responsive (not to mention less expensive). You'll read more about PIC projects in Chapter 10.

Listing 3.10 The logic probe.

```
hilo con 8
open con 9
puls con 10
ptest con 6
probe con 7
output hilo
output open
output puls
laststate var byte
laststate=2  ' no idea what previous state is/was
loop:
output ptest
low ptest
if in7<>0 then notopen
high ptest
if in7<>1 then notopen
' open
laststate=2
low hilo
high open
low puls
goto loop
notopen:
low open
input ptest
if in7=1 then one
```

Listing 3.10 The logic probe. (Continued)

```
' zero
low hilo
if laststate<>1 then loop
high puls ' light pulse LED
laststate=0
goto loop
one:
high hilo
if laststate<>0 then loop
high puls
laststate=1
goto loop
```

Automated Cable Tester

Another useful tool is an automated cable tester. Suppose you want to test a 9-pin serial cable. You could use a Stamp pin to send a signal down the cable and use more Stamp pins to monitor the results. However, that would require 18 pins, and you'd probably want some sort of result LED to tell if the cable is okay or not. You can't get 18 pins without going to a BSIIP, so you should really think about how many pins you actually need.

The circuit in Figure 3.15 only tests eight of the nine lines. The nineth line has a simple green LED that turns on when you make the connection. You can wire the two DB9 sockets (socket A and socket B) straight, or cross the connections to match a cross-cable configuration.

The other eight lines have a simple pull-up resistor and an LED. The Stamp can exercise each line (see Listing 3.11) and compare the inputs to the expected pattern. If there are any shorts or opens, the input will be different. That includes if the nineth pin is shorted to any other pin.

After the test cycle, you'll find one of three conditions. If the red LEDs are off and the green LED is on, the cable is okay. If the green LED is off, or if any red LED remains on, the cable is bad.

You repeat the resistor/LED circuit for each of the eight pins using P1 and P9 for the second pin, P2 and P10 for the third pin, and so on. The cable connects to the two open dots near the center of the circuit.

Figure 3.15 This cable tester uses a tricky design to minimize the number of pins required.

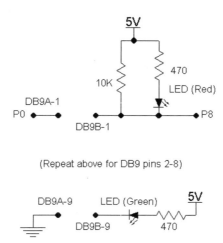

(Repeat above for DB9 pins 2-8)

Under the Hood

The pull-up and LED circuit repeats for eight of the nine conductors. The code cycles a 0 on each pin. At each stage, only one input should be 0 and the remainder should be 1s. Any deviation indicates an error.

To keep the code simple, the count runs from 0 to 7, and a bit mask is shifted on each iteration. Before output occurs, the code inverts the bits using the XOR operator and $FF. This simply changes all 1 bits to 0s and vice versa.

As written, the code stops after a successful test. You might want to make it test continuously to help nail down intermittent failures.

Listing 3.11 The program for the cable tester.

```
' cable tester -- williams
DIRL=%11111111   ' 0-7 outputs



i var byte
bits var byte
testval var byte
```

Listing 3.11 The program for the cable tester. (Continued)

```
top:
bits=1
for i=0 to 7
  testval = bits ^ $FF
  OUTL=testval
  if INH<>testval then badcable
  bits=bits<<1
next
OUTL=$FF   ' or goto top for continuous testing
badcable:
END
```

Summary

The Stamp is quite adept at handling digital inputs and outputs. While expanding the amount of available I/O is possible, it takes a good bit of effort and some expense as well. You'll be happier if you can design around the available I/O, sharing pins where possible.

Although the Stamp is primarily a digital device, it is possible to use it to measure and generate certain analog quantities as you'll see in the next chapter. Of course, you can always use traditional digital I/O to interface to an A/D or D/A converter — special chips that convert voltages to numbers and numbers to voltages, respectively.

Exercises

1. In the LED Counter, what hardware change could simplify the code?
2. In the LED Counter, can you think of another way to simplify the code without changing the hardware?
3. In the PWM project (Listing 3.4), what happens if you use the same temporary variable for both BUTTON commands?
4. Rewrite the Merlin Program in Listing 3.5 for the Stamp II.

For answers to the exercises, see the Answer Key, page 426.

Chapter 4

A Digital Power Supply: Analog Output

Digital things are very modern and trendy, but humans are still basically analog devices. When I was a kid, there was no such thing as a digital watch. When the old-fashioned LED watches appeared, it seemed it would spell the end of teaching kids about the big hand and the little hand. The LCD display, with its lower power requirements and more pleasing appearance, seemed an even surer winner.

Today, you still find as many analog timepieces as digital. The same goes for automobile dashboards. In many applications, people prefer analog instruments. As a circuit designer, you may prefer digital to analog design. Digital hardware is usually more logical, following an exact set of rules. Analog, on the other hand, requires a different discipline. Things don't have exact values like 1 and 0 in analog circuits. A 220Ω resistor is only approximately 220Ω. Even in the same circuit, the value changes with temperature, age, and other factors.

Surprisingly, the Stamp — a decidedly digital device — is actually quite capable in the analog world. By using some subterfuge, the Stamp can produce voltages from 0 to 5V (with 8-bit resolution), and create tones (including telephone touch tones). In the following chapter, you'll see that you can even read analog quantities to some extent.

211

In this chapter, I'll show you how to exploit these capabilities to create a digitally-controlled power supply. In later chapters, I'll show you how to expand this design.

Of course, if you want industrial-strength analog output, you'll want to use a special IC known as a *D to A converter* (or, more simply, a *D/A* or *DAC*). There are several types (see "Traditional D/A" on page 220) that use a serial interface and are very easy to interface with the Stamp. However, with some planning, you'll find you rarely even need to use these; the Stamp's built-in analog capabilities are adequate for many tasks.

Sound and Tone Generation

Making sounds come out of the Stamp could hardly be simpler — if you don't mind putting everything on hold while you make the tone. The Stamp I has the SOUND command which generates a square wave on any pin you want. The equivalent command on the Stamp II is FREQOUT. The FREQOUT command has a similar intent to SOUND, but its internal operation is different. Instead of generating a simple square wave, FREQOUT generates a train of pulses that have a certain average frequency. When filtered, these pulses form a close approximation to a sine wave. This is a form of *Pulse Width Modulation* (PWM). Because of this, the Stamp II can generate two tones at once, if you like. Of course, you can also generate a single tone.

A common use for two tones mixed together is to generate touch tones for telephone signaling. Each number on your phone's keypad generates two specially selected frequencies. There are also four other keys that don't appear on normal phones, so there are 16 touch tone frequency pairs. Because this is so common, the Stamp II has a special command, DTMFOUT, just for this purpose.

Simple Speaker Circuits

Probably the simplest way to hear sound from a Stamp, is to directly connect a small piezoelectric speaker directly to the Stamp pin. These speakers have a very high impedance, so they don't draw much power from the Stamp. However, they also don't sound very good and they are not very loud. Still, for a warning beep, or just for experimenting, you can't get anything simpler.

When you are shopping for a piezoelectric speaker, be sure to get one that is actually a speaker. Some piezoelectric elements only produce one frequency (these are more like buzzers than speakers). Radio Shack's 273-091 is suitable for use with a Stamp, for example.

The other option is to use a regular speaker. Although a normal speaker generally sounds better than a piezoelectric speaker, they also require some extra circuitry. The problem is that a normal speaker has a coil that has a very low resistance. Because of this, you need a capacitor to block DC current from flowing through the coil. A typical speaker has an 8Ω coil. If you pass 5V through 8Ω you draw 625mA — well beyond the Stamp's drive current limits!

For best results, you'll want to place a 10µF electrolytic capacitor between the Stamp and the speaker (see Figure 4.1). Be sure the + end of the capacitor points towards the Stamp. An 8Ω speaker will still require more current than is safe, so it is best to use a speaker that is at least 32Ω. Unfortunately, these speakers are hard to find. Some electronics distributors carry them, or you can often find them in less-expensive transistor radios. If all else fails, you can take a normal 8Ω speaker and wire a 33Ω resistor in series. This effectively gives you a 41Ω speaker, but at the expense of quite a bit of volume.

Figure 4.1   Connecting a speaker to a Stamp I.

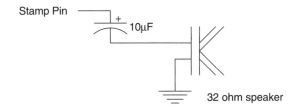

Because the Stamp II uses PWM to generate sound, you'll find that just using a simple speaker connection results in a lot of high-frequency noise on the output audio. For some applications, this isn't very important, but you can filter the noise very simply (see Figure 4.2). Of course, this filtering cuts down on the output volume.

Figure 4.2   Connecting a speaker to a Stamp II.

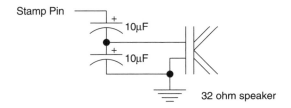

Experimenting with PWM Noise

Build the circuit in Figure 4.2 using a solderless breadboard. Write a program that uses FREQOUT to generate a 1kHz tone. While the tone is playing, remove the filter capacitor (the one that connects to ground) and note the difference. If you have access to an oscilloscope, look at the output with and without the filter capacitor.

Amplifiers

The truth is that none of these methods will produce much volume anyway. If you really want to hear the Stamp, you'll want to feed the input to an amplifier stage of some sort. For experimenting, you might just get a signal tracer, or other small amplifier (like Radio Shack's 277-1008, for instance). You can also try feeding the Stamp's output to the center pin of a cheap transistor radio's volume control.

Of course, for a real project, you'll want to build your own amplifier. Although you can do this with discrete transistors, there are now single-chip audio amplifiers that perform much better than anything else you could build for the price. An LM386 IC will cost you around a dollar, and requires only one or two capacitors (and a speaker, of course) to form a complete amplifier.

You'll also want a filtering network between the Stamp and any amplifier. You can find a schematic in Figure 4.3. If you want to use an amplifier that is already built, just build everything up to pin 3 of the IC and replace the IC and its circuitry with your amplifier.

Figure 4.3   Driving an amplifier.

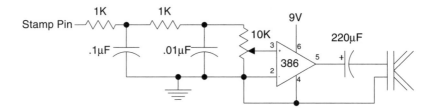

Connecting to the Phone Line

Connecting to a phone line can be very difficult. The phone system has many peculiar requirements and, if you are selling your product, you'll need FCC approval for any hookup you make. Most designers simply buy a *DAA* (*Data Access Arrangement*) that is already FCC approved. However, these can be hard to acquire in small quantities.

If you just want to experiment, you have several options. First, you can gut a cheap telephone and wire to its microphone element. You can also build a simple phone line interface (see Figure 4.4). This interface is available from Parallax and is not too difficult to build. However, it does use some parts that may be hard to obtain. As a last ditch effort, you could acoustically couple the speaker to a cheap phone like old-fashioned modems did. Acoustically couple is just a fancy way of saying, stick the speaker next to the microphone. For traditional handsets, a canned drink insulator (most people call them cuzzies or snuggies) work well for coupling the speaker to the phone's microphone.

Figure 4.4 A telephone interface.

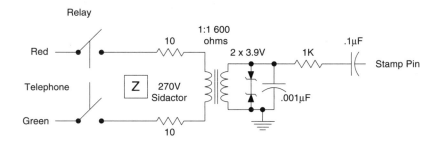

An Example

If you really want to see a large example that uses sounds, check out the Merlin game in Chapter 3 (beginning on page 169). Of course, it does lots of different things like read buttons and light LEDs, too.

For a simpler example, consider a home alarm system. If the system detects a break in, the alarm will call your numeric pager to alert you. Of course, the system could detect anything — water in your basement (we don't have basements in Texas, but I'm told they get water in them), or a power outage. Anything you could detect with a Stamp could trigger the pager call.

The code in Listing 4.1 could hardly be simpler. The program watches for input on pin 0. If it detects a rising edge on that pin, it calls the pager number by emitting touch tones on pin 7. Pin 6 controls a relay that takes the phone off the hook.

Listing 4.1 Dialing the phone.

```
   LOW 6    ' make sure phone is on the hook
Top:
  IF in0=0 then Top
  HIGH 6   ' take phone off hook
  DTMFOUT 7,[5,5,5,1,2,1,2]
  GOTO Top
```

It is easy to take a telephone on and off the hook. When the phone device is inactive, it simply presents an open circuit to the phone line. This is most easily done with a relay as you can see in Figure 4.4. If you don't like the idea of a relay, keep in mind that when the phone rings, the line can have around 100V on it, so be sure whatever you are using can withstand the ring voltage.

Generating Voltages Using PWM

One of the most interesting things the Stamp can do is use PWM to generate a voltage. The idea is to use a capacitor to average the voltage coming out of the Stamp over time. Take a look at Figure 4.5. If the Stamp pin stays at ground level (logic 0), it is clear that the output voltage will be 0V. It should be just as plain that if the pin goes to a logic level 1, the capacitor will eventually charge up and the output voltage will be at 5V.

Figure 4.5   PWM output circuit.

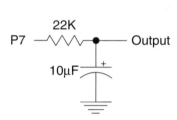

The magic happens when you switch the voltage rapidly. Suppose that 50% of the time the pin is at a logic 1 and 50% of the time the pin is at 0V. The capacitor then charges and discharges repeatedly. The average voltage will be 2.5V (half of 5V). If the pin were at a logic 1 level for 25% of the time (and 0 for 75%), the output voltage will be 1.25V. You'd think the Stamp would use nice even cycles, but it doesn't. If you look at the output on a scope, you'd find the frequency varies depending on the duty cycle. But the average time on and off will still be correct.

The Stamp II, for example, generates pulses about 4µS wide. So if the duty cycle is 50%, the pin will be high for 4µS and low for 4µS. If you select 4% (well, $1/255$ actually), there will be a 4µS high pulse, followed by 1.02mS low.

The Stamp can vary the duty cycle of the PWM output from 0 to 255 (1 byte's worth). That means that you can output voltages using this scheme ranging from 0 to 5V in 255 steps — which works out to just under 20mV (0.02V) per step. Not bad for two extra components that cost a few pennies each.

So what's the downside? The voltage remains stable as long as the Stamp keeps the pin cycling at the specified duty cycle. The problem is, the Stamp can only do one thing at a time. As soon as the Stamp does something else, the capacitor will start to lose charge. If the Stamp froze the pin in a steady state, the capacitor would very quickly charge up to 5V or discharge to 0V.

Luckily, the Stamp is smarter than that. It changes the pin to an input when it no longer wants to maintain a voltage. However, the input does form a very high resistance to ground, so there is some leakage. Besides, no capacitor is perfect. Internal leakage will claim some voltage over time. The big problem though isn't the Stamp or the imperfect capacitor. It is the load.

Presumably, if you are generating a voltage, you want to do something with it. Suppose you breadboard the circuit in Figure 4.5 and connect a voltmeter to it. If you program the Stamp to generate, for example, 100mS of PWM, you'll find the voltage stays for a long time (at least several seconds) after the program stops. That's because the meter has a high resistance. The Stamp's input pin and the capacitor's leakage resistance is high too.

Now consider if you connect a light bulb to the capacitor. Varying the PWM duty cycle will directly affect the brightness of the lamp. However, when the program stops pulsing the pin, there is a significant load on the capacitor (the bulb). This will discharge the capacitor very quickly.

Exactly how much load the capacitor can handle (and for how long) depends on the value of the capacitor and the capacitor's construction. Larger values will hold their charge longer than smaller values. However, larger values also require more time to charge to their desired value, so it is a trade off.

You'll almost never be able to use the PWM voltage as it is because of the effect of a load. However, you can directly drive, for example, an op amp or comparator input since they don't present much of a load (you'll see an example of this in the next chapter). This suggests a solution to the problem. You can use an op amp buffer to isolate the Stamp's PWM capacitor from the actual load. While you are at it, you could even multiply the voltage (provide gain) or offset it.

Of course, when you multiply the voltage, you also multiply the step size you can take. If you use an amplifier with a gain of two, your step size increases to around 40mV. You'll find some example buffer amplifiers in Figure 4.6. (You can also read about op amps in the sidebar, "Op amp basics" on page 218.) One important note about op amps: *you usually can't get the output to reach the supply voltages.* That means if you want to supply 5V from an op amp, you'll want to power the op amp from a voltage greater than 5V. Many op amps also require a negative voltage. Then you'll want to build a traditional power supply to generate the negative voltage. You can also use two batteries to obtain positive and negative voltages (see Figure 4.7).

Figure 4.6   Op amp circuits.

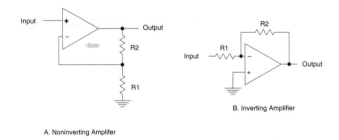

A. Noninverting Amplifer

B. Inverting Amplifier

Figure 4.7   Using two 9V batteries with an op amp.

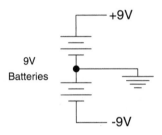

Use your battery

If you are powering your Stamp from a 9V battery, you can use the battery to supply the positive voltage to an op amp or comparator. You usually won't need to regulate the voltage because the op amp doesn't mind variations in voltage.

No matter how well isolated your capacitor is, you still have to recharge it periodically. Exactly how long depends on the type of capacitor you are using, the value of the capacitor, and your total loading. You'll have to experiment to find how long you can wait between PWM commands. Just remember that your voltmeter does not supply a sufficient load for testing.

Op amp basics

Op amps are very simple to deal with, if you take the right approach. A good way to think about op amps is to imagine that it will make its output do whatever it takes to make its inputs equal, if possible. Of course, this assumes that the output is connected to the input and the voltages required are within the op amp's ability.

Why is this helpful? Consider the amplifier in Figure 4.6A. Suppose you put 5V on the + input. We know the op amp will do whatever it can to also put 5V on the − input. If R1 and R2 are the same value, they form a 50% voltage divider, right? So if the center of the voltage divider is at 5V, it stands to reason that the input of the divider (the output of the op amp) is at 10V. That's exactly right. The gain in this configuration is two.

If the voltage divider ratio was 25%, the gain would be four. Of course, putting 5V on the input would require the output to be 20V. That wouldn't be possible unless the op amp's supply voltage was greater than 20V to start with.

The gain of this type of amplifier is always $1 + R2/R1$. What if you want an amplifier with a gain of one? Just wire the output directly to the − input. Because the output will try to make the − voltage the same as the + voltage, you'll have a gain of one. Why is this important? Suppose you want to generate a PWM voltage using an RC network (described in the text). The op amp's + terminal will draw practically no power, which is good for PWM. The op amp's output, on the other hand, can source quite a bit of power (depending on the op amp). The power drawn from the op amp's output will not affect the charge on the capacitor.

These amplifiers output a positive voltage if you input a positive voltage, so they are *noninverting*. An *inverting* amplifier reverses the sign of a voltage, changing a negative to a positive and vice versa. You can see an example of this sort of amplifier in Figure 4.6B. The gain for this sort of amplifier is $−R2/R1$.

The analysis of inverting amplifiers is a bit trickier than the earlier example. You have to realize that the + terminal is at 0V. Therefore, the op amp will try to make the − terminal 0V (often called a *virtual ground*). Suppose you put 2V at the input terminal at R1 and that R1 is 10K. Further assume that R2 is a 20K resistor. If the − terminal of the op amp is at 0V, the current through R1 must be $(2 − 0)/10K$ or 0.2mA. That means there must be −0.2mA also flowing through R2 (you can ignore the tiny currents through the op amp). A −0.2mA current flowing through 20Ks results in −4V.

Once you get used to dealing with op amps, there isn't much to them. With modern devices, the input resistance is so high you can safely ignore them in all but the most precise applications.

Trying PWM

Build the circuit in Figure 4.5 using a 0.1F capacitor. Run the program below and see how long it takes the 5V output to drop to 4.5V. Then put a 10F electrolytic capacitor in parallel with the 0.1F unit (the – terminal to ground, of course). Measure the time to discharge now. The program consists of two lines:

```
PWM 0,255,1000
Stopit: GOTO Stopit ' don't use END to avoid sleep mode
```

Try the same experiment, but add a 100K resistor across the capacitor to simulate a load. Remember, 100K at 5V is only 50A, which is a very small load. Try a 1K resistor (5mA).

Other Uses for PWM

PWM can do more than just generate voltages. For example, hook up an LED and a resistor directly to Stamp Pin 0. If you run the program in Listing 4.2, you'll see the LED's brightness vary up and down.

Listing 4.2   Varying an LED.

```
Top:
FOR b1=0 to 255
  PWM 0,b1,500
NEXT
GOTO Top
```

Although PWM is a common way to control motor speeds, the Stamp's PWM command is not well suited for this because you can't keep generating PWM while doing other things. However, you can get third-party modules that use PWM to control motor speed (see Chapter 8).

Traditional D/A

Of course, for high precision and speed, there is no substitute for a dedicated D/A converter (sometimes known as a *DAC*). These are specialized ICs that convert a digital number into a voltage. There are a wide variety of DACs available, but the ones you will want to use with the Stamp have serial inputs. This allows you to connect to the Stamp using only a few I/O pins.

A prime example of a serial DAC is an LTC1257 (from Linear Technology). This is a 12-bit DAC, so you can vary the output voltage from 0 to 5V in about 1.2mV steps. Like an op amp, the DAC can't provide a voltage as high as its supply voltage, so you'll certainly want to connect the Vcc pin to a higher supply (like a 9V battery).

The 1257 requires a Vref input that sets the maximum voltage output. The Stamp's regulated 5V output makes a great input to Vref. You can see a typical circuit in Figure 4.8.

Figure 4.8   Using a serial DAC.

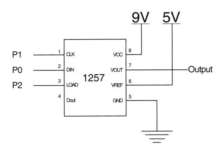

Software to operate the 1257 is simple. The idea is that you send the DAC 12 bits, and then pulse the LOAD pin to convert that number into a voltage. The voltage stays on the output until you pulse the LOAD line again (presumably to load a new number). You simply shift 12 bits out on the data pin (most significant bit first). For each bit, you pulse the clock line. For the Stamp I, you can use a loop like this:

```
' assume data is in W0
' data pin is pin 0
' clock pin is pin 1
' load pin is pin 2
FOR b5 = 1 to 12
  Out0=Bit11
  PULSOUT 1,5
  W0=W0*2
NEXT
PULSOUT 2,5
```

On the Stamp II, just use SHIFTOUT. Once you send the data to the DAC, you pulse the LOAD pin to store the number you sent into the analog output buffer. If you need multiple output voltages, you can daisy chain multiple 1257s together. Just tie all the CLK and LOAD pins together. The master DAC receives data from the Stamp on the Din pin. The master's Dout pin connects to the first slave's Din pin. The first slave can connect to another slave by connecting their Dout and Din pins together.

If you daisy chain DACs like this, you have to send all the bits you want to load together, sending the data for the last slave first. You'll read more about this type of serial communications in Chapter 6.

The 1257 isn't the only serial DAC in town. The Maxim MAX521, for example, is an 8-bit serial DAC that uses the I2C protocol (see Chapter 6 for more about the I2C protocol).

A Digital Power Supply

Using a DAC or a PWM is not usually a good way to produce power. Even with an op amp buffer, you can't draw much power from most DAC circuits. In this chapter and the next three chapters, you'll see the development of a power supply that a Stamp controls. The first stage of the project is to simply develop sufficient power from a Stamp PWM output so that you can use it as a power supply. From that simple beginning, you can have a power supply that uses digital controls (that is, up and down buttons) to set the output voltage. Future chapters will add closed loop control, RS-232 control, and an LCD display.

Designing a proper power supply isn't as easy as you might think. If everything works as you expect, it isn't that difficult — a single transistor will do the job. However, what happens if the load circuit draws too much current? Or if you accidentally short circuit the output? What will happen when the circuit overheats?

Luckily, there are integrated circuits that account for all of these problems and more. They are inexpensive and readily available. Of particular interest is the LM317, an adjustable three-terminal regulator. The 317 allows you to input an unregulated voltage and a reference voltage. The output of the regulator will be 1.25V above the reference voltage.

TIP

Be extra careful about the LM317's pinout. Unlike most three-terminal regulators, the 317's metal tab is connected to the output (on a 7800-series regulator, the tab is ground). The pin out itself is unusual too. The input voltage is on pin 3, the output is on pin 2, and the adjustment voltage is on pin 1.

As a first attempt, consider the circuit in Figure 4.9. This is simply a PWM circuit directly feeding the adjustment terminal. This works — sort of. Suppose you set the PWM duty cycle to 90 by using a command like this:

```
top:
PWM 0,90,100
GOTO top
```

You'd expect the PWM output to be 1.76V and since the LM317 outputs 1.25V above the reference, the output should be 3V. However, this isn't the case. The output will be actually 4V. This is because the voltage regulator sends current out the adjust pin and this current develops voltages in the PWM network.

Figure 4.9   A simple power supply.

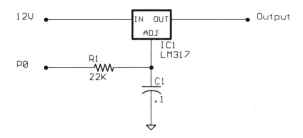

Still, for some cases this wouldn't be a problem. I plotted a few values of output vs. input (see Figure 4.10) and determined that the output (Y) corresponded to the PWM count (X) in a linear fashion described by:

$$Y=0.0193X + 2.29$$

Notice that the slope (0.0193) is nearly what you'd expect from the 8-bit PWM since $5/256 = .0196$. Of course, the LM317 introduces a 1.25V offset so 1.04V of the offset is due to the stray current flowing through the PWM circuit.

Figure 4.11 shows another circuit that doesn't have this problem. With the unity gain op amp (IC2, and LM324 op amp), the output impedance is so low that the regulator's stray current is not significant. Of course, the maximum output from the Stamp is 5V, so the regulator tops out at about 6.25V.

Figure 4.10   PWM vs. voltage output.

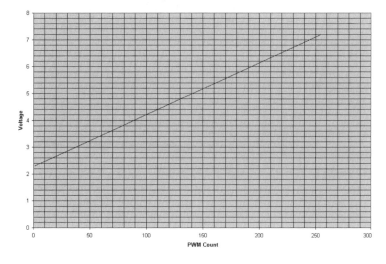

Figure 4.11 A 1.25 to 5V power supply.

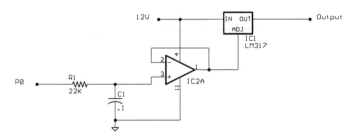

The answer to this problem is to scale the output of the PWM using an op amp that shows gain. So if you use an op amp circuit with a gain of two, you could output 1.25 to 10V (and each step would be roughly 40mV instead of 20mV). A gain of three would allow 1.25–15V. You can find a circuit in Figure 4.12 that uses two op amps — one that shows gain and another that isolates the whole circuit from the effects of the regulator. The ratio (R2+R3)/R2 sets the gain of the op amp so that using equal resistors will set the gain to two.

Adding two buttons (see Figure 4.12) allows you to step the voltage up and down using the program that appears in Listing 4.3.

Figure 4.12 A 1.25 to 10V power supply.

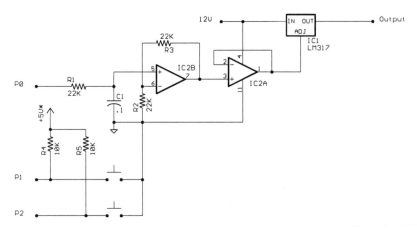

Listing 4.3 This simple code steps the power supply's output voltage up or down.

```
volt var byte
btn1 var byte
btn2 var byte


volt=0
btn1=0
btn2=0



top:
pwm 0,volt,200
button 1, 0, 5, 5, btn1, 1, voltup
button 2, 0, 5, 5, btn2, 1, voltdn
goto top

voltup:
  volt=volt+1
  goto top

voltdn:
  volt=volt-1
goto top
```

Summary

Even though the Stamp is primarily a digital device, it is possible to output analog quantities with it — at least to some extent. With the use of an outboard DAC, of course, the Stamp can generate very precise voltages easily. Although DACs are not very inexpensive, there is no substitute when you need something precise.

If you read other books about more traditional microprocessors, you may run across inexpensive DAC substitutes, but these are probably not the right thing to use with the Stamp. For example, it is easy to build a network of resistors (commonly called an *R2R network*) that converts a digital number into a voltage. While these work well (and are quite inexpensive), they require the data in parallel form. For eight bits of precision, you'd need all the pins on a Stamp I and half of the pins on a Stamp II.

While many people (especially programmers) naturally understand digital design, analog electronics can be a little frustrating at first. The cookbook op amp and amplifier circuits in this chapter should help you get started. In reality, op amps are not hard to understand, but they do require some study. A little time spent learning fundamentals will save a lot of time down the road.

Exercises

1. Write a program that allows you to connect an analog voltmeter to a Stamp pin (with a resistor and capacitor as in Figure 4.5) and cause the voltmeter's needle to sweep like a metronome.

2. Using three buttons, make a toy organ that plays notes on a speaker as you press buttons (you can use the Stamp activity board for this purpose). Add more buttons if you have them available.

3. Design an op amp to buffer the Stamp's PWM output so that you can create a voltage from 3V to 11V. You may need more than one op amp.

For answers to the exercises, see the Answer Key, page 431.

Chapter 5

A Recording Voltmeter: Analog Input

When I was in high school, I had a math teacher named Mr. Harder. Mr. Harder was probably one of the best mathematicians I've ever met. His approach to teaching high school was off-beat (but memorable).

What really impressed me about Mr. Harder was his problem-solving skills. If you are a programmer or an engineer, you know that this is one of the hardest things to teach. Some people seem to be better at solving problems than other people. I'm not sure anyone knows why.

One thing that Mr. Harder used to constantly say was, "You have to use what you know to get to what you don't know." This should be the motto of every digital computer that tries to measure analog quantities. Nearly always, the computer will convert the analog quantity into something it can understand. A pulse width, for example, is easy to measure digitally. If you could convert an analog quantity (say a resistance) into a pulse width, you could measure it very simply. That's exactly what the Stamp does.

In this chapter, I'll use the Stamp's analog input capabilities to build:

- a capacitance meter and
- a recording Voltmeter.

Before tackling these projects, I'll explain how the Stamp can measure analog signals by converting the analog quantity into pulses that the Stamp can easily measure. I'll also show you some other important techniques that allow you to read data that isn't digital in nature.

In Chapter 4, you saw that the Stamp could produce analog values, but for heavy-duty applications, you probably wanted an external piece of hardware known as a DAC. The same is true of analog input. In many cases, you can use the Stamp's built-in commands. In other cases, you'll want an external *analog to digital converter* (A/D or ADC) for the extra precision and ease of use.

Careful What You Ask For

The number one thing you have to ask yourself when you want to make an analog measurement is, "What is it that I really want to measure?" In many common cases, you don't really want to read a voltage, even though it might seem like it at first glance. For example, suppose you have a potentiometer connected across a 9V battery. When the pot is all the way in one direction, the voltage on the wiper is 0V or 9V (depending on the direction). If the pot is at the midway position, the voltage on the wiper is 4.5V.

It is true that you could measure the voltage to determine the position of the pot. However, the Stamp has very simple-to-use commands for reading the charge and discharge of a capacitor through a resistor. It does not have an easy way to measure voltage directly. Therefore, if you can change your question from, "What's the voltage on the wiper of the pot?" to "What's the position of the pot?," you can save a lot of time and energy. Because the Stamp can read a pulse width, anything you can convert to a frequency is a candidate for measurement that way.

Reading Resistance or Capacitance

The Stamp has built-in commands for measuring the amount of time it takes for a capacitor to charge or discharge through a resistor (the RCTIME and POT commands; see Chapter 2). There are many ways you can capitalize on these features. Obviously measuring a potentiometer's position can be a useful thing to do. Real-world sensors that change resistance and capacitance abound. Thermistors measure temperature, hygristors measure humidity, strain gauges measure force (or weight, if they measure the force of gravity). Many proximity sensors change capacitance as do certain motion sensors.

All of these are simple to read with the Stamp. You can find the details in Chapter 2. The trick, of course, is to realize that by fixing either the resistance or the capacitance, you can determine the other value easily.

There are several tricky things you can do using the POT or RCTIME commands. For example, the Stamp manual shows a way to read multiple switches with one Stamp pin. The idea is that each switch controls a resistor so that the total resistance depends on the button pushed (see Figure 7.2 in Chapter 7). By measuring the total resistance, the Stamp can deduce which button is down (if any).

A Capacitance Meter Project

Here is a poor man's capacitance meter (although you could use it for reading a resistive transducer like a thermistor). In Chapter 7 you'll see how to use alphanumeric LCD displays, but what if you only need numbers? The idea of this project is to use a digital voltmeter for the output (along with the Stamp's PWM command). For experimenting, you can just use a digital multimeter. For real projects, you might consider one of the inexpensive digital voltmeter modules that many vendors sell.

The simple circuit is in Figure 5.1 (the code is in Listing 5.1). With the values and code shown, you can measure capacitance from about 0.02µF to over 10µF. You could change the component values (and recalibrate) to make the device to work on nearly any range of values. You may need to recalibrate depending on your construction if you want the best accuracy because my setup and yours may have different amounts of stray capacitance.

Figure 5.1   The capacitance meter.

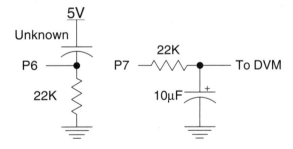

The hardest part of the software is converting the nonlinear RCTIME result to engineering units, and then to PWM-scale units. I measured several known-value capacitors and used the DEBUG command to examine the raw counts they generated. I then used the GAUSFIT program to generate a third order polynomial function to fit my data. This program is part of Parallax's Application Note #7 (available on their web site or on the CD-ROM). Of course, if you have a decent scientific calculator, it will fit curves too.

Of course, a curve fit program will generate real number coefficients. There are two problems with this: (1) the Stamp only does integer arithmetic, and (2) you have to ensure that the intermediate results will not overflow or underflow in the range you are interested in calculating.

Here's the calculation that came close to fitting my curve:

$$Y = 0.78 \times 10^{-6} \times X^3 - 0.0005263 \times X^2 + 0.5838454 \times X + 0.4225229$$

Well, that doesn't work well for the Stamp! So first, I rewrote it as a bunch of fractions like this:

$$Y = \frac{8 \times (X^3) - 5263 \times (X^2)}{10000000} + \frac{58 \times X + 42}{100}$$

Which is a little better, but still has some very big numbers in it. However, if you play with enough algebra, you can come up with:

$$Y = \frac{\dfrac{8 \times X - 5263}{100} \times X}{1000} \times \frac{X}{100} + \frac{58 \times X + 42}{100}$$

Now we are getting somewhere! The code's only other trick — to preserve as much accuracy as possible, it scales small raw counts up by multiplying them by 10 until they are greater than 300. This prevents small numbers from underflowing and avoids some problems with negative numbers. Of course, the answer must be scaled back down by the same number of divisions by 10.

This formula converts, for example, 10μF into 1,000 and 0.2μF into about 20. The PWM command's counts, however, must range 0–255, and each one represents about 20mV of voltage ($1/255$V). By allowing 20mV to represent 0.2μF, 1V represents 10μF. This is not only pleasing to the eye, but pleasing to calculate as well.

If you use a fixed-value capacitor, the resistor could vary and you could measure that instead.

Listing 5.1   The capacitance (or resistance) meter.

```
'RCMETER code by Al Williams AWC
'http://www.al-williams.com/awce.htm
raw var word      ' raw counts
eu var word       ' Engineering units
scalect var byte ' Conversion scaling
pwmv var word     ' PWM voltage output
```

Listing 5.1   The capacitance (or resistance) meter. (Continued)

```
output 6
output 7
top:
high 6
pause 1
rctime 6,1,raw     ' Read capacitor value
' EU Convert (see text)
gosub scale
eu=8*raw-5263/100*raw/1000
eu=eu*(raw/100)+((58*raw+42)/100)
gosub unscale
' adjust to PWM units... about 20/mv per unit
pwmv=eu/20
pwm 7,pwmv,50
goto top
scale:
scalect=0
if raw=0 then xret   ' don't scale zero!
scaleloop:
if raw>300 then xret
scalect=scalect+1
raw=raw*10
goto scaleloop
xret:
return
unscale:
if scalect=0 then xret
scalect=scalect-1
eu=eu/10
goto unscale
```

Converting from some raw numbers to meaningful quantities is often called *EU* or *engineering unit conversions*. You'll find that you nearly always have to perform some calculation to convert sensor data into human-readable values.

Using an ADC

Sometimes there is no substitute for reading an analog voltage. In those cases, you'll want to use an external circuit to convert the voltage to a digital quantity. Of course, because pins are scarce on the Stamp, you should use an ADC that has serial output. For example, the LTC1298 is a 12-bit dual-channel ADC. This chip is very similar to the LTC1257 DAC from Chapter 4, except it reads voltages instead of generating them. You can find a sample circuit in Figure 5.2. There are many serial ADCs you can use instead of the LTC device. For example, the Maxim MAX111 is a 14-bit dual-channel serial ADC.

Figure 5.2   Using the LTC1298.

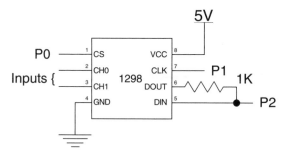

The software required to read the LTC1298 ADC is very similar to that required for the DAC in Chapter 4. The only major difference is that you have to send the device a command to tell it what type of sampling you want to perform. The 1298 can sample one of two channels, or it can read the differential voltage between the two channel inputs. Assuming you have symbols defined for the CLK (clock), DATAP (the data pin), and CS (chip select) pins, your code might look like this:

```
' assuming Stamp II -- use Symbol for Stamp I
CLK con 1
CS con 0
DATAP var in2
DATAPN con 2
Dly con 5
Result var Word
BitCtr var nib      ' could use byte here


Result=0        ' assume 0 counts
LOW CLK
DATAP=1         ' start bit
LOW CS
PULSOUT CLK,Dly
DATAP=1             ' single end mode
PULSOUT CLK,Dly
DATAP=0         ' channel 0 (or use 1)
PULSOUT CLK,Dly
DATAP=1       ' select MSB first (preferred)
PULSOUT CLK,Dly
INPUT DATAPN
FOR BitCtr=0 to 12    ' must read 0 start bit so 13 reads
   Result=Result<<1 + DATAP   ' For Stamp I use Result*2+DATAP
   PULSOUT CLK,Dly
NEXT
HIGH CS
' Counts now in Result
```

Of course, you could use SHIFTOUT and SHIFTIN if you remember to use the correct number of bits (four output bits and 13 input bits).

Keep in mind that the ADC does not return the value of the voltage. Instead, it returns a number that represents the percentage of the reference voltage present at the input. So %111111111111 is 5V, and %100000000000 is 2.5V. The reference voltage, by the way, is the chip's power supply, so your accuracy is only as good as the power supply regulation.

When selecting an ADC, you should be aware that the conversion timing for different types of ADCs can vary considerably. The fastest (and most expensive) ADCs use a technique called *flash conversion*, which compares the input voltage to a number of reference voltages. This is very fast, but for 8-bit operation, it requires 256 reference voltages and comparators.

A less expensive (but slower) technique is *successive approximation*. Here, the ADC guesses a voltage (usually using an internal DAC) and compares it to the input voltage. This is like playing the old children's game, "High/Low." Later in this chapter, you'll see how to construct this type of ADC from scratch. The LTC1298 uses successive approximation. However, when you request a reading, it freezes the input (storing the voltage in an on-board capacitor) so that it gets the correct value even if the input changes before the chip finishes guessing.

Averaging Readings

If you've ever built an A/D converter into a Stamp project, you've probably found out that these devices aren't the clean digital text book devices you'd like them to be. There will always be noise present — from the power supply, from the Stamp clock, and from the A/D's clock.

The problem is especially bad when you are measuring small voltages. Consider an 8-bit A/D. If you use a 5V reference, then each LSB (least significant bit) is worth $5/255 = .0196$ (about). That assumes that 0V gives 0 counts and 5V gives 255 counts. Call it 20mV per step, just to have a round number.

But what happens if you use a smaller reference? Suppose you are using a 2.6V reference? Now each step is .0094V — just under 10mV. With a 1.2V reference you drop to around 5mV. Each step down makes your noise that much more apparent.

There are many hardware methods to reduce noise. Careful ground layouts, decoupling capacitors, etc. However, you can also perform some software tricks to get better response from an A/D.

Since noise tends to be random, you'd expect errors that add to the true reading will be as prevalent as errors that subtract from the true value. Therefore, averaging can reduce noise quite a bit. In fact, noise can help by using a technique called dithering.

Dithering averages many samples to get even better resolution then the A/D's hardware allows. Consider this example. Suppose you are measuring a 2.35V signal with an A/D that uses a 4.096V reference (that's 16mV/LSB). You really should get 146.875 counts, but that's not possible. In theory, you'll get a count of 146 (or maybe 147 depending on the converter's methods). In practice, noise will cause the LSB to swing around anyway, so you'll get values ranging from 145 to 147 and —

this is the important part — the average value will be 146.875 (assuming the noise is truly randomly distributed).

So if you average enough samples, you should get 146.875, which is more accurate than 146 or 147. Of course, no amount of averaging on the Stamp will give you 146.875 because the Stamp only handles integers (unless you add a floating point math coprocessor like the PAK-I you'll read about in Chapter 6 or its big brother, the PAK-IX, which combines an A/D converter and floating point math).

The code in Listing 5.2 uses some tricks to get a better average from an ADC08034 A/D. This is an 8-bit converter with four channels you can use single ended, or you can use them as two differential pairs. The chip has a built-in 2.6V reference, which sounds great until you find out that there is no standard for how accurate that reference is. National privately admitted to me that they don't provide that spec on purpose. Each part will range between 2.5 and 2.7V (from my experience). The reference is pretty stable at whatever voltage it happens to be, but if you really want 2.6V, you'll have to screen the parts, which is not practical for production quantities, or calibrate each A/D individually.

Still, this is a common converter and you can always use an external reference if you like. If you have an external reference or you don't mind calibrating each device, you might want to give these parts a try.

Here are a few things to look for in the code:

- The `xvert` code takes the actual reading (a byte in `adin`).
- The `convert` routine adds up all the `adin` values into a word variable `acc`.
- The `VREF` constant is in tenths of a volt (decivolts), so 26 is really 2.6V.

Listing 5.2 Averaging A/D readings.

```
' A/D example -- Williams
VREF con 26        ' VREF in decivolts
sample con 25
adin var byte
acc var word
volts var byte


' change to suit your setup to the chip
cs con 0        ' Chip select on pin 0
do con 1        ' Data out on pin 1
di con 2        ' Data in on pin 2
aclk con 3      ' Clock on pin 3
```

Listing 5.2   Averaging A/D readings. (Continued)

```
' AD channels for flow and temp
' You can reverse these and also reverse
' the polarity of the jacks if you wish
' %1000 = 0+,1-
' %1001 = 2+,3-
' %1010 = 0-,1+
' %1011 = 2-,3+
'


convert:
  acc=0
  for i=1 to sample
    gosub xvert
    acc=acc+(10*adin)
  next
  adin=acc/sample+5/10
  volts = adin * VREF / 255
  return

' Talk to ADC0834
xvert:
  low cs
  shiftout di,aclk,MSBFIRST,[%1010\4]   ' 0-, 1+
  shiftin do,aclk,MSBPOST,[adin]
  high cs
  return
```

The Stamp's lack of real math is a slight problem here. Suppose you set sample to 5 and you get the following readings:

127 126 129 128 128

The average (integer-only) is 127, but the true average is 127.6, which is closer to 128. To fix this, the convert routine multiplies each input value by 10 (essentially converting the units from counts to decicounts). Now the average is 1,276!

To get back to counts, we round the number to the nearest 10 position and divide by 10:

adin=acc/sample+5/10

The +5 changes 1,276 to 1,281 and dividing by 10 goes back to 128. So with a simple trick, you can get a better average — of course, floating point math would be more precise, but this answer is good enough.

Be careful when selecting how many samples you average or you may overflow the Stamp's 16-bit math. Consider five samples. The maximum value of acc is 2,550 × 5 = 12,750 — no problems. With 25 samples, you get 2,550 × 25 = 63,750. Getting close to the limit there. If you try 26 samples, you'll find that 2,550 × 26 = 66,300 — too much for 16 bits. This kind of problem can be hard to track because it only occurs when you get large values. So be careful!

A Homebrew ADC

An ADC IC like the LTC1298 represents the ultimate in convenience. You connect it and it does all the work. However, with a little ingenuity, you can homebrew your own ADC with surprisingly effective results.

How about using a 99¢ comparator chip to get four analog input channels? The downside? Reasonably slow conversion, and accuracy of about ±0.1V at 0–5V. The specs won't knock your socks off, but this circuit is certainly good enough for many purposes.

The heart of this homebrew ADC is a LM339 comparator chip. You can find the schematic in Figure 5.3. None of the resistor values are critical. The circuit will work for either Stamp.

Figure 5.3   The homebrew ADC.

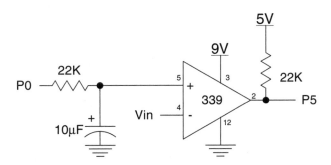

How does it work? The idea is to use PWM to generate a voltage at the + lead of the comparator. Really, any reasonable op amp ought to work here. However, the 339 is inexpensive, has an open collector output, and runs off a single positive power supply. When the PWM voltage matches the input voltage, the Stamp knows the input voltage is the same as the PWM voltage. Pin 5 will go high when the Stamp passes from lower than the input voltage to higher. If you like it the other way, reverse the + and − leads.

Notice that the 339 has an odd pinout (power is on pin 3 and ground is on pin 12). The supply input to the IC is +9V not +5V. This allows the device to measure right up to 5V. If you connect the supply to 5V, you can only measure 4V or so. The Stamp doesn't care because the output is open collector. It either outputs 0V or leaves its output floating (that's why there is a pull-up resistor on the output). You could use any voltage up to the chip's limit (36V). A good place to get this voltage is from the PWR pin of the Stamp.

Want to measure more than one voltage? Great! There are three more comparators in the same package. Just tie the + leads together and pull up the outputs with a 10K resistor. No need to duplicate the RC network. That means you can measure four analog voltages with five Stamp pins. Not too bad. Here's the simplest possible code to read the voltage:

```
for w1=0 to 255pwm 0,w1,1
  if vin=1 then done
next w1' overflow here
done:
  w2=w1*50/255 ' convert to decivolts (10 decivolts=1 volt)
```

Of course, it takes longer to convert 5V than it does to convert 0.1V because you have to count higher. On the other hand, you can easily convert all four channels at once.

The maximum conversion time is $5mS \times 255 = 1,275mS = 1.275S$ (each test is about 5mS). Testing three more comparators won't add much to that time. You might think about using a binary search algorithm to speed things up. The problem is you need a comparator with three states (high, low, and equal) to do this.

However, you can do a modified binary search by testing for each bit individually. First, try 128. The result is either too high or too low. If it is low, leave the value at 128, add 64, and try again. If 128 is too high, just try 64. Keep going until you've done all eight bits. Then you can do the conversion in roughly 40mS. That's fast enough for many applications. The code is a bit harder to understand, but it is much faster. Of course, if you are doing more than one channel you have to repeat the steps for each channel. You'll find code for this method in Listing 5.3 and 5.4.

Listing 5.3   Stamp I A/D code.

```
' Quick and dirty A/D -- Binary search method
' Al Williams
' http://www.al-williams.com/awc/awce.htm
symbol vin=pin5
symbol result=w1
symbol mask=w3
symbol endv=b10
symbol i=w2

output 7
input 5
input 0

agn:
result=128
mask=128
for i=1 to 8
  pwm 0,result,1
  if vin=0 then toolow
  result=result-mask ' clear bit
  toolow:
  mask=mask/2    ' shift right
  result=result+mask
next i


' We now know the voltage as a count from 0-255
' let's break it into an integer and tenth fraction
' I could have done this in less variables
' but I wanted to see each result for debugging

found:
w2=result*50/255  ' convert to decivolts
w5=w2/10       ' get whole number
w3=w5*10       ' get even # of decivolts
```

Listing 5.3   Stamp I A/D code. (Continued)

```
w4=w2-w3        ' subtract leaving fractional part


' Write rawcount : voltage on a line to PC
' This assumes 2400 baud inverted communications
serout 7,n2400,(#result,":",#w5,".",#w4,13,10)
goto agn   ' Keep on keeping on
```

Listing 5.4   Stamp II A/D program.

```
' A/D Converter for Stamp II
' Al Williams
' http://www.al-williams.com/awc/awce.htm
vin var in5
result var word
mask var word
i var word
whole var word
frac var word
output 0
input 5

agn:
result=128
mask=128
for i=1 to 8
  pwm 0,result,1
  if vin=0 then toolow
  result=result-mask  ' clear bit
  toolow:
  mask=mask/2  ' shift right
  result=result+mask
next
result=result*50/255
whole=result/10
frac=result-(whole*10)
serout 16,84,[dec whole,".",dec frac,cr]
goto agn
```

The Recording Voltmeter

Armed with any of the A/D circuits discussed in this chapter, it is easy to monitor the output voltage of the power supply in Chapter 4. Listing 5.5 shows the result of merging the power supply code (Listing 4.3) with the homebrew A/D code from Listing 5.4. Because the A/D and the power supply both use pin 0, I moved the A/D's pin 0 to pin 5.

Listing 5.5   Recording power supply voltage.

```
vin var in5
result var word
mask var word
i var word
whole var word
frac var word

volt var byte
btn1 var byte
btn2 var byte

volt=0
btn1=0
btn2=0

output 6
input 5

top:
pwm 0,volt,200
gosub convert     ' output current voltage
button 1, 0, 5, 5, btn1, 1, voltup
button 2, 0, 5, 5, btn2, 1, voltdn
goto top

voltup:
  volt=volt+1
  goto top
```

Listing 5.5   Recording power supply voltage. (Continued)

```
voltdn:
  volt=volt-1
goto top

convert:
result=128
mask=128
for i=1 to 8
  pwm 6,result,1
  if vin=0 then toolow
  result=result-mask    ' clear bit
  toolow:
  mask=mask/2   ' shift right
  result=result+mask
next
result=result*50/255
whole=result/10
frac=result-(whole*10)
  debug dec whole,".",dec frac,cr
return
```

Voltage to Pulse Conversion

It is possible to convert a voltage to a pulse. There are specific voltage to frequency chips that can do this (like National's LM331), or you can use the 555 timer IC (see Figure 5.4). This technique usually requires field calibration because the exact pulse width will depend on the components used.

The 555 is a well-known IC often used for creating timers. The chip is nothing more than a few comparators and some associated circuitry. You can build many things using the functional blocks that this device supplies. In this case, the 555's operation is governed by the charging and discharging of the capacitor between 5V and the unknown voltage (which has to be greater than 5V for the circuit to operate).

Figure 5.4   Using a 555 for A/D.

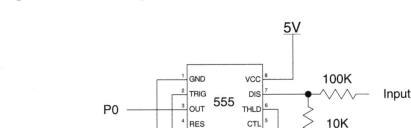

Once you have the circuit generating a train of pulses that correspond to the voltage, it is a simple matter to measure their width. The PULSIN command will measure the width and you'll have to correlate that to the voltage you want to sense.

You can also use a portion of a 4046 Phase Locked Loop (*PLL*) chip for the same purpose. PLLs have a *Voltage-Controlled Oscillator (VCO)* and a phase comparator. In this application, you'd only use the VCO. Because the VCO has a logarithmic response, it can smooth out nonlinear inputs (like thermistors). You can read more about using a 4046 in this type of application in Parallax's Stamp Application Note #5 (included with the Stamp manual on the CD-ROM).

The Simplest Analog Input

If you have very modest needs, you may be able to let the Stamp input serve as an analog input. This works because the Stamp recognizes voltages below a certain level as a 0 and above that level as a 1. The Stamp IISX has a threshold of 2.5V. The other Stamps have 1.5V (approximate) threshold.

How can you use this? Suppose you want to detect when a 9V battery drops below 8V. It would be a simple matter to devise a voltage divider that would transform 8V to about 1.5V (use a 200K and a 47K resistor, for example). Now the Stamp will see a 1 if the battery voltage is good, and a 0 if it low. Is this very accurate? No, it isn't extremely accurate, but it is good enough for many applications.

Another way you might use this to your advantage is to perform rudimentary timing functions. Consider the circuit in Figure 5.5. You could easily write software to make this a simple combination lock. The relay (simulated with an LED in this case) will only energize when someone presses the correct keys in the correct order.

Figure 5.5 The combination lock.

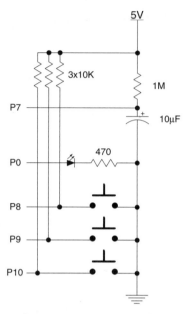

However, what happens if someone stops and pushes a few buttons and leaves? Now when you go to operate the lock, you have no way to know what buttons you should press. The answer is to incorporate a timeout so that if a certain amount of time passes without input, the lock resets and starts looking for the code at the beginning again.

There are several ways you could do this timeout. For example, you could maintain a counter and give up after it reaches a certain number. However, the count might vary depending on what the program is doing, how long you hold keys down, and so forth. This is an even bigger problem if the Stamp is doing anything other than monitoring buttons.

Another alternative is to use a capacitor and a resistor to set the time period. You can find the code to do this in Listing 5.5.

There are a few interesting points in the code: first, the switches are active low, so a zero in the corresponding bit means the button is down. The inc variable reads four bits from pin 8 to 11. This way the code can sample all three switches at the exact same time. It is more intuitive to work with active true buttons, so the code flips the sense of the bits. It also rearranges things so that the code returned in the switch variable is 0 for no button pushed, or 1, 2, or 3 to correspond with the active button.

The main loop simply resets the timer and waits for a key. When it detects a key, it compares it to the current code digit. If the key is correct, it advances to the next code digit and reenters the loop. If it is incorrect, the lock sequence starts again. If you are in the middle of a key entry and the timeout expires, that also restarts the lock sequence.

With the values given, you have about six seconds to enter each key. Any keystroke resets the timer, of course. You could vary the R and C values to change the timeout, of course.

The timeout is really the interesting part to this circuit. Normally the capacitor charges through the resistor to 5V. However, the software can change the sense pin (pin 7) to an output, set it low, and drain the capacitor. The 1MΩ charging resistor is large, so the Stamp has no problem overriding it. Once the capacitor drains, the program changes pin 7 to an input again. If you watch pin 7 with a voltmeter, you will see it slowly rise in voltage at this point. When the voltage exceeds the Stamp's logic 1 threshold, the timer has expired. Don't forget that the Stamp IISX has a different threshold than the Stamp II, so if you change chips, your time period will change also.

There are many times you might want to know when a certain period has elapsed without keeping a count through a loop. This is especially true if your loop has many paths of different durations. This simple circuit is just the solution.

Listing 5.6   Combo lock.

```
' Combo lock demo by Al Williams
' Shows how to use an RC network for generating
' a timeout
rctrig con 7 ' pin connected to capacitor
codelen con 5 ' length of combo
lockrelay con 0 ' turns on when unlocked
timeout var in7
current var byte
switch var byte
test var byte
output lockrelay
low lockrelay ' locked!


top:
current=-1 ' before 1st digit
' The code jumps here to advance to the next test digit
```

Listing 5.6 Combo lock. (Continued)

```
advance:
current=current+1 ' look at next digit
if current=codelen then unlock ' or, if done, we got em all
gosub resettimer ' reset timer on good key
loop:
gosub readsw ' read switches
if switch=0 then testtime ' no switches? Look for timeout
' get current key to compare for
lookup current,[3,3,1,2,3],test
if switch=test then advance ' right! Advance to next
debug "bad code",cr ' could make an obnoxious beep here
goto top ' Start over from beginning
testtime:
if timeout=0 then loop ' still time, so keep looking
if current=0 then top ' don't complain if no entry
debug "timeout",cr
goto top
unlock:
debug "unlocked",cr
high lockrelay
goto top ' go again for debugging purposes
'Read combo switches to switch variable
' You could customize this in many ways
' SWITCH will equal 0 (no key)
' or 1, 2, 3 for the 1, 2, or 3 keys
readsw:
switch=inc & 7 ' only 3 switches
switch=switch ^ 7 ' reverse sense (active low->active high)
if switch=0 then noread ' nothing
if switch<4 then readsw_ret ' correct switch 3
switch=3 ' top most switch
readsw_ret:
' now switch=0, 1, 2, or 3
pause 25 ' debounce
readloop:
if inc <> 15 then readloop ' wait for keys to go up
```

Listing 5.6   Combo lock. (Continued)

```
pause 25 ' debounce
debug ?switch
noread:
return
' Reset RC timer
resettimer:
output rctrig
low rctrig ' discharge capacitor
pause 100 ' give it time
input rctrig
return
```

Summary

Although there are some limitations, the Stamp can read analog quantities in many cases with very little external hardware. The trick is to remember what you actually want to read — don't get stuck assuming you must measure a voltage.

For cases where you do need to read a voltage, you can often get away with a simple circuit like the homebrew ADCs in this chapter. Of course, there are times when you need an honest-to-goodness ADC to precisely measure voltages. The Stamp can handle those too.

Exercises

1. How would you change the homebrew ADC in Figure 5.3 to read 0–12V?

2. Write a program that sets one of four LEDs based on the position of a potentiometer. In other words, when the pot is to the left, the left-most LED should be on. As you advance the pot, the LED extinguishes and the next LED lights. This continues until the pot is to the right and the right-most LED is the only one on.

3. Design a circuit that uses a LM339 to detect four voltage levels: 1.4V, 2.1V, 3.5V, and 5V. [Hint: A silicon diode will produce a good 0.7V reference.]

For answers to the exercises, see the Answer Key, page 433.

Chapter 6

Stamp to Internet: Serial I/O

Like a lot of hard core computer guys, I've spent more than my share of time using the UNIX operating system. These days, UNIX receives a lot of criticism for its cryptic command language. For example, to request a list of files, you issue an `ls` command. One way to view a file is to use `cat`. The `cp` command copies you get the idea.

I've often said that anyone who complains that this is cryptic never had to dial into a remote computer at 110 baud on an old-fashioned teletype. At 110 baud, `ls` is the soul of wit. Modems are an example of a serial device. They transmit data one bit at a time (serially) using some prearranged scheme to reassemble the bits into bytes. Contrast this with a parallel printer, for example. A printer that uses a parallel port receives data a byte at a time.

Back in those days, it was common to speculate on when there would be a computer in most homes. That day came earlier than most people expected, but in a surprising way. The average family began buying computers unknowingly in their microwave ovens, their TV sets, and their phones. You can scarcely find a piece of consumer electronics that doesn't have a computer in it now.

Of course, today many homes have "real" computers (or even a Macintosh — sorry, I just can't resist). Even then, these are often little more than really fancy teletypes that connect to the Internet via a modem. It is clear that serial communications — in this case, communications via a modem — has become far more important than anyone expected.

The Stamp's built-in serial commands make it easy to take advantage of serial I/O in your application. In this chapter, I'll explain the basics of the most common serial protocols and show you how to use serial techniques to build some useful tools. Specifically, you'll learn how:

- the most common serial protocols work,
- the processor uses the IC2 serial protocol to communicate with other chips,
- to build a data logger that uses EEPROM to store data,
- to build a Frequency Counter, and
- to connect a Stamp to the web.

Serial communications are especially important to Stamp developers because of the Stamp's limited number of I/O pins. In earlier chapters, you've already seen A/D and D/A that communicate serially. These are ideal for the Stamp because they take two or three I/O pins to connect. A conventional 8-bit A/D chip would require at least eight (and probably nine or 10) I/O pins. A Stamp I only has eight pins to begin with! Even on the Stamp II, wasting nine or 10 pins for one device is usually unacceptable.

Definitions

You can broadly divide serial I/O protocols into two categories: *synchronous* and *asynchronous*. A *synchronous protocol* usually requires a clock and a data line. The devices transfer data in step with the clock. This makes for very simple software, but it has the disadvantage of requiring multiple I/O lines. *Asynchronous protocols* (like RS232, for example) don't require a clock. Instead, the receiver synchronizes on the sender's start bit. Also, there must be at least one stop bit to allow the receiver time to resynchronize. So while an asynchronous transmission only requires one wire (in theory), the sender must transmit at least two extra bits for each byte. This reduces the overall speed of the communications channel.

When discussing serial protocols (especially asynchronous ones), it is common to discuss baud rate. Without splitting hairs, you can think of the *baud rate* as the number of bits per second the protocol allows (for RS232, this is a sufficient definition). Remember, there are at least two extra bits per byte, so a 9,600 baud link can transfer, at maximum, about 960 characters per second.

When dealing with synchronous protocols, it is more common to specify the minimum clock width or the maximum clock frequency that you can use. This also determines the amount of information you can send. Of course, for a synchronous protocol, there are usually no extra bits. So if the maximum clock frequency is 16kHz, you can transfer about 2,000 characters per second.

You might decide that asynchronous communications is a better fit for the Stamp because it requires fewer I/O lines. This isn't always the case. First, in practical use, the transmitter or receiver may require extra lines to inform the other that it isn't ready (handshaking lines). Also, the receiver must constantly watch for start bits so as not to miss any transmissions. The Stamp can only do one thing at a time, so it requires careful design to be sure you receive all serial transmissions.

Simple Serial Protocols

There is code in Chapters 4 and 5 that deals with serial A/D and D/A converters. These converters appear as a shift register to the Stamp. To write to a device like this, you place data on the data line and pulse the clock line. Of course, you have to agree with the device if the data is valid when the clock is high or low, and if the least-significant or most-significant bit is first.

Devices like this are so common that the Stamp II has special commands (SHIFTIN and SHIFTOUT) just for dealing with these devices. Of course, even with the Stamp I, it is simple enough to mimic the operation of the commands.

Some devices extend the idea of this simple protocol to gain extra functionality. For example, the PAK series coprocessors from AWC use a modified synchronous protocol to provide functions like floating point math or concurrent I/O operations. By using a synchronous protocol, the Stamp can continue working while the coprocessor performs operations.

Interfacing with the PAK-I

The PAK-I is a good example of a device that uses a synchronous protocol that is very similar to SPI (the Serial Peripheral Interface). The chip has five pins that may connect with the Stamp (although you only need two in most cases). By using the shift instructions, the Stamp can command the PAK-I to do floating point math.

The PAK-I has separate input and output data pins to accommodate microprocessors that don't allow you to change I/O pin directions. However, the output is open collector, so you can connect the input and output pins together when you use it with a Stamp. Because the output is open collector, you'll need a pull-up resistor on it in any case. For basic operation, you can just wire the input and output pin to a Stamp pin, and wire the clock line to another Stamp pin.

Some operations you might perform with the PAK-I can take some time to execute. All lengthy commands output a return byte, and that byte will always begin with a 0 bit. This allows the Stamp to check to see if the PAK is ready to respond. If the Stamp is waiting for a response and the data line is high, the PAK is busy. The Stamp can wait until the data is available, or it can do something else and check again later.

The Stamp can also reset the PAK by using a special sequence on the clock and data lines. Normally, when the clock goes high, the data line will remain stable until the clock drops again. If the Stamp changes the data line while the clock is high, the PAK understands that this is a reset and returns to a known state.

However, there are cases where you might want more than one PAK connected to the Stamp at the same time. In this case, you can wire all the clock and data lines to the same Stamp pins. You'll also use a separate Stamp pin to enable each PAK individually. This line can also reset the PAK, and the PAK can signal its readiness over the same line.

The fifth pin the PAK provides is an alternate busy indicator. If you ground this pin before the PAK powers up, it understands that you want to use the enable line as a busy indicator. In this case, you tie a pull-up resistor to the enable line. To disable the PAK, pull the enable line low. If the PAK is busy, it will pull the enable line low.

For some processors, it is difficult to treat a single pin as both an input and an output. In this case, you can install a pull-up resistor on the alternate busy indicator. Then, the PAK will signify its ready state on that pin, and only read the enable pin. You shouldn't use this mode with the Stamp because it wastes an extra I/O pin.

The circuit in Figure 6.1 shows a typical PAK-I setup. Because there is only one PAK connected, the Stamp doesn't use the enable or the alternate busy indicator pins. The code in Listing 6.1 calculates square roots using Newton's method and prints them on the debugging terminal (this is a nice example, but the PAK-II, a more capable coprocessor, actually computes square roots in hardware, so you probably wouldn't do this in real life). (Discussion continues on page 261.)

Figure 6.1   Typical connections for the PAK-I.

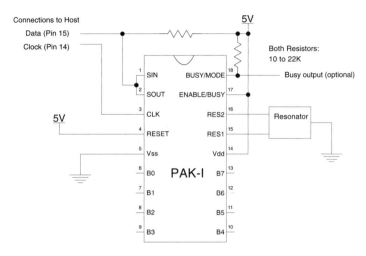

Listing 6.1   Calculating square roots with the PAK-I.

```
' Change these to suit your setup
datap con 15    ' Data pin (I/O)
datapin var in15
clk con 14      ' Clk pin (output)

' Constants for options
FSaturate con $80
FRound con $40


output clk
output datap


fpstatus var byte    ' FPSTATUS
fpx var word         ' Integer used by some routines
fpdigit var byte     ' Digit returned from DIGIT
fpxlow var word      ' The X register low & high
fpxhigh var word
fpb var byte         ' Temporary byte
' The X register in bytes
fpxb0 var fpxlow.lowbyte
```

Listing 6.1 Calculating square roots with the PAK-I. (Continued)

```
fpxb1 var fpxlow.highbyte
fpxb2 var fpxhigh.lowbyte
fpxb3 var fpxhigh.highbyte

gosub freset        ' always reset!

' Square root table
i var word
for i=1 to 1000
fpx=i    ' number
gosub floadint
gosub fsqrt
fpx=2
Debug dec i, "  -  "
gosub fdump
debug "  Error="
gosub fswap
fpx=i
gosub floadint
gosub fswap
gosub fsquare
gosub fsub
fpx=1
gosub fdump
debug cr
next
end


' Reset the Pak1
FReset:
LOW DATAP
LOW CLK
HIGH CLK
HIGH DATAP
LOW CLK
```

Listing 6.1 Calculating square roots with the PAK-I. (Continued)

```
return

' Wait for +,-,*,/,INT,FLOAT, & DIGIT
Fwaitdata:
input DATAP
if DATAPIN=1 then Fwaitdata
return


'Absolute Value
FAbs:
fpb=17
FSendByte:
  Shiftout datap,clk,MSBFIRST,[fpb]
  return

' Store0
FSto0:
fpb=18
goto FSendByte

'Store1
FSto1:
fpb=$92
goto FSendByte

'Rcl0
FRcl0:
fpb=19
goto FSendByte

'Rcl1
FRcl1:
fpb=$93
goto FSendByte
```

Listing 6.1 Calculating square roots with the PAK-I. (Continued)

```
' Load X with fpxhigh, fpxlow
FLoadX:
Shiftout datap,clk,MSBFIRST,[1,fpxb3,fpxb2,fpxb1,fpxb0]
return

' Load Y
FLoadY:
Shiftout datap,clk,MSBFIRST,[2,fpxb3,fpxb2,fpxb1,fpxb0]
return


' Load X with 0
FZeroX:
Shiftout datap,clk,MSBFIRST,[1,0,0,0,0]
return

' Load Y with 0
FZeroY:
Shiftout datap,clk,MSBFIRST,[2,0,0,0,0]
return

' Load an integer from FPX to X
FLoadInt:
Shiftout datap,clk,MSBFIRST,[1,0,0,fpx.highbyte,fpx.lowbyte]
' Convert to Int
Shiftout datap,clk,MSBFIRST,[7]
goto fpstat

' to int
FInt:
Shiftout datap,clk,MSBFIRST,[11]
gosub Fwaitdata
Shiftin datap,clk,MSBFIRST,[fpstatus]
if fpstatus<>0 then FInterr

' Read the X register
```

Listing 6.1   Calculating square roots with the PAK-I. (Continued)

```
FreadX:
fpb=3
gosub FSendByte
ShiftIn datap,clk,MSBPRE,[fpxb3,fpxb2,fpxb1,fpxb0]
fpx = fpxlow
FInterr:
return


' Swap X and Y
FSwap:
fpb=4
goto FSendByte


' X=X*Y
FMult:
fpb=12
fpstats:
gosub FSendByte
fpstat:
gosub FWaitdata
Shiftin datap,clk,MSBPRE,[fpstatus]
return ' status

' X=X/Y
FDiv:
fpb=13
goto fpstats

' X=X+Y
FAdd:
fpb=15
goto fpstats

' X=X-Y
```

Listing 6.1 Calculating square roots with the PAK-I. (Continued)

```
FSub:
fpb=14
goto fpstats

' Get Digit (fpx is digit #) return in fpdigit
FGetDigit:
Shiftout datap,clk,MSBFIRST,[5,fpx]
Fgetdigw:
gosub fwaitdata
ShiftIn datap,clk,MSBPRE,[fpdigit]
return


' Dump a number fpx is # of digits before decimal point
' Assumes 6 digits after decimal point
FDump:
fdj var byte
fdnz var bit
fdjj var byte
fdjj=fpx
fpx=0
fdnz=0
gosub FgetDigit
' Remove this line to print + and space
if fpdigit="+" or fpdigit=" " then Fdumppos
Debug fpdigit
Fdumppos
for fdj=1 to fdjj
  fpx=fdjj+1-fdj
  gosub FgetDigit
  if fpdigit="0" and fdnz=0 then FdumpNext
  fdnz=1
  Debug fpdigit
Fdumpnext
next
Debug "."
```

Listing 6.1   Calculating square roots with the PAK-I. (Continued)

```
for fpx=$81 to $86
  gosub FgetDigit
  Debug fpdigit
next
return


' Set options in fpx
' $80 = saturate
' $40 = round
FOption:
  Shiftout datap,clk,MSBFIRST,[$10,fpx]
  return


FXtoY:
  fpb=$17
  goto FSendByte


FYtoX:
  fpb=$18
  goto FSendByte



' Square Root, set tolerance below
fsqrt:
gosub fsto1    ' R1=target
    ' guess half the original #
fpxhigh=$8000
fpxlow=0
gosub floady
gosub fdiv
gosub fsto0    ' R0=guess
goto fsqrterr
freguess:
gosub frcl0    ' get guess
gosub fsquare      ' square it
gosub fswap    ' put it in Y
```

Listing 6.1   Calculating square roots with the PAK-I. (Continued)

```
gosub frcl1    ' get target
gosub fswap    ' x=guess squared; y=target
gosub fsub     ' subtract
gosub freadx   ' get x to fpxhigh,fpxlow
gosub frcl0    ' get guess
gosub fswap    ' y=guess
fpx=2          ' x=2
gosub floadint
gosub fmult    ' x=2*guess
gosub fswap    ' y=2*guess
gosub floadx   ' x=guess squared - target
gosub fdiv     ' x=x/y
gosub fswap    ' y=x/y term
gosub frcl0    ' x=guess
gosub fsub     ' x=guess-term
gosub fsto0    ' new guess
fsqrterr:
gosub fsquare
gosub fswap
gosub frcl1
gosub fsub
gosub fabs
' Select your error tolerance
' more precise values may fail to converge or take a long time
' check for error<.01
fpxhigh=$7823
fpxlow=$D70A
' check for error <.001
'fpxhigh=$7503
'fpxlow=$126f
' check for error<.0001 - warming may not converge
'fpxhigh=$7151
'fpxlow=$B717
gosub floady
gosub fsub
fpx=0
```

Listing 6.1   Calculating square roots with the PAK-I. (Continued)

```
gosub fgetdigit
if fpdigit="+" then freguess
' Found it!
gosub frc10
return
End


' X=X**2 ; does not destroy Y, but destroys fpxlow/fpxhigh
Fsquare:
   gosub fswap        ' get y
   gosub freadx       ' save it
   gosub fytox        ' y->x
   gosub fmult        ' x=x*y
   gosub floady       ' restore old y
   return
```

Notice that the code uses subroutine calls to load values, do multiplication, and other operations. At the heart of these subroutines is the simple SHIFTIN and SHIFTOUT commands — coupled with the busy indication logic, where appropriate.

The PAK-I's big brothers, the PAK-II and the PAK-IX, add various features. For example, the PAK-II has more storage space and handles advanced functions like logarithms, sine, cosine, and others. It also includes 16 spare I/O bits instead of eight. The PAK-IX is just like a PAK-II except it only has eight spare I/O bits. However, in place of the missing eight bits, this PAK has five channels of 10-bit A/D. The PAK can automatically read multiple readings and provide a floating point average (see Chapter 5 for more about averaging A/D readings). Luckily, communicating with these devices is exactly the same as talking to a PAK-I. You simply have extra commands you can issue.

The I2C Bus

The PAK-I protocol is versatile (well, I think so, but then again, I designed it), and well-suited for the Basic Stamp. However, it is hardly unique. There are other protocols, not necessarily designed for the Stamp, that allow you to connect multiple devices to a few microprocessor pins. One of the most popular of these is the Interface for Integrated Circuits (IIC or I2C) bus. This bus originated at Phillips, and there are many devices from a variety of vendors that utilize it. There are other similar standards including Microwire and SPI, but if you can understand I2C, you'll have no trouble with the others.

I2C is a synchronous protocol that uses only two wires and can communicate at 100 kbits/second (or 400 kbits/second in some cases). Some devices are *masters* — they initiate communications — and others are *slaves* (slaves only respond to masters). It is possible for a device to be both a master and a slave. It is also possible to have more than one master. This means that the I2C protocol has a complex algorithm for arbitrating disputes among masters.

To correctly implement an I2C master or slave takes quite a bit of work. Luckily, for most Stamp designs, you can assume that the Stamp is the only possible master and that the devices it wants to talk to are slaves. This can greatly simplify your code.

If you plan on using I2C, you should consider using the Basic Stamp IIP. It has commands that allow you to read and write I2C devices with no effort at all. In addition, it can do the same trick with Dallas 1-Wire devices, another type of serial bus.

I2C Basics

The I2C protocol uses two lines. One (SDA) is for data and the other (SCL) is for a clock. The master device drives the clock while the data line is bidirectional. However, slave devices can affect the clock to slow the master down, as you'll see shortly. Also, it is possible for more than one master to exist, in which case the masters must cooperate to prevent problems.

Each I2C line normally floats, and an external pull-up resistor brings the lines high. Devices (either masters or slaves) always pull the lines low to send a zero, and allow them to float to represent a logic 1. This is important because much of the cooperation between devices depends on the ability for multiple devices to drive the lines low.

To transmit a bit on the bus, the transmitter (which may be a master or a slave) must set the SDA line to the proper state while the SCL line is low. Once the SCL line goes high, the state of SDA must remain stable until SCL goes low again. You always transfer data eight bits at a time, most significant bit first.

Of course, you can't just start sending bits whenever you want. When a master wants to communicate with a slave, it generates a *start sequence*. This sequence sets the SDA line high, raises the SCL line, and then, while SCL is still high, drops the SDA line to a low logic state. This is clearly not a data bit because data bits must remain stable while SCL is high.

When slaves see a start sequence, it is their cue to listen to the SDA line to see if the master wants to speak to them. Each slave has an address that must be unique on the bus. Some devices allow you to select part of their address with jumpers so you can avoid collisions between devices.

Usually, the first byte following the start sequence selects the slave the master wishes to use. This byte will contain a 7-bit address and a single bit that selects reading (1) or writing (0). If the address byte is 0, the master is broadcasting to all slaves. There are other possible ways to address some I2C components (for example, there is an extension for 10-bit addresses). However, for Stamp projects, the 7-bit address convention is almost always adequate.

After a transmitter sends eight bits, the receiver usually has to send a single 0 bit to acknowledge receipt of the byte. If the receiver is, for example, too busy to process the byte, it can fail to acknowledge (which looks like a 1 because of the pull-up resistor), and the master then knows that the slave is not listening.

The exception to the acknowledgement bit rule is when a master is receiving and a slave is transmitting. Then, the master acknowledges all but the last byte it wants to receive from the slave.

Ending a Transmission

When the master no longer wishes to communicate with a particular slave, it may generate another start sequence and switch to another slave. If the master no longer needs the bus, it can issue a stop sequence.

A *stop sequence* is simply the reverse of the start sequence. The master holds SDA and SCL low. Then it raises SCL to indicate a valid clock. While the clock is still high, the master then raises SDA.

Slow Slaves

The master always generates the SCL clock. That means that the master can pace the transaction to suit its own purposes. However, there is always a danger that the slave will require more time than the master's clock allows.

For example, suppose you have an I2C slave that writes data to a floppy disk. When the master sends a byte of data, the slave needs some time to write the data out before the next data byte starts. It also might need time to be sure the disk operation succeeds before issuing an acknowledge.

The slave can easily pull the clock line low when it wants more time. The master will detect this condition and be unable to cycle the clock until the clock goes high again. Therefore, the width of the pulse is determined by the master, but the time between clock pulses depends on the slowest device participating in a transaction.

The hypothetical floppy disk slave can allow clocks to operate normally until it reaches the last data bit. By pulling the clock line low, the slave can hold off the next clock pulse from the master (the one that will clock the slave's acknowledge bit) until it is ready to respond.

Arbitrating Multiple Masters

Before a master can create a start condition, it must be sure the bus is not in use. That means masters must monitor start and stop conditions on the bus to track when the bus is in use.

Of course, it is possible that two or more masters will attempt to assert a start at the exact same time (or close enough that they can't detect each other). Remember, each master only drives SDA low. To send a 1, the master simply lets SDA float (so that the pull-up resistor drives the line high).

This is the key to detecting bus collisions. When SCL is high (indicating stable data), and the master is sending a 1, the master must sample the SDA line itself to make sure that SDA is really in a logic 1 state. If it isn't, this indicates that another master is active. The master sending the 1 must relinquish control of the bus with no further action (the losing master is allowed, but not required, to continue sending clock pulses until the end of the byte).

This is an elegant solution. When multiple masters are active, any one that sends a 0 while other masters are sending a 1 wins out over the other masters. Eventually, only one master is left. That master is completely unaware that arbitration occurred. There is no need to resend data or take any special action whatsoever.

Of course, if a master also functions as a slave, it must process the aborted transaction as a slave. After all, the winning master might be calling the losing master's slave device. As you can see, this can get complicated rather quickly.

Luckily, when using the Stamp and I2C devices, you'll usually only have one master (the Stamp) and a few slave devices. Further, you can almost always assume that the Stamp will be slower than the slowest I2C slave. If these two statements are true, you can write much simpler code that still works.

I2C Plans

For most Stamp projects, all you really need is a simple master. Here's the plan:
- Keep SCL and SDA pins as inputs.
- When ready, bring the SDA line low, this initiates a start sequence.
- Bring SCL low.
- Place each bit of the slave address (and read/write bit) on the SDA pin and pulse SCL from low to high and back to low.
- When expecting a response from the slave, make SDA an input and sample while SCL is high.
- Bring SDA high, then SCL, and bring SDA low to generate a start condition.

The Stamp doesn't need to see if anyone else is using the bus because it is the only master. This is the same reason the Stamp can place a 1 on the SDA bit. Technically, it should switch the SDA bit to an input to make it a high (and check for bus arbitration). However, with only a single host, this isn't necessary.

Interfacing to an I2C EEPROM

Perhaps the most common I2C device that you might add to a Stamp design is a EEPROM. Sure the Stamp has EEPROM already, but there isn't much of it, and you share it with your program. If you have a lot of data to store, the Stamp's EEPROM doesn't go far.

Another reason you might use an external EEPROM is for portability of data. For example, suppose you had a device that read temperatures from a thermistor, converted them to Centigrade, and stored them for later analysis. You could design the device so that it reads conversion factors from an external EEPROM and then stores the results in the same EEPROM. When the EEPROM is full, someone could simply remove it from a socket and replace it with a fresh one (possibly with updated conversion factors). The old EEPROM returns home where you could download its data to a PC, for example. Then you reprogram it and put it back in the system next time. With clever mechanical design, you could house the EEPROM in a way that it was easy to install and remove like a smart credit card, or PCMCIA card housing.

Regardless of why you want an EEPROM, you'll have to use a complex serial protocol to communicate with it. As an example, consider the circuit in Figure 6.2. This simple circuit will serve as a Morse code message generator. You load the program in Listing 6.2 and use it to set the message in the EEPROM. Then you download the program in Listing 6.3 which will replay the message. (Discussion continues on page 275.)

Figure 6.2   The Morse code generator.

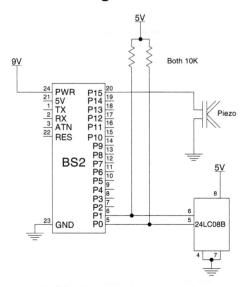

Listing 6.2   Setting the Morse code message.

```
' CW Ider Storage by WD5GNR

scl con 1
sda con 0
sdain var in0
sclin var in1


i2cackbit var bit   ' Ack bit -- should be zero after operations
i2craw var byte     ' I2C in or out byte
eeadr var word      ' EEPROM address
eedata var byte     ' EEPROM data in or out



eeadr=0
Serout 16,84,["Enter dots, dashes, blanks, $ to end",13,10]
top:
Serin 16,84,[eedata]
if eedata<>"$" then eew
' convert . to 0
```

Listing 6.2   Setting the Morse code message. (Continued)

```
eedata=0
eew:
gosub eewrite
eeadr=eeadr+1
goto top


' Begin I2C Code

' Set up a start condition
' Could hang if bus stays busy; could remove i2cbusy and the if
' following it if you are the only master
i2cstart:
  input sda
  input scl
i2cbusy:
  if (sdain and sclin)=0 then i2cbusy
  low sda
  low scl
  return

' Set up stop condition
i2cstop:
  low sda
  input scl
  input sda
  return

' Read ack bit
i2cack:
  input scl
await:
  if sclin=0 then await  ' wait for clock stretch
  i2cackbit=sdain
  low scl
  return
```

Listing 6.2 Setting the Morse code message. (Continued)

```
' Write 8 bits to I2C bus
' For multi-master, should perform arbitration
' Should also perform clock sync
i2cwrite:
  shiftout sda,scl,1,[i2craw\8]
  input sda
  return


' Read 8 bits from I2C bus
' Should perform clock sync
i2cread:
  shiftin sda,scl,4,[i2craw\8]
  return

' Begin EEPROM address
' Set EEPROM address -- common to read and write
eesetadr:
  gosub i2cstart
  i2craw=$A0 | ((eeadr>>7) & $E)
  gosub i2cwrite
  gosub i2cack
  if i2cackbit=1 then eeerr
  i2craw=eeadr & $FF
  gosub i2cwrite
  gosub i2cack
  if i2cackbit=0 then eeret
eeerr:
  ' NACK error
eeret:
  return

' Write byte to EEPROM
eewrite:
  gosub eesetadr
```

Listing 6.2   Setting the Morse code message. (Continued)

```
  i2craw=eedata
  gosub i2cwrite
  gosub i2cack
  if i2cackbit=0 then writeok
  ' NACK error
writeok:
  goto i2cstop  ' hidden return

' Read byte to EEPROM
eeread:
  gosub eesetadr
  gosub i2cstart    ' Abort write command
  i2craw=$A1 | ((eeadr>>7) & $E)
  gosub i2cwrite
  gosub i2cack
  gosub i2cread
  eedata=i2craw
  gosub i2cack
  goto i2cstop  ' hidden return

' Check for write complete
eecheck:
  gosub i2cstart
  i2craw=$A0
  gosub i2cwrite
  goto i2cack    ' hidden return

' Wait for write operation to complete
eepoll:
  gosub eecheck
  if i2cackbit=1 then eepoll
  return
```

Listing 6.3   Morse code playback.

```
' CW Ider by WD5GNR
spkr con 15
key con 8
ptt con 9

scl con 1
sda con 0
sdain var in0
sclin var in1

i2cackbit var bit  ' Ack bit -- should be zero after operations
i2carb var bit     ' Arbitration -- should be zero
i2craw var byte    ' I2C in or out byte
i2ci var nib       ' I2C bit counter
eeadr var word     ' EEPROM address
eedata var byte    ' EEPROM data in or out

mindelay con 5   ' 5 minutes
pttdelay con 50 ' delay to let transmitter key
ditlen con 80   ' set morse code speed
f con 1000       ' frequency for speaker

dotdash var byte
i var byte
output spkr
output key
output ptt
high ptt   ' unkey xmit
high key   ' unkey cw keying
top:
eeadr=0
low ptt    ' key transmitter
pause pttdelay  'wait for xmit to settle
loop:
gosub eeread
```

Listing 6.3 Morse code playback. (Continued)

```
dotdash=eedata
eeadr=eeadr+1
' element must be 0 (end), blank, dot, or dash
if dotdash=0 then wait1
if dotdash=" " then cspc
if dotdash="-" then dash
low key
freqout spkr, ditlen, f
high key
goto elspc
dash:
low key
freqout spkr, ditlen*3,f  ' dash is 3*dit
high key
elspc:         ' space each element
pause ditlen
goto loop
cspc:          ' space between characters
pause ditlen*4
goto loop
wait1:         ' done! wait for next time
pause pttdelay
high ptt
for i=1 to mindelay
  pause 60000            ' 60 seconds
next
goto top               ' do it again!
' Begin I2C Code

' Set up a start condition
' Sets i2carb=1 if busy
i2cstart:
  input sda
  input scl
  i2carb=0
  if (sdain & sclin)=1 then i2crdy
```

Listing 6.3 Morse code playback. (Continued)

```
i2cnoarb
  i2carb=1
  return
i2crdy:
  low sda
  low scl
  return

' Set up stop condition
i2cstop:
  low sda
  input scl
  input sda
  return

' Read ack bit
i2cack:
  input scl
i2cawait:
  if sclin=0 then i2cawait  ' wait for clock stretch
  i2cackbit=sdain
  low scl
  return

' Write 8 bits to I2C bus
i2cwrite:
  for i2ci=1 to 8
    if (i2craw & $80)<>0 then i2conewr
    low sda
    goto i2cwrbit
i2conewr:
    input sda
    if sdain=0 then i2cnoarb ' arbitration lost!
i2cwrbit:
    input scl
i2cwrclk:
```

Listing 6.3   Morse code playback. (Continued)

```
    if sclin<>1 then i2cwrclk  ' wait for clk sync
    low scl
    i2craw=i2craw<<1
 next
  input sda
  return



' Read 8 bits from I2C bus
i2cread:
  i2craw=0
  for i2ci=1 to 8
    input scl
i2crdclk:
    if sclin<>1 then i2crdclk  ' wait for clk sync
    i2craw=(i2craw<<1)+sdain
    low scl
  next
  return


' Begin EEPROM address
' Set EEPROM address -- common to read and write
eesetadr:
  gosub i2cstart
  if i2carb=1 then eesetadr  ' if we lose arbitration, try again
  i2craw=$A0 | ((eeadr>>7) & $E)
  gosub i2cwrite
  gosub i2cack
  if i2cackbit=1 then eeerr
  i2craw=eeadr & $FF
  gosub i2cwrite
  gosub i2cack
  if i2cackbit=0 then eeret
eeerr:
  ' NACK error -- what to do?
eeret:
```

Listing 6.3   Morse code playback. (Continued)

```
      return

' Write byte to EEPROM
eewrite:
  gosub eesetadr
  i2craw=eedata
  gosub i2cwrite
  gosub i2cack
  if i2cackbit=0 then writeok
  ' NACK error
writeok:
  goto i2cstop  ' hidden return

' Read byte to EEPROM
eeread:
  gosub eesetadr
  gosub i2cstart    ' Abort write command
  i2craw=$A1 | ((eeadr>>7) & $E)
  gosub i2cwrite
  gosub i2cack
  gosub i2cread
  eedata=i2craw
  gosub i2cack
  goto i2cstop  ' hidden return

' Check for write complete
eecheck:
  gosub i2cstart
  i2craw=$A0
  gosub i2cwrite
  goto i2cack   ' hidden return

' Wait for write operation to complete
```

Listing 6.3 Morse code playback. (Continued)

```
eepoll:
  gosub eecheck
  if i2cackbit=1 then eepoll
  return
```

The I2C code is different in the two listings. In Listing 6.2, I've assumed that the Stamp is the only master and that the EEPROM will always operate more quickly than the Stamp. These are good assumptions and the code is much simpler. There is no worry about arbitrating multiple masters, nor is there any provision for the EEPROM to slow the Stamp down.

Compare the I2C code in Listing 6.2 with the code in the next listing. Here, the I2C code attempts to arbitrate with multiple masters and allow the slave to slow the transfer down. The code is much more complicated. Of course, in this case, it isn't necessary to do these things, so you could easily replace the code in the second listing with the subroutines from the first with no ill effects. Even with this improved code, there is potential for failure in a multimaster system because the Stamp can't always monitor the bus. The only way to really support multiple masters is to employ interrupts, something the Stamp can't do.

A BS2P Datalogger

An external I2C EEPROM is a good place to store lots of data the Stamp collects. With the BS2P's built-in I2C support, it is even easier to connect an I2C EEPROM to your circuit.

I decided to make a simple data logger with the BS2P. I used an I2C EEPROM for external storage and a resistive sensor for data input. I just used a pot, but you could replace the resistor with a thermistor or light dependent resistor, for example.

The circuit logs data (from the resistor "sensor") to the EEPROM periodically until you push the button. The period in the example is 30 seconds. When you push the button, it dumps the data to the serial port and resets data collection. I didn't go to the trouble of handling the case where the EEPROM is full (there is room for 2,048 samples). The schematic appears in Figure 6.3.

Figure 6.3 A simple data logger.

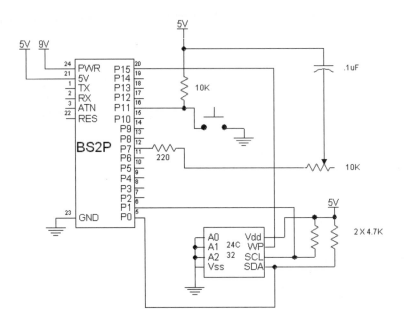

The BS2P requires the I2C devices to connect to P0/P1 (as shown) or P8/P9. You can't use other pins. The I2CIn and I2COut commands work like SERIN and SEROUT. You specify the first pin number (0 or 8) and the device code. Each I2C device has a unique device code. In the case of EEPROMs like the 24C32, the code is $A0 (for writing) or $A1 (for reading). In addition, the EEPROM uses the A0, A1, and A2 pins to allow multiple devices on the same bus. Since all of these pins are 0 in the example, the code doesn't change. However, suppose I tied A0 to 5V instead of ground. Then the codes would be $A2 and $A3. This allows you to daisy chain up to seven EEPROMs by giving each a unique 3-bit code on the A0–A2 pins.

The 24C32 needs two bytes of address data, and the I2CIn and I2COut commands allow this by placing the high byte first, followed by a backslash, followed by the low byte of the address. That means you have to break apart the address into two parts. That's easy enough though. If you have an address, AD, you can write:

```
I2COUT 0, $A0, AD>>8\AD&$FF,[whatever]
```

The WP pin allows you to write protect the EEPROM. I didn't really use this feature — you could simply ground the WP pin if you wanted to save a Stamp pin. The BS2P has a special command that lets you redirect the READ and WRITE commands to a different program bank. That means you could use unused program space as EEPROM and not even use an external chip. The STORE command allows you set the bank that READ and WRITE use.

Instead of querying the switch constantly, I used the polling interrupt feature to watch for a switch closure. The POLLIN command lets me specify the pin number (P11) and the desired state (0 is a switch closure). POLLRUN tells the Stamp to run a different program when the pin set by POLLIN reaches the desired state.

Polling isn't enabled by default, however. You have to call POLLMODE to set polling on and specify an action. This is easily the most confusing part to using polling. In this case I set POLLMODE to 4 (although 3 would work just as well). This activates polling and allows POLLRUN to work.

The modes are a bit tricky:

0	Turn off polling and clear all polling setup
1	Turn off polling, but remember all polling setup
2	Turn on polling, allowing POLLOUTPUT and POLLWAIT to work
3	Turn on polling, allowing POLLRUN to work
4	Turn on polling, allowing all commands (POLLOUTPUT, POLLWAIT, and POLLRUN) to work
5	Clear POLLINPUT setup
6	Clear POLLOUTPUT setup
7	Clear both POLLINPUT and POLLOUTPUT setup

Modes 3 and 4 automatically switch to mode 1 or 2 when triggered. This prevents them from retriggering in an endless loop. Modes 5–7 don't actually change the mode, they just clear the action and maintain the current mode.

I didn't use polled output in this example, but you can set modes 8–15 to make the outputs latch instead of following the input state when using polled output.

If all that was confusing, don't feel bad. It is easier to look at the sample code in Listings 6.4 and 6.5. There are three lines at the start of the program. The POLLIN command tells the Stamp to watch the switch and, when it goes to 0, to generate a polled event. The POLLRUN command tells the Stamp that the action you want to take is to run a new program when the event occurs. Finally, the POLLMODE command turns polling on. It stays on forever, so even though the POLL commands only execute once, their effect goes on for the duration of your program. As soon as the Stamp sees the push button turn on, it will run program #1.

Since the Stamp only checks the polled input pins between instructions, it is important not to use a long PAUSE statement. Instead, break your pause statements up into smaller pauses like the example does. This allows the Stamp to check for polled input often. There is also a POLLWAIT which puts the Stamp in low-power mode until a polled event occurs. You can set how often the Stamp wakes up to check the polled inputs.

There are two programs. The first is the main program (see Listing 6.4) and the second (Listing 6.5) is the push button response program. Notice that it waits for the button to release before it resumes execution of the first program. This prevents immediately executing the push button program again.

Notice there is no easy way to go back to exactly the point you were at when the polled event occurs. In this case, I simply restart the main program which is okay.

I didn't use the automatic assignment of variables because that makes it difficult to share variables between banks. Instead, I name variables manually. For example:

```
adctr     var     w0
```

This causes the program to use w0 as the adctr variable. This makes it easier to share and also to keep from clobbering another program's variables. Just remember that if you use w0 is the same as b0 and b1. The w1 register is the same as b2 and b3, and so on. You can't use w0 and, for example, b1 without causing problems.

Listing 6.4   Program for bank 0.

```
' This is program 0 of the logging example
' Requires a BS2P -- Williams
WCTL CON 15 ' EEPROM WCTL (not actually necessary)
RC CON 7 ' RC input
DUMP CON 11 ' Button goes low for data dump


low WCTL ' Enable EEPROM write (could tie low)


adctr var w0 ' address counter (shared with pgm 1)
state var w1 ' current state
i var b4 ' gp counter


adctr = 0 ' start at 0


' When DUMP button goes low, run program 1 right away
POLLIN DUMP,0
POLLRUN 1
POLLMODE 4
debug "Running...",cr
```

Listing 6.4   Program for bank 0. (Continued)

```
loop:
' Read sensor
HIGH RC
PAUSE 10
RCTIME RC,1,state
' Write to EEPROM
i2cout 0,$A0,adctr>>8\adctr&$FF,[state>>8,state&$FF]
adctr=adctr+2
for i=1 to 60 ' delay 30 seconds in 1/2 second ticks
   pause 500
next
goto loop
```

Listing 6.5   Datalogging program part 2 (bank 1).

```
' Program 1 for the Logging Example
' Requires BS2P -- Williams
DUMP CON 11 ' DUMP button
adctr var w0 ' shared address counter
state var w3 ' non-shared state variable
ad var w4 ' non-shared address counter

' Dump all data
for ad=0 to adctr-2 step 2
   ' read from EEPROM
   i2cin 0,$A1,ad>>8\ad&$FF,[state.highbyte,state.lowbyte]
   debug hex ad, ":", hex state,cr
next
waiting: if in11=0 then waiting ' wait for button release
pause 1 ' wait for bounce
run 0 ' restart log
```

Asynchronous Communications

The chief reason you'll want to do RS232 communications is to talk to a PC via its standard serial port. However, there are other devices that require RS232 (for example, the serial LCDs in Chapter 7). Another reason you might want to perform serial I/O is to communicate with another Stamp over a wire, or a modem. You can also use a modem to dial a phone — perhaps to dial a pager number when some condition occurs.

RS232 Basics

RS232 ports usually use a male 25-pin connector (a DB25) or a male 9-pin connector (a DB9). Therefore, you'll need to connect using a female connector. Terminals, PCs, and similar devices are usually wired as Data Terminal Equipment (DTE). This means that they transmit on pin 2 and receive on pin 3 (at least, on a DB25). DCE (Data Communication Equipment) transmits on pin 3 and receives on pin 2. Every pin that is an input for a DTE device is an output on a DCE device and vice versa (see Table 6.1). Modems and printers are often DCE devices.

You can easily connect a DTE and a DCE device with a straight cable — that is, one that connects every pin to the same pin on the other side of the cable. A cross cable crosses the inputs and outputs.

Table 6.1 shows that there are many signals on the 25-pin connector. However, most devices don't use all of the pins. Commonly, pins 1–8 and pin 20 will take care of nearly all devices. Many cheap cables only wire these pins anyway.

Some devices really don't require any pins except for the send and receive (along with a ground). This leads to three-wire cables (which may be straight or crossed, of course). Some three-wire cables have fake handshaking connections — they just short each side's inputs to the same side's outputs.

If it sounds like getting a good connection between devices is difficult, it is! There are lots of combinations of cables and connections you may have to try. This isn't a problem peculiar to the Stamp — it is part of using RS232. You can purchase a *break out box* (sometimes known as a *BOB*) that lets you monitor the signals on the cable. This can be a big help in troubleshooting. Many BOBs also let you selectively reroute signals so you can experiment with various cross cable configurations.

For RS232 data transfer to work, you must meet several conditions:

- The baud rates must match.
- The number of stop bits, data bits, and parity must match.
- The signal polarity must match.
- The transmitter's voltage levels must be acceptable to the receiver.

- The transmitter's output must connect to the receiver's input and vice versa.
- Any necessary handshaking signals must be enabled.

Table 6.1   RS232 connections.

Signal	Pin (25)	Pin (9)	DTE Direction	Description
PG	1	N/A	N/A	Frame or protective ground
TX	2	3	Out	Transmit data
RX	3	2	In	Receive data
RTS	4	7	Out	Request to send
CTS	5	8	In	Clear to send
DSR	6	6	In	Data set ready
GND	7	5	N/A	Signal ground
CD	8	1	In	Carrier detect
DTR	20	4	Out	Data terminal ready
RI	22	9	In	Ring indicator

The Stamp has a limited number of baud rates, stop bits, data bits, and parity settings. That means you'll usually have to adjust the other device to match the Stamp. Voltage and polarity, however, are more of a hardware issue.

A correctly-designed RS232C device (RS232C is the most common RS232 variant) will produce –12V for a logic 1 and +12V for a logic 0. Of course, the Stamp doesn't usually have a supply of ±12V so this could present a problem.

The Stamp II's built-in RS232 port assumes that when it is sending data, the other side will not be talking (a good assumption because the Stamp can't listen and talk at the same time anyway). It, therefore, feeds the –12V from the serial input back to the output for a logic 1. When it wants to generate a 0, it forces the serial output to 5V.

Of course, 5V isn't the normal value for an RS232 0, but most receivers will accept it and it is within the RS232 spec. In fact, most RS232 receivers will work with 5V and 0V, so you can directly connect a Stamp pin to an RS232 input and it will almost always work. The operative word, is almost. If it doesn't work, the equipment manufacturer is not at fault because this is not a standard value for RS232.

Of course, if you do connect 0 and 5V directly to an RS232 input, you'll need to invert the output bits. The Stamp allows you to do this by changing the baudmode parameter to the SEROUT command (see Chapter 2). For example, using 84 on the Stamp II selects 9,600 baud normal mode and 16,468 selects 9,600 baud inverted.

This is somewhat confusing because normal RS232 data is inverted (–12V is a 1). However, line drivers typically invert the logic signal for you. So a direct connection is inverted, while a connection through a line driver (which inverts the signal) is non-inverted (because the two inversions cancel each other out).

You can receive data directly from an RS232 port, too. The Stamp's input protection diodes will bleed off the excess voltage from the RS232 port. Of course, the diodes will look like dead shorts, so you'll want to put a series resistor (22K or so) between the Stamp pin and the RS232 output. This prevents the short circuit from damaging the RS232 port. Again, you need to invert the bits in software with this method (using an inverted baudmode parameter to SERIN).

If you don't want to resort to these kind of tricks, you can use a level converter. The classic converters are the 1488 and 1489 ICs. However, these require ±12V supplies. A more popular alternative is the MAX232 from Maxim. This chip requires four capacitors and uses them in a charge pump to generate ±12V from the 5V supply. The Dallas Semiconductor DS275 is another driver for 5V systems. This chip uses circuitry similar to what you'll find on the Stamp II to route the –12V from the RS232 port back to the input. It then supplies 5V for a logic 0.

For production designs you really should use a chip like the 1488/1489, MAX232, or DS275. However, for your own purposes, it is often very useful to use direct connection or other methods that don't generate the appropriate voltage levels.

The final piece to the RS232 puzzle is handshaking (sometimes called flow control). Suppose you are trying to send data to a PC via the RS232 port. You start Hyperterminal (the standard Windows terminal program) and you don't see any data. Of course, if your wiring or programming is wrong, you won't see anything. But what if everything seems to be correct (including the points already mentioned like baud rate), but you still get no results? Perhaps Hyperterminal is expecting hardware handshaking. That means that it expects certain voltage levels on RS232 pins (most hardware using DTR, CTS, RTS, and DSR for handshaking). If the program doesn't see the correct signals, it won't send or receive data.

You can fake the correct signals, of course (and some cables do this automatically by shorting, for example, CTS to RTS and DSR to DTR). However, the easiest answer is to simply tell Hyperterminal to use no handshaking. Exactly how you do this depends on your terminal software. For Hyperterminal, bring up the properties for the connection and select None in the Flow Control section.

Software handshaking (also known as XON/XOFF handshaking) relies on a special character to tell the other device to stop sending (XOFF). Later, the device will send an XON to enable the device to resume transmission. The Stamp is poorly suited for using this type of flow control. In real life, when you send an XOFF, there may be several characters still on the way to you before the other device stops sending. Because the Stamp can't handle input asynchronously, you can only use XON/XOFF in certain situations.

Hardware handshaking fundamentals

Different devices may use hardware handshaking lines differently. For example, a simple serial printer may only use DSR to indicate if it is ready or not. However, you can usually expect handshaking to work something like this:

Action	Meaning
DTE asserts DTR	I am on-line and ready
DCE asserts DSR	OK I'm ready too
DTE asserts RTS	I'm ready to go
DCE asserts CTS	I'm ready to go too
DCE/DTE exchange data	
DCE lowers CTS	Buffer is full — DTE must stop sending
DCE asserts CTS	Ready again
DCE/DTE exchange data	

Use a constant for baudmode and pin numbers

You should rarely if ever specify a fixed number for the baudmode parameter in the SEROUT and SERIN commands. Instead, use a constant value. That way if you have to change how your program works, you can make one or two easy changes instead of having to edit every serial I/O command. So instead of:

```
SEROUT 16,84,[w1]
```

Try:

```
SERPIN con 16
BAUDRATE con 84
SEROUT SERPIN, BAUDRATE,[w1]
```

Open Collector Async

You'll notice that the Stamp's baudmode parameters can be set to an open collector mode. This can be useful where you want to network multiple Stamps together. Of course, all the Stamps can't talk at one time, so you need some software control. However, with open collector outputs, you can connect all the pins together (along with a single pull-up resistor) and not worry about short circuits damaging the Stamp pins.

As an example of software control, suppose you had one Stamp acting as a master. It might transmit a byte that selects an active slave Stamp. The slave can then send data back to the master until the master selects another slave.

A PC Frequency Counter

There are many ways to measure frequency with a Stamp. Why measure frequencies? Many real-world sensors provide frequency outputs (tachometers, for example). You also might need to measure tones for data communications or control purposes.

You can measure frequency with the COUNT command or the PULSIN statement. COUNT counts the number of pulses in a given amount of time. PULSIN measures the width of a single half-cycle.

PULSIN measures the amount of time a pulse remains high or low. On the Stamp II, the result of the PULSIN command is the length of the pulse (in 2S units). So if the command returns 10, the pulse width is really 20S. This is just the width of a half-cycle. If the duty cycle is 50%, you can multiply the answer by 2. Otherwise, you need to measure a positive and negative cycle and add the results. Of course, this assumes the signal is repetitive (which is usually true).

If you want to convert the raw counts to Hertz (cycles per seconds), you need to multiply by 2 (to get S) and divide by 1,000,000 (to convert to seconds), then take the reciprocal. The problem is that the Stamp is not good at doing this kind of math. The Stamp only does integer math and can only handle numbers to 65,535.

Of course, the reciprocal of $x/1,000,000$ is $1,000,000/x$ no matter what x is. Because the Stamp can't divide by 1,000,000, you need to factor the expression. Rewrite $1,000,000/x$ as $50(20,000/x)$ and you are in business (because 50 and 20,000 are both numbers that can fit in a word variable). You can find the code for both Stamps in Listing 6.6 through 6.8. The Stamp I code is very similar to the Stamp II code except that the Stamp I measures pulses in 10S units.

Listing 6.6   Basic Stamp I frequency counter.

```
input 8
loop:
pulsin 8,1,w1    ' measure 1/2 cycle
pulsin 8,0,w2    ' measure 1/2 cycle
w3=(w1+w2)*10      ' total cycle time
```

Listing 6.6 Basic Stamp I frequency counter. (Continued)

```
' You could do a variety of things here
' including calculate the resistance of R
' or the capacitance of C (if you are using
' the sample oscillator)
' We will calculate the frequency in Hz
w4=(50000/w3)*20  ' convert to engineering units
       ' obviously the lowest we can resolve
       ' is 20hz this way
       ' although the basic precision is much higher
       ' however with integer only math this is a problem
debug #w4, "Hz", cr
goto loop
```

Listing 6.7 Basic Stamp II frequency counter.

```
v1 var word ' time for 1 cycle
v0 var word ' time for 0 cycle
v var word  ' total time of cycle
f var word  ' computed frequency
input 8
loop:
pulsin 8,1,v1   ' measure 1/2 cycle
pulsin 8,0,v0   ' measure 1/2 cycle
v=(v1+v0)*2     ' total cycle time
' You could do a variety of things here
' including calculate the resistance of R
' or the capacitance of C (if you are using
' the sample oscillator)
' We will calculate the frequency in Hz
f=(50000/v)*20  ' convert to engineering units
       ' obviously the lowest we can resolve
       ' is 20hz this way
       ' although the basic precision is much higher
       ' however with integer only math this is a problem
debug dec f, "Hz", cr
goto loop
```

Listing 6.8 PC interface frequency counter.

```
v1 var word ' time for 1 cycle
v0 var word ' time for 0 cycle
v var word  ' total time of cycle
f var word  ' computed frequency
input 8
loop:
pulsin 8,1,v1    ' measure 1/2 cycle
pulsin 8,0,v0    ' measure 1/2 cycle
v=(v1+v0)*2      ' total cycle time
serout 16,84,[dec v, 13,10]
goto loop
```

If you don't have a frequency source handy you can easily build one with simple parts (for example the LM339 comparator used in the A/D converter in Chapter 5). You can find an example oscillator in Figure 6.4. Just connect pin 2 of the comparator to the Stamp input (pin 8 in the example code). You can vary the resistor or capacitor to vary the frequency. Try touching the capacitor leads and then observe the effect. You could use this circuit as a touch switch. Try replacing the resistor with a sensor that changes with temperature, light, or some other external stimulus.

Figure 6.4 Sample oscillator.

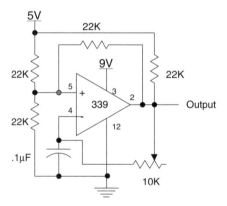

If you want to read frequency on a PC, consider the code in Listing 6.8. This is more or less the same code from the previous listing, but it uses SEROUT instead of DEBUG. Also, this code doesn't convert the raw counts to Hertz because the PC does a better job of this. You can find a VB program that reads the frequency in Listing 6.9

and a Visual C++ program in Listing 6.10. Either program will display the frequency in a digital display (see Figure 6.5).

Figure 6.5   The digital display.

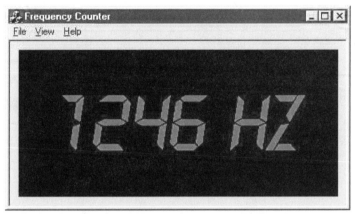

Both programs use the MSCOMM ActiveX control from Microsoft. This ActiveX control makes it very simple to use the RS232 port from your programs. When data arrives, the MSComm1_OnComm event fires and it is simple to read the data using the control's Input property. (Discussion continues on page 294.)

Listing 6.9   VB program for the frequency counter.

```
VERSION 5.00
Object = "{648A5603-2C6E-101B-82B6-000000000014}#1.1#0";"Mscomm32.ocx"
Begin VB.Form Form1
   Caption         =   "Frequency Counter"
   ClientHeight    =   3195
   ClientLeft      =   60
   ClientTop       =   345
   ClientWidth     =   5175
   LinkTopic       =   "Form1"
   ScaleHeight     =   3195
   ScaleWidth      =   5175
   StartUpPosition =   3  'Windows Default
   Begin MSCommLib.MSComm MSComm1
      Left         =   3720
      Top          =   2400
```

Listing 6.9   VB program for the frequency counter. (Continued)

```
        _ExtentX        =    1005
        _ExtentY        =    1005
        _Version        =    327680
        CommPort        =    2
        DTREnable       =    -1   'True
        RThreshold      =    250
    End
    Begin VB.Label Label2
        Caption         =    "You have to change the COM port using VB for this Demo.
By default, it uses COM2"
        Height          =    735
        Left            =    240
        TabIndex        =    1
        Top             =    2280
        Width           =    2895
    End
    Begin VB.Label Label1
        BackColor       =    &H00000000&
        Caption         =    "0000HZ"
        BeginProperty Font
            Name        =    "Crystal"
            Size        =    72
            Charset     =    0
            Weight      =    400
            Underline   =    0    'False
            Italic      =    -1   'True
            Strikethrough =  0    'False
        EndProperty
        ForeColor       =    &H0000FF00&
        Height          =    1815
        Left            =    240
        TabIndex        =    0
        Top             =    240
        Width           =    4575
    End
End
```

Listing 6.9   VB program for the frequency counter. (Continued)

```
Attribute VB_Name = "Form1"
Attribute VB_GlobalNameSpace = False
Attribute VB_Creatable = False
Attribute VB_PredeclaredId = True
Attribute VB_Exposed = False
Private Sub Form_Load()
MSComm1.PortOpen = True
End Sub

Private Sub MSComm1_OnComm()
If MSComm1.InBufferCount <> 0 Then
    InpString = MSComm1.Input
   For i = 1 To Len(InpString)
      c = Mid(InpString, i, 1)
      If c = Chr(13) Or c = Chr(10) And aValue <> "" Then
        If aValue <> 0 Then
           Label1.Caption = Int(1000000# / aValue) & "HZ"
        Else
           Label1.Caption = "-0-"
        End If
        aValue = ""
      Else
        aValue = aValue & c
      End If
   Next
End If
End Sub
```

Listing 6.10 Excerpts from a C++ program
to read frequency.

```
// FreqCtrView.cpp : implementation of the CFreqCtrView class
//

#include "stdafx.h"
#include "FreqCtr.h"
```

**Listing 6.10 Excerpts from a C++ program
to read frequency. (Continued)**

```cpp
#include "FreqCtrDoc.h"
#include "LedDisplay.h"
#include "FreqCtrView.h"

#ifdef _DEBUG
#define new DEBUG_NEW
#undef THIS_FILE
static char THIS_FILE[] = __FILE__;
#endif

/////////////////////////////////
// CFreqCtrView

IMPLEMENT_DYNCREATE(CFreqCtrView, CFormView)

BEGIN_MESSAGE_MAP(CFreqCtrView, CFormView)
//{{AFX_MSG_MAP(CFreqCtrView)
ON_WM_TIMER()
ON_COMMAND(IDM_COLOR, OnColor)
//}}AFX_MSG_MAP
// Standard printing commands
ON_COMMAND(ID_FILE_PRINT, CFormView::OnFilePrint)
ON_COMMAND(ID_FILE_PRINT_DIRECT, CFormView::OnFilePrint)
ON_COMMAND(ID_FILE_PRINT_PREVIEW, CFormView::OnFilePrintPreview)
END_MESSAGE_MAP()

/////////////////////////////////
// CFreqCtrView construction/destruction

CFreqCtrView::CFreqCtrView()
: CFormView(CFreqCtrView::IDD)
{
//{{AFX_DATA_INIT(CFreqCtrView)
m_freq = _T("");
```

Listing 6.10 Excerpts from a C++ program to read frequency. (Continued)

```
//}}AFX_DATA_INIT
// TODO: add construction code here


}


CFreqCtrView::~CFreqCtrView()
{
}


void CFreqCtrView::DoDataExchange(CDataExchange* pDX)
{
CFormView::DoDataExchange(pDX);
//{{AFX_DATA_MAP(CFreqCtrView)
DDX_Control(pDX, IDC_MSCOMM1, m_comm);
DDX_Text(pDX, IDC_FREQ, m_freq);
//}}AFX_DATA_MAP
}


CFreqCtrDoc* CFreqCtrView::GetDocument() // non-debug version is inline
{
ASSERT(m_pDocument->IsKindOf(RUNTIME_CLASS(CFreqCtrDoc)));
return (CFreqCtrDoc*)m_pDocument;
}
#endif //_DEBUG


/////////////////////////////
// CFreqCtrView message handlers
BEGIN_EVENTSINK_MAP(CFreqCtrView, CFormView)
    //{{AFX_EVENTSINK_MAP(CFreqCtrView)
//}}AFX_EVENTSINK_MAP
END_EVENTSINK_MAP()
```

Listing 6.10 Excerpts from a C++ program to read frequency. (Continued)

```cpp
void CFreqCtrView::OnInitialUpdate()
{
int port;
CFormView::OnInitialUpdate();
LED.SubclassDlgItem(IDC_FREQ,this);
port=((CFreqCtrApp *)AfxGetApp())->m_comport;
m_comm.SetCommPort(port);
m_comm.SetSettings("9600,N,8,1");
m_comm.SetInputLen(0);
m_comm.SetHandshaking(0); // no handshaking
m_comm.SetRThreshold(0);  // no events
m_comm.SetInBufferSize(4096);
m_comm.SetPortOpen(TRUE);
SetTimer(1,50,NULL);
ResizeParentToFit(TRUE);
}


void CFreqCtrView::OnTimer(UINT nIDEvent)
{
if (m_comm.GetInBufferCount())
{
  VARIANT inputv;
  char* input;
  inputv=m_comm.GetInput();
  int ct=m_comm.GetInBufferCount();
  // got to convert BSTR to CString here
  int len=m_comm.GetInBufferCount();
  input=(char *)inputv.bstrVal;


  while (len--)
  {
  if (*input=='\x0d' || *input=='\x0a')
```

Listing 6.10 Excerpts from a C++ program
to read frequency. (Continued)

```
{
if (!value.IsEmpty())
{
unsigned v=strtoul(value,NULL,10);
if (v!=0)
{
float f=1000000.0f/v;
m_freq.Format("%d HZ",(int)f);
}
else
m_freq="-0-";
}
  value.Empty();
}
else
{
  if (*input>='0' && *input<='9') value+=*input;
}
  input+=2; // skip hi byte of UNICODE characters
  }
}
UpdateData(FALSE);
CFormView::OnTimer(nIDEvent);
}




// Set colors
void CFreqCtrView::OnColor()
{
CColorDialog dlg(LED.m_Color);
```

Listing 6.10 Excerpts from a C++ program to read frequency. (Continued)

```
if (dlg.DoModal()==IDOK)
LED.m_Color=dlg.GetColor();
LED.Invalidate(NULL);
}
```

More Power Supply

The last two chapters have contained a Stamp-controlled power supply project. It might seem simple to add RS-232 control to the power supply. However, since the Stamp can only do one thing at a time, including listening for RS-232 input, this takes careful design.

Consider the simple program that appears in Listing 6.11. This is more or less the same power supply program that appears in Chapter 4 but instead of using push buttons, it looks for a + or – character from an RS-232 terminal.

If you run this program you'll notice that not all of the + or – characters you enter will have any effect. That's because while the Stamp is executing the PWM command it is not listening to the serial port. You can reduce the time the PWM command executes, but that is only useful to a point. Even if you don't build the hardware, try running this program and observe the results on the debug terminal. Then you can experiment with the effect different PWM durations and SERIN timeouts have on the program.

Listing 6.11 This RS-232 controlled power supply has limitations.

```
volt var byte
btn1 var byte
btn2 var byte
cmd var byte

volt=0
btn1=0
btn2=0


top:
pwm 0,volt,200
serin 16,84,200,top,[cmd]
if cmd="+" then voltup
if cmd="-" then voltdn
```

Listing 6.11 This RS-232 controlled power supply has limitations.

```
goto top

voltup:
  volt=volt+1
debug ?volt
  goto top

voltdn:
  volt=volt-1
debug ?volt
goto top
```

One thing to notice about the program is that it uses a serial timeout. Without this, the Stamp would stop processing until you pressed some key. The PWM capacitor would eventually sag, and the voltage output of the supply would droop. Again, this is because the Stamp does exactly one thing at a time. It is either listening for RS232 input, or it is generating PWM. The timeout on the SERIN statement allows the Stamp to periodically generate PWM even when there is no serial input.

Extending PC I/O

One of the main reasons you'll want to interface a Stamp to a PC is so you can have the best of both worlds. The Stamp excels at low-level I/O processing. It can measure pulses, do PWM, and other things that are difficult to accomplish on the PC. On the other hand, the PC is fast and has very comprehensive user interface capabilities. Besides that, the PC does floating point math, has access to networks, disk drives, and printers. Wouldn't it be great if the PC could do all the things it can do, plus do the things the Stamp can do?

The code in Listing 6.12 lets you do exactly that. This is a Stamp program that allows you to send serial commands to the Stamp and the Stamp will follow your instructions. The Stamp will act as a *proxy* for the PC, giving it full access to its 16 I/O ports and some other features, as well. Listing 6.13 shows a Visual Basic class module that makes it easy to work with the Stamp from a VB program. Of course, you could do the same thing in Visual C++ or any language that allows you to send and receive data from the serial port. Unlike the last example, this project requires data to flow in both directions.

The Stamp code is pretty simple (see Listing 6.12). It waits for a 5-byte packet at 9,600 baud. The packet contains one command byte and two 16-bit arguments (MSB first). Different commands use the arguments differently.

When you design a protocol between the PC and the Stamp, you need to take into account the Stamp's limitations. For example, not all packets use all five bytes. However, the Stamp is not able to read a byte, look at it, and then read another byte (unless the sending program pauses between bytes). A fixed-size packet is easiest for the Stamp to read.

Table 6.2   PC interface commands.

	Command	Description	Inputs	Outputs
1	PINS: Performs I/O	Sets given output bits; returns input bits	Word 1= Mask Word 2 = Value	INS register
2	DIRS: Sets/reads the DIRS register (see page 297)	Sets and returns direction bits	Word 1 = Mask Word 2 = Value	DIRS register
3	INPUT	Same as normal Stamp command	Word 1 = Pin	None
4	OUTPUT	" " " "	Word 1 = Pin	None
5	REVERSE	" " " "	Word 1 = Pin	None
6	LOW	" " " "	Word 1 = Pin	None
7	HIGH	" " " " "	Word 1 = Pin	None
8	TOGGLE	" " " "	Word 1 = Pin	None
9	PULSIN	" " " " "	Word 1 = Pin Word 2 = State	Result
10	PULSOUT	" " " " "	Word 1 = Pin Word 2 = Duration	None
11	SHIFTIN	" " " " "	Byte 1 = Cpin Byte 2 = Dpin Byte 3 = Mode Byte4 = Bits	Result
12	SHIFTOUT	" " " " " (Use 12 or the mode bit *32)	Byte 1 = Cpin Byte 2 = Dpin Word 2 = Data X1 = Bits (see SETHI)	None
13	COUNT	" " " " "	Word 1 = Pin Word 2 = Period	Result
15	PWM	" " " " "	Byte 1 = Duty Byte 2 = Pin Word 2 = Period	None

Table 6.2   PC interface commands. (Continued)

	Command	Description	Inputs	Outputs
16	RCTIME	" " " " "	Word 1 = Pin Word 2 = State	Result
17	FREQOUT	" " " " "	Word 1 = Pin Word 2 = Duration X1 = Note 1 X2 = Note 2 (see SETHI)	None
18	DTMFOUT	" " " " "	Byte 1 = Tone Byte 2 = Pin Byte 3 = On time Byte 4 = Off time	None
19	WRITE	" " " " "	Word 1 = Address Word 2 = Value	None
20	READ	" " " " "	Word 1 = Address	Value
30	SETHI (see page 297)	Set extra words used by FREQOUT, SHIFTOUT	WORD1 = X1 WORD2 = X2	None
31	ALIVE	Returns AA55 if connected	None	AA55

Most of the commands are straightforward. The PINS and DIRS command take a mask and a value so you can set or clear any bits you like. If you set the mask to zero, these commands are useful for reading input or the state of the DIRS pins. Where the previous table says X1 or X2, it means you must call SETHI first to initialize X1 and X2. These values never clear, so if you can use them more than once, you don't have to keep calling SETHI.

Every command emits a 3-byte response packet. The first byte is always status where 0 is success and FF is failure. Currently, the only failure possible is to pass an unrecognized code to the Stamp. It would be possible, however, to check for invalid arguments (like pins $\geq$ 16, etc.) and return errors for these as well.

TIP

Designing serial protocols

This example shows a good way to design a serial protocol using the Stamp and a PC. Notice that every command consists of five bytes from the PC followed by three bytes from the Stamp. This design allows the Stamp to easily read the 5-byte packet. It also signals the PC when the Stamp is ready for more packets.

In cases where five bytes was not sufficient to hold all the arguments, the program requires you to send multiple packets. Of course, you could make the packet size larger, but that would affect all commands equally. The length of five was a good compromise — although some commands waste some of the packet space, it wastes less space than making the packet the maximum required size.

While this design is not very efficient in terms of bandwidth, it does make life easier when programming the Stamp.

Obviously, you could add as many commands as you wanted. For example, I didn't include code for XOUT. You might want to have a single command generate a series of pulses in a predefined sequence. Just remember that while the Stamp is doing something else, it isn't listening for your commands. This is especially a problem when you use Stamp commands that take awhile to complete. For example, if you try to send commands every half second and you use a PWM command with a duration of 5,000mS, you will have problems!

The other thing to remember is that the speed of this is limited by the serial port speed. You can't write a PC-based oscilloscope with this technique (well, you could, but it would be very slow). If you want to do fast processing, you are probably better off doing it on the Stamp. Of course, you could use a special command to initiate a subroutine and another command to retrieve the results. (Discussion continues on page 306.)

Listing 6.12 I/O code.

```
' PC/BS2 Interface
' Allows the BS2 to function as an I/O port for the PC
'
' Williams -- AWC http://www.al-williams.com/awce.htm
' This code doesn't use named symbols
' so that it can overlay variables
top:
W12=0
Serin 16,84,[B5,B7,B6,B9,B8]
```

Listing 6.12 I/O code. (Continued)

```
B4=B5 & $1F  ' B4 is command
' Could save space by puttin these on one line,
' but... doesn't show up nicely on the Web
' Like that
Branch B4, [ERR,CMDPINS,CMDDIRS,CMDINPUT,CMDOUTPUT,CMDREVERSE,CMDLOW]
Branch B4-7,[CMDHIGH,CMDTOGGLE,CMDPULSIN,CMDPULSOUT,CMDSHIFTIN]
Branch B4-12,[CMDSHIFTOUT,CMDCOUNT,ERR,CMDPWM,CMDRCTIME]
Branch B4-17,[CMDFREQOUT,CMDDTMFOUT,CMDWRITE,CMDREAD,ERR,ERR,ERR,ERR]
Branch B4-25,[ERR,ERR,ERR,ERR,ERR,CMDSETHI,CMDALIVE]
ERR:
B23=$FF
GOTO Fin
FINOK:  ' Finish with ok status
B23=0
FIN:
' Output status codes in B23/B24/B25
Serout 16,84,[B23,B24,B25]
Goto Top
CMDPINS:  ' Pins set pins with mask and return current
OUTS=(OUTS  & (W3^$FFFF)) | (W3 & W4)
W12=INS
Goto FINOK
CMDDIRS: ' Dirs set with mask and return current
DIRS=(DIRS & (W3^$FFFF)) | (W3 & W4)
W12=DIRS
Goto FINOK
CMDINPUT: ' INPUT
Input B6
Goto FINOK
CMDOUTPUT: ' OUTPUT
Output B6
GOTO FINOK
CMDREVERSE: ' REVERSE
Reverse B6
GOTO FINOK
CMDLOW: ' LOW
```

Listing 6.12 I/O code. (Continued)

```
Low B6
GOTO FINOK
CMDHIGH: ' HIGH
High B6
GOTO FINOK
CMDTOGGLE: ' TOGGLE
Toggle B6
GOTO FINOK
CMDPULSIN:
Pulsin B6,B9,W12
Goto FINOK
CMDPULSOUT:
Pulsout B6,W4
Goto FINOK
CMDSHIFTIN:
ShiftIn B6,B7,B9,[W12\B8]
Goto FINOK
CMDSHIFTOUT:
B22=(B5 & $F0)/32
ShiftOut B6,B7,B22,[W4\B9]
Goto FINOK
CMDCOUNT:
COUNT B6,W4,W12
Goto FINOK
CMDPWM:
PWM B6,B7,W4
Goto FINOK
CMDRCTIME:
RCTime B6,B8,W12
Goto FINOK
CMDFREQOUT:
if W10=0 then FZ
Freqout B6,W4,W9,W10
Goto FINOK
FZ:
Freqout B6,W4,W9
```

Listing 6.12 I/O code. (Continued)

```
Goto FINOK
CMDDTMFOUT:
DTMFOUT B6,B9,B8,[B7]
GOTO FINOK
CMDWRITE:
WRITE B6,B9
GOTO FINOK
CMDREAD:
READ B6,B25
GOTO FINOK
' Set high words for some commands
CMDSETHI:
W9=W3
W10=W4
GOTO FINOK
' See if the BS2 is alive
CMDALIVE:
W12=$AA55
Goto FINOK
```

Listing 6.13 The VB class module for the I/O
extender.

```
VERSION 1.0 CLASS
BEGIN
  MultiUse = -1  'True
END
Attribute VB_Name = "Stamp"
Attribute VB_GlobalNameSpace = False
Attribute VB_Creatable = True
Attribute VB_PredeclaredId = False
Attribute VB_Exposed = False
' Class module to interface PC to Stamp
' Williams - AWC
' http://www.al-williams.com/awce.htm
Option Explicit
```

Listing 6.13 The VB class module for the I/O extender. (Continued)

```
Private comm As Object
Public RawResult    ' If you want the raw result
' Call this function first
Public Function Start(ByVal port As Integer) As Boolean
' Dynamic creation of an MSComm object -- how about that!
Set comm = CreateObject("MSCommLib.MSComm")
comm.CommPort = port
comm.Handshaking = comNone
comm.InputLen = 8
comm.InputMode = comInputModeBinary
comm.Settings = "9600,N,8,1"
comm.PortOpen = True
Start = comm.PortOpen
' Purge buffer
Do While comm.InBufferCount <> 0
  comm.Input
Loop
End Function
Public Function Shutdown() As Boolean
comm.PortOpen = False
Shutdown = True
End Function
Private Function StampResult() As String
Dim s
Dim timeo As Date
timeo = DateAdd("s", 20, Now)
Do While comm.InBufferCount <> 8
  If timeo < Now Then
    MsgBox "Timeout"
    Exit Function
  End If
Loop
s = comm.Input
If Left(s, 1) = Chr(0) Then
```

Listing 6.13 The VB class module for the I/O extender. (Continued)

```
  MsgBox "Unexpected " & Hex(Asc(Left(s, 1)))
End If

RawResult = Right(s, 3)
StampResult = RawResult
End Function
' Common code for simple commands
Private Sub Cmd0(ByVal n, ByVal pin)
comm.Output = Chr(n) + Chr(0) + Chr(pin) + Chr(0) + Chr(0)
StampResult
End Sub
' Some binary helpers
Private Function lowbyte(ByVal n) As String
n = n And 255
lowbyte = Chr(n)
End Function
Private Function hibyte(ByVal n) As String
n = n / 256
n = n And 255
hibyte = Chr(n)
End Function
Private Function ReturnWord(ByVal s) As Long
ReturnWord = 256# * Asc(Mid(s, 3, 1)) + Asc(Mid(s, 2, 1))
End Function
Private Function Word(n) As String
Word = hibyte(n) & lowbyte(n)
End Function
Public Function Stamp_SetIO(mask, value) As Long
  comm.Output = Chr(1) + Word(mask) + Word(value)
  StampResult
  Stamp_SetIO = ReturnWord(RawResult)
End Function
Public Function Stamp_ReadInputs() As Long
Stamp_ReadInputs = Stamp_SetIO(0, 0)
```

Listing 6.13 The VB class module for the I/O extender. (Continued)

```
End Function
Public Function Stamp_SetDIR(mask, value) As Long
  comm.Output = Chr(2) + Word(mask) + Word(value)
  StampResult
  SetDIR = ReturnWord(RawResult)
End Function
Public Function Stamp_ReadDIRS() As Long
ReadDIRS = SetDIR(0, 0)
End Function
Public Sub Stamp_Input(pin)
Cmd0 3, pin
End Sub
Public Sub Stamp_Output(pin)
Cmd0 4, pin
End Sub
Public Sub Stamp_Reverse(pin)
Cmd0 5, pin
End Sub
Public Sub Stamp_Low(pin)
Cmd0 6, pin
End Sub
Public Sub Stamp_High(pin)
Cmd0 7, pin
End Sub
Public Sub Stamp_Toggle(pin)
Cmd0 8, pin
End Sub
Public Function Stamp_Pulsin(pin, state)
comm.Output = Chr(9) + Chr(0) + Chr(pin) + Chr(0) + Chr(state)
StampResult
Stamp_Plusin = ReturnWord(RawResult)
End Function
Public Sub Stamp_Pulsout(pin, dur)
comm.Output = Chr(10) + Chr(0) + Chr(pin) + Word(dur)
StampResult
```

Listing 6.13 The VB class module for the I/O extender. (Continued)

```
End Sub
Public Function Stamp_ShiftIn(dpin, cpin, mode, bits) As Long
End Function
Public Sub Stamp_ShiftOut(dpin, cpin, mode, bits, value)
End Sub
Public Function Stamp_Count(pin, period) As Long
comm.Output = Chr(13) + Chr(0) + Chr(pin) + Word(period)
StampResult
Stamp_Count = ReturnWord(RawResult)
End Function
Public Sub Stamp_PWM(pin, duty, dur)
comm.Output = Chr(15) + Chr(duty) + Chr(pin) + Word(dur)
StampResult
End Sub
Public Function Stamp_RCTime(pin, state) As Long
comm.Output = Chr(16) + Chr(0) + Chr(pin) + Chr(0) + Chr(state)
StampResult
Stamp_RCTime = ReturnWord(RawResult)
End Function
Public Sub Stamp_FreqOut(pin, dur, t1, t2)
Stamp_HiSet t1, t2
comm.Output = Chr(17) + Chr(0) + Chr(pin) + Word(dur)
StampResult
End Sub
Public Sub Stamp_DTMFOut(pin, ondur, offdur, tone)
comm.Output = Chr(18) + Chr(tone) + Chr(pin) + Chr(offdur) + Chr(ondur)
StampResult
End Sub
Public Sub Stamp_Write(ad, value)
comm.Output = Chr(19) + Chr(0) + Chr(ad) + Chr(0) + Chr(value)
StampResult
End Sub
Public Function Stamp_Read(ad) As Long
comm.Output = Chr(20) + Chr(0) + Chr(ad) + Word(0)
StampResult
```

Listing 6.13 The VB class module for the I/O extender. (Continued)

```
Stamp_Read = Asc(Mid(RawResult, 3, 1))
End Function
Public Sub Stamp_HiSet(x, y)
comm.Output = Chr(30) + Word(x) + Word(y)
StampResult
End Sub
Public Function Stamp_Alive() As Boolean
comm.Output = Chr(31) + Word(0) + Word(0)
StampResult
Stamp_Alive = RawResult = Chr(0) & Chr(&HAA) & Chr(&H55)
End Function
```

Stamps on the Net

Can a Basic Stamp connect to the Internet? Perhaps not in the traditional sense, but with another computer acting as an intermediary, the Stamp can interact with a network. There are small computers specifically designed for this type of service, but you might want to consider using a PC as a gateway.

Don't be too quick to dismiss using a PC as a slave to a Stamp. The PC doesn't have to be very modern. Older PCs are very inexpensive and plentiful. Also, one PC can handle many Stamps, so the cost per Stamp could be less than using a dedicated Internet connection solution.

There are commercial programs that allow the PC to interpret data and send it over the Internet (like my company's NetPorter software, for example). However, it is simple enough to write a dedicated program using Visual Basic.

There are two Visual Basic components that make this relatively easy. First, you can use the MSCOMM control to read data from a serial port. You've seen this component in the previous project. The other component is the Microsoft Internet Transfer Control. This control can handle HTTP and FTP transfers with a minimum of fuss.

Neither of these controls show up automatically. You have to use the Project | Components menu item to add them to your tool palette. When you place them on your VB form, you'll only see a small icon. The user sees nothing. These components are for your internal use — they don't present a user interface.

Figure 6.6 shows the program in action. You simply set your FTP user ID and password along with the other parameters. The program assumes 9,600, 8, *n*, 1 for communications parameters. When you make entries, the program remembers them for next time in the registry (except for the password).

Figure 6.6 The Internet bridge program in action.

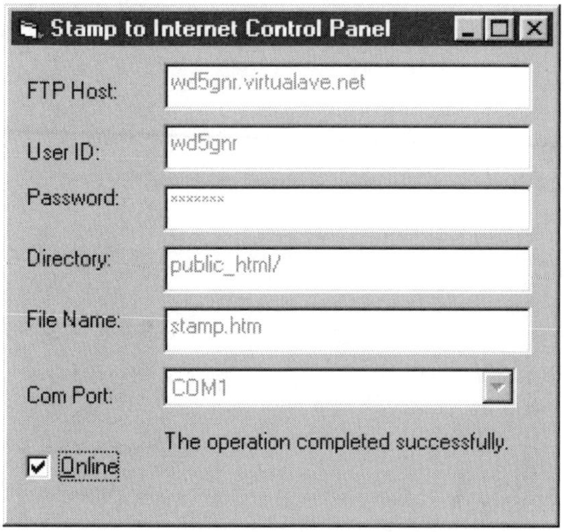

Once everything is set up, you click Online and the program starts its work. Internet transfers can be slow, so if any errors occur, the program keeps working, but displays any error messages near the bottom of the window. The test Stamp program sends data every five seconds and I didn't have any problems but your mileage may vary.

The only parts of the VB code (Listing 6.13) that may not be obvious are the parts that read the Stamp's data and the FTP code. The way the COM port component is set up, the MSCOMM1_OnComm function fires when characters arrive. The logic in this function stores partial strings and uses a carriage return (chr(13)) to mark the end of a data packet. Each data packet is processed through WriteHTML.

The WriteHTML function creates a temporary file (using the same name your provide on the main form) and writes an HTML file using the data from the Stamp. You could do any post processing you want here and you can add (as I did) server-specific code, formatting, etc. You could even remember, for example, the last 10 values, and show more than one value here.

Once the temporary file is constructed, the program uses the transfer control's Execute method to FTP the data to the server. Error handling is critical here because it is possible for the last operation to still be pending. (Discussion continues on page 311.)

Listing 6.14 The Internet bridge software (Visual Basic).

```
Dim regName As String ' name for registry settings

Private Sub Form_Load()
regName = "StampNet"
MSComm1.Settings = "9600,n,8,1"
MSComm1.RThreshold = 1
Host.Text = GetSetting(regName, "FTP", "Host", "")
UID.Text = GetSetting(regName, "FTP", "UID", "")
' do not save password for security reasons
dir.Text = GetSetting(regName, "FTP", "DIR", "public_html/")
FN.Text = GetSetting(regName, "FTP", "FN", "stamp.htm")
Combo1.ListIndex = GetSetting(regName, "Comm", "Port", 1) - 1
End Sub


Private Sub WriteHTML(s As String)
' If things are still executing, we will get errors here
On Error GoTo WriteErr
' Open temporary file
Open FN.Text For Output As #1
Print #1, "<HTML><HEAD><TITLE>Basic Stamp Data</TITLE>"
Print #1, "</HEAD>"
Print #1, "<BODY BGCOLOR=GRAY>"
' specific for VirutalAve
Print #1, "<!--virtualavenuebanner-->"
Print #1, "<P><FONT COLOR=RED>"
Print #1, "Value="; s
Print #1, "</FONT></P>"
Print #1, "</BODY></HTML>"
Close #1
Inet1.Execute "FTP://" & UID.Text & ":" & PW.Text & "@" & Host.Text, "PUT " &
FN.Text & " " & dir.Text & FN.Text
GoTo EndWrite
WriteErr:
  ' don't worry about it, but try to close file
```

Listing 6.14 The Internet bridge software (Visual Basic). (Continued)

```vb
   On Error Resume Next
   Close #1
EndWrite:
End Sub


Private Sub Inet1_StateChanged(ByVal State As Integer)
Response.Caption = Inet1.ResponseInfo
End Sub

Private Sub MSComm1_OnComm()
Static inraw As String
Dim inline As String
Dim n As Integer
' when characters are available...
If MSComm1.CommEvent = comEvReceive Then
   Do
     inraw = inraw & MSComm1.Input
     ' find end of line
     n = InStr(inraw, Chr(13))
     If n <> 0 Then
       inline = Left(inraw, n - 1)
       inraw = Mid(inraw, n + 1)
       WriteHTML inline
     Else
       Exit Do
     End If
   Loop While Len(inraw) <> 0
End If

End Sub

Private Sub Online_Click()
If Online.Value = 1 Then
```

Listing 6.14 The Internet bridge software
(Visual Basic). (Continued)

```
  Combo1.Enabled = False
  Host.Enabled = False
  UID.Enabled = False
  PW.Enabled = False
  FN.Enabled = False
  dir.Enabled = False
  Response.Caption = ""
  MSComm1.PortOpen = True
Else
  MSComm1.PortOpen = False
  Combo1.Enabled = True
  Host.Enabled = True
  UID.Enabled = True
  PW.Enabled = True
  FN.Enabled = True
  dir.Enabled = True
End If
End Sub

Private Sub Host_Change()
SaveSetting regName, "FTP", "Host", Host.Text
End Sub
Private Sub UID_Change()
SaveSetting regName, "FTP", "UID", UID.Text
End Sub

Private Sub dir_Change()
SaveSetting regName, "FTP", "DIR", dir.Text
End Sub

Private Sub FN_Change()
SaveSetting regName, "FTP", "FN", FN.Text
End Sub
```

Listing 6.14 The Internet bridge software (Visual Basic). (Continued)

```
Private Sub Combo1_Change()
MSComm1.CommPort = Combo1.ListIndex + 1
SaveSetting regName, "Comm", "Port", Combo1.ListIndex + 1
End Sub
```

Of course, you also need a Stamp program to generate data for the Internet. You could use the circuit in Figure 6.3 and the simple program in Listing 6.15.

Listing 6.15 A test program for the Internet bridge.

```
top:
high 7
pause 1
rctime 7,1,w1
serout 16,84,[dec w1,cr]
pause 5000
goto top
```

Summary

You'll use serial I/O to communicate with PCs, RS232 devices, and other peripherals. Making RS232 work need not be a black art, although you do need a logical, methodical approach when things don't go right.

Using serial communications can open the door to complex networked designs as well as designs that use coprocessors, modems, EEPROMs, or those that communicate with a PC. PC communication is especially useful. Imagine a Stamp reading sensors and passing the readings to a PC program which updates a Web page. Of course, you could also store data in a database or a comma-delimited file for input to a database.

Exercises

1. Change the code in Listing 6.1 so that it doesn't use SHIFTIN and SHIFTOUT. Instead, replace it with the same logic using HIGH, LOW, and PULSOUT.

2. Change the PC Frequency Counter in this chapter to connect directly to an ordinary Stamp pin. What changes do you need to make to the Stamp code? What changes, if any, does the PC software require?

3. Design a PC-controlled pattern generator using the I2C EEPROM circuit in this chapter. The Stamp accepts commands from a terminal program on the PC. Allow commands to set specific EEPROM addresses and the maximum address you want to use. When the PC user issues a RUN command, the Stamp will cycle through the EEPROM from address 0 to the maximum address transferring the byte in EEPROM to eight output pins (monitor these with LEDs or a scope). After the Stamp reaches the maximum EEPROM address, it starts over at address 0. If you don't have an external EEPROM, you could use a portion of the Stamp's built-in EEPROM to complete this exercise. This could be the basis for a useful test instrument that could simulate various input sequences for a system under test.

For answers to the exercises, see the Answer Key, page 435.

Chapter 7

A Pong Game:
LCDs and Keypads

Have you ever noticed that if you pick any old saying, you can usually find another one that contradicts it? For example, consider, "A fool and his money are soon parted," versus "Penny wise, pound foolish." How about, "Fools rush in where angels fear to tread" versus "He who hesitates is lost."

I like an old saying as well as the next person. But sometimes I think some of these old sayings aren't as true as they could be. The worst offender? "A picture is worth a thousand words." I think they need to rewrite this one to be, "A detailed picture is worth a thousand words. But a 32-pixel square icon is worth about 25 cents." There are many times that I've run a program and wondered what the toolbar button with two squiggly lines and a pizza means. It would be much easier if it just said, "Lights Off" or whatever.

The same holds true for microcontroller projects. Sure, you can wire up lights and switches all you want, but that often doesn't tell people exactly what they want to know. Sometimes there is no substitute for text and numbers and labeled keys.

Sure, you can connect a Stamp to the PC and have all the character I/O you want, but that isn't always possible. Many Stamp projects will operate far away from a PC, and you'll want something that is just as portable.

In this chapter, I'll introduce you to some input devices that work conveniently with the Stamp. As a demonstration of basic techniques, I'll show you how to build the classic video pong game for a Stamp with a limited graphics display.

Of course, you can get numeric output with seven-segment LEDs, but for the Stamp, this isn't usually a great idea. LED displays require a lot of I/O lines and constant multiplexing. You can get display chips that handle some of the work for you — but for less work and about the same money, you can often use an LCD display. These displays are more flexible, consume less power, and in some cases, even do graphics.

When it comes to keyboards, you might think about wiring a PC keyboard directly to the Stamp. This sounds like a good idea, but in reality, it isn't very practical. The keyboard uses a synchronous protocol and it generates the clock which is quite fast. While you can interface a PC keyboard with extra hardware, you'll find a PC keyboard is not as useful on a Stamp as it is on a PC. But there are many ways to use smaller keypads (or even just switches) to good advantage.

Serial LCDs

The easy way to interface to an LCD is to use a module that takes serial input and displays it on an LCD. You can buy modules that include the LCD, or single ICs that drive an LCD that you supply. These devices are as simple as can be to use. You just use SEROUT to send the strings you want to display. Most of the LCD controllers will accept control characters to allow you to perform different functions. These may vary between different vendors.

Scott Edwards Electronics is probably the best-known manufacturer of serial LCDs with their line of LCD Backpacks. You can use a Control-L character ($0C), for example, to clear the LCD. Later in this chapter, you'll see a Scott Edwards display that can even do graphics.

LCD Interfacing

Serial LCDs have a lot going for them — they usually require a single I/O pin from the Stamp and they are easy to use. However, this simplicity comes at a price. Literally, a price because the modules that run the LCDs are not inexpensive, especially those that incorporate their own LCD.

Prime LCDs will cost you a lot if you buy them from the usual distributors. However, there are many sources for surplus LCDs that are very inexpensive. If you only need a few displays for a particular project, you can get a bargain if you shop around.

Of course, these LCDs don't have the serial interface that you'd like them to have. So you'll need to control them directly. Some surplus LCD modules have a proprietary interface and are practically useless to you. However, the good news is that the vast majority of LCD displays have a common 14-pin interface and all work the same way. That's because most LCD displays use a Hitachi HD44780 controller (or something that acts like a 44780).

Table 7.1 shows the standard 14-pin layout for the LCD displays you are likely to find. You may have to do some detective work to figure out which pin is pin 1 (although it will probably have a mark of some kind if you look carefully). A few LCDs arrange the 14 pins in a straight row which is easy enough to figure out. Most, however, have two rows of seven pins. These are made for insulation displacement connectors with ribbon cable to attach to them. That means that if you find pin 1, pin 2 is directly below it in the same column. To the side of pin 1 is pin 3, and pin 4 is directly below pin 3.

Table 7.1   Standard LCD pin out.

1 - GND	2 - +5	3 - Vcontrast	4 - RS	5 - R/W	6 - E	7 - DB0
8 - DB1	9 - DB2	10 - DB3	11 - DB4	12 - DB5	13 - DB6	14 - DB7

You'll notice in Table 7.1 that there are eight data pins (DB0-DB7). So you'd think you could not run an LCD from a Stamp I, and that it would take up more than half the I/O on a Stamp II, right? Wrong. If you know how to program the LCD correctly, you can shift it into a 4-bit mode where you only use four data bits (DB4-DB7). You'll also need to control the RS and E pins for a total of six I/O pins. In 4-bit mode, you can ground DB0-DB3, and you can usually ground the R/W pin as well because the Stamp generally only wants to write to the LCD.

TIP

Straight line LCDs
Sometimes you'll find an LCD with a ribbon cable connected to 14 holes straight across on the PC board. These are great finds. Remove the wire carefully with solder wick or a pump (or both) and solder a right-angle header into the holes. Now you can plug the LCD directly into the breadboard. Not only is this handy, it just looks neat!

Once you have figured out the LCD's pins, you can apply 5V to pin 2 and ground pin 1. Just as a quick test, try connecting pin 3 to ground or 5V and see if you can see faint boxes where the character appears. Some LCDs work fine with the contrast voltage fixed at a particular level. If you don't see any boxes, put a variable resistor (say a 10K) between power and ground and connect the wiper to the contrast voltage. Then you can adjust the contrast correctly. If you don't see any characters, the LCD may be bad, or you may have a unit that expects a negative contrast voltage.

For the example programs in this chapter, connect Stamp pins P0 to P3 to DB4 through DB7 (ground DB0 to DB3). Also ground pin 5 ($^R/_W$). As I mentioned before, you might be able to just ground pin 3, but you might need a pot (say 10K) tied between pins 1 and 2 with the wiper to pin 3 to adjust contrast. Pin 6 of the LCD (enable or E) connects to pin 5 of the Stamp. Finally connect RS (pin 4 on the LCD) to the Stamp's P4.

The BSIIP

Since LCDs are so popular with Stamp projects, Parallax added LCD interfacing to the BSIIP chips. There are three commands: LCDCMD, LCDIN, and LCDOUT. Although these commands accept a pin number as an argument, they really require seven pins to connect to the LCD. Also, you can only specify pin 0, 1, 8, or 9 as the pin argument.

If you specify pin 0 or 1, then that pin becomes the LCD's E pin. Pin 2 will be the $^R/_W$ pin, and pin 3 will connect to the LCD's RS pin. Then you'll use pins 4–7 to connect to the LCD's data bus (DB4–DB7). The BSIIP does not handle 8-bit mode. You can also elect to use pin 8 or 9 as E. Then pin 10 will be R/W, pin 11 is RS, and the data bus connects to pins 12–15.

The remainder of this chapter assumes you are directly programming the LCD. However, if you are using the BSIIP you can send commands with the LCDCMD instruction. To write data to the LCD you use LCDOUT, of course. LCDIN reads data from the LCD, which is not always necessary (however, the Stamp uses the RW pin, so you can't use it for anything else easily).

LCD Commands

The Hitachi LCD controller responds to several 8-bit commands when the RS bit is low (see Table 7.2). Remember, in 4-bit mode, you must chop these commands into two pieces (most significant four bits first).

The LCD commands are straightforward but require some bit manipulation. For example, to move the cursor to location 40 ($28; the first character of the second line), you'd need to send the command $A8 ($80+$28).

Table 7.2   Selected LCD Commands

Command (binary)	Description
00000001	Clear display and set cursor home
0000001X	Return cursor to home position X = don't care
000001DS	Sets cursor direction (D = 1 for increment; D = 0 for decrement) and shift mode (S)
00001DCB	D = 0 display off; C = 0 cursor off; B = 1 blink cursor
0001SRXX	S = 1 shift display; S = 0 move cursor; R = 1 move right; R = 0 move left; X = don't care
001LNFXX	L = 1 8-bit interface; L = 0 4-bit interface; N = 1 for 2 lines; N = 0 for 1 line; F = 1 use 5×10 font; F = 0 use 5×8 font
1AAAAAAA	Set cursor address to AAAAAAA

LCD Software

The software to drive the LCD is not too hard to understand (see Listing 7.1). The i_LCD routine initializes the LCD to 4-bit mode. The routine assumes you have a two-line display. You can change the initialization code to 0 if you have only one line or want to use a single line in a dual line display.

If you are using the BSIIP, you could use this code to initialize the LCD:

```
InitLCD:
    PAUSE 1000 ' Wait for LCD to power up
    LCDCMD 1, 48 'Send 3 wakeup commands
    PAUSE 10
    LCDCMD 1, 48
    PAUSE 1
    LCDCMD 1, 48
    PAUSE 1
    LCDCMD 1, 32 'Set data bus to 4-bit mode
    LCDCMD 1, 40 'Set to 2-line mode with 5x8 font
    LCDCMD 1, 8 'Turn display off
    LCDCMD 1, 12 'Turn display on without cursor
    LCDCMD 1, 6 'Set to auto-increment cursor (no display shift)
    LCDCMD 1, 1 'Clear the display
```

Once the LCD is active, you simply place data (four bits at a time) on the data lines, and pulse the E pin (or use the LCDOUT command on the BSIIP). The high-order bits are first, followed by the low-order bits. This is a good place to remember that you can address the P0 to P3 pins as a single 4-bit port named OUTA. If the RS pin is high, the LCD treats the data as a character to display. If RS is low, the LCD understands that the data is a command (see Table 7.2). You can use wr_LCD to write normal characters to the LCD and cmd to write command bytes.

There are a few other useful routines in the LCD code. The wr_worddec routine writes a 16-bit word in decimal to the LCD. For bytes, use wr_bytedec instead. The clear and setcursor commands allow you to clear the screen or set the cursor position.

The cursor position on LCDs may not match your expectations. All LCDs think they have 40 characters per line, even if they don't. Therefore, the first character of the second line is always at position 40 regardless of the number of columns the LCD displays. (Discussion continues on page 322.)

Listing 7.1   The LCD driver software.

```
' 4 bit LCD interface for BS2
' Williams
' Assumes LCD is connected to P0-P3
E con 5  ' LCD Enable bit
RS con 4 ' LCD Reg Select

char var byte   ' char to LCD
inum var word    ' number to write
j var byte     ' gp variable
nozero var bit  ' set to 1 for zero supression
cursor var byte

pw con 1    ' Pulse width

' Set up the Stamp's I/O lines and initialize the LCD.
begin:
  GOSUB i_LCD

  i var word
  k var word
  k=100
```

Listing 7.1 The LCD driver software. (Continued)

```
msg:
  cursor=40      ' set cursor to line 2
  gosub setcursor
  i=0
ploop:           ' Write out the company name
  LOOKUP i,["AWC",0],char
  if char=0 then main
  gosub wr_LCD
  i=i+1
  goto ploop

' Main program loop:
main:
  pause 1000    ' wait a second

ctloop:
  gosub clear   ' clear LCD
  inum=k        ' k starts at 100
  nozero=1
  gosub wr_worddec   ' Write out K with zero suppress
  k=k-1
  cursor=39      ' move cursor to far left
  gosub setcursor
  LOOKUP k//4,["*","+","-"," "],char   ' make spinner
  gosub wr_LCD
  goto msg


' Write the ASCII character in char to LCD.
wr_LCD:
  outA =  char.NIB1 ' OR the first 4 bits in
  pulsout E,pw ' Blip enable pin.
  outA = char.NIB0
  pulsout E,pw ' Blip enable.
  return
```

Listing 7.1 The LCD driver software. (Continued)

```
' Write a word in decimal
wr_worddec:
   j=5
   goto wr_dec

' Write a byte in decimal
wr_bytedec:
   j=2
wr_dec:
   char=inum DIG j +"0"
' Supress zeros
   if j<>0 AND char="0" and nozero=1 then digz
   gosub wr_LCD
   nozero=0  ' turn off suppression so we don't turn 102 into 12
digz:
   if j=0 then nowr
   j=j-1
   goto wr_dec
nowr:
   return




' Initialize the LCD in accordance with Hitachi's instructions for 4-bit inter-
face.
i_LCD:
   outA = 0 ' Clear the output lines
   LOW E
   LOW RS
   dirA = %1111 ' 7 outputs.
   pause 200 ' Wait 200 ms for LCD to reset.
' force 8-bit op - repeating to be sure it resets
   outA = %0011
   pulsout E,pw
   pulsout E,pw
   pulsout E,pw
```

Listing 7.1   The LCD driver software. (Continued)

```
  outA = %0010  ' Set to 4-bit operation from 8 bit.
  pulsout E,pw

' could remove this line if you wanted to
  outA = %0010  ' Set to 4-bit operation from 4 bit.
  pulsout E,pw
' if you want 1 line, you could comment out the next line
  outA = %1000  ' 2 line - use 0 for 1 line
  pulsout E,pw

  char = 14 ' Set up LCD in accordance with
'  char = 15  ' blinking cursor (use 14 for non-blink)
  gosub wr_LCD ' Hitachi instruction manual.
  char = 6 ' Turn on cursor and enable
  gosub wr_LCD ' left-to-right printing.


clear:
  char = 1 ' Clear the display.
  gosub cmd ' Write instruction to LCD.
  return

cmd:
  low RS
  gosub wr_LCD
  high RS
  return

setcursor:
  char=$80 + cursor
  gosub cmd
  return
```

Scanning a Keypad

Depending on your needs, you may only need a few buttons that you can handle like you always do (that is, by reading the input or using the BUTTON command from Chapter 3). Of course, sometimes you need a larger number of keys, and the Stamp's limited number of I/O pins gets in the way.

For example, suppose you want 16 keys on a Stamp II. To wire them up as single buttons would consume the entire I/O capacity of the Stamp II. Clearly, you need a better way to handle large numbers of buttons.

You can buy dedicated keyboard controller ICs (like the 74C922 used in Stamp Application Note #3). However, there is no reason you can't simply use the Stamp itself to do the same work that a dedicated chip would do.

The most traditional way to scan a keyboard is to organize the keys into rows and columns (see Figure 7.1). There are several ways you can arrange to scan the keys by arranging the row lines as outputs and the column lines as inputs (or vice versa). The idea is to bring each output bit low while monitoring the inputs.

Figure 7.1   Scanning a keypad.

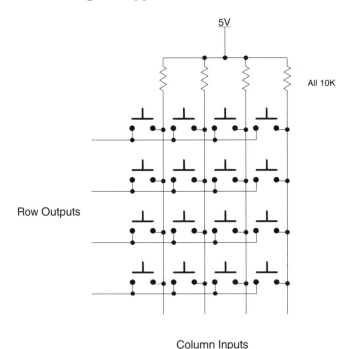

As an example, suppose you depress the key connected to row 1 column 0. The Stamp writes $E (%1110) to the row lines. Because none of the keys in the first column are down, the input from the column lines will be %1111. Next, the Stamp writes %1101 to the row lines. Now the column 0 line will drop to a logic 0 because the Stamp's output can easily override the pull-up resistor. When the Stamp reads the column inputs, it will find %1110. It is a simple matter of correlating the current row (1) and the active column (0) to determine which key is down.

Here is a small piece of code that will do the job (assuming OUTA contains the output pins and INB contains the inputs):

```
DIRS=$F0
OUTA=$F  ' all lines on
scani var nib
scan var nib
key var nib


' your code here
readkey:
  for scani=0 to 3
      lookup scani,[7,11,13,14],scan
      OUTA=scan
      if INB=$F then nextscan
      key=15  ' more than one key?
' key now has row or 15
      lookdown scan,[7,11,13,14],key
      if key=15 then nextscan


      ' column in scani and row in key (inverted)
    scan=key ^ $FF
    scani=scani ^ $FF   ' invert
    ' assume keys go up by row
    key=scani<<4+scan
    ' if keys arranged by column, use key=scan<<4+scani
    return
nextscan:
  next
goto readkey
```

Because only one line is active at once on both the inputs and outputs, you could use a multiplexer and demultiplexer to save pins. Another idea would be to use a counter and demultiplexer to generate the scanning signal. Then you'd need an I/O pin to clock the counter and another to clear it. Of course, if you are adding all this hardware, you might just as well use a keyboard chip like the 74C922. This chip lets you use five pins to read 16 keys. The chip uses a row and column scanning technique much as the Stamp code above does. However, it does it all in hardware.

The chip signals the Stamp when the user presses a key and makes the key number (0–15) available on four output pins for the Stamp to read. You can find more about this chip in Stamp Application Note #3 from Parallax (you can also find it in the Stamp Manual on the CD-ROM).

Analog Keypads

Using eight pins to get 16 keys is acceptable, but its still a heavy price to pay — a full 50% of the Stamp II's I/O capacity. However, using a bit of analog trickery, you can read a number of keys with only one pin!

The trick is to devise a resistor network that varies its value based on what switch the user pushes (see Figure 7.2). Essentially this is nothing more than a potentiometer that uses push buttons to set the total resistance. Using the RCTIME command (or the POT command on the Stamp I), it isn't hard to deduce which key the user pressed. Of course, you'll need to calibrate by reading the value each switch produces. By using large enough resistors (and programming in a wide tolerance), you should be able to use one set of calibration numbers even if you make more than one keyboard.

Figure 7.2   A resistor network keypad.

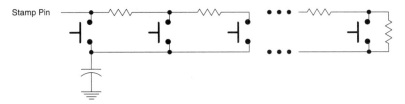

The Stamp II's LOOKDOWN command is well-suited for this type of keyboard because you can specify a comparison operator to use when searching the list. For example, suppose that for four buttons you determine, the threshold values are 900, 600, 400, and 200:

```
LOW keypin      ' discharge capacitor
RCTIME keypin,1,W2
B1=-1
LOOKDOWN W2,>[1200, 900, 600, 400, 200],B1
```

Once you know the number of the key, it is a simple matter to use LOOKUP to convert it into a character. Of course, you may be satisfied to simply know the number of the key.

This sounds almost too simple. That's because it is too simple. There are several problems. First, a variety of factors combine to prevent you from getting rock-solid readings. The counts will vary a bit each time you measure the button array. Because the measurement is very fast (compared to the speed people press keys), it is a good idea to average two to four samples before comparing the numbers.

Another problem is that when you push the button, the Stamp may be in the middle of measuring the resistance. In this case, you'll get erroneous values. To combat this, make sure you can get the same key three or four times in a row before you report it to the program. Errors caused by push buttons are transient in nature, and if you get the same key three times in a row, you can bet that was the key pressed. You'll find an example of this technique in the Answer Key for this chapter on page 441.

Making the Most of Limited Keys

When you first start thinking about a project, it is tempting to plan for a huge keyboard. However, if you've ever set a digital alarm clock, you know you can do a lot with only a few buttons, if you want.

For example, with an LCD display, you might devise a menu system. You could use one button to move forward in the menu and another button to move back in the menu. A third button could act as a select button. If you need to enter a string or a number, you can use the same idea, using two buttons to move forward and backward, and a third button to select the value you want. You'll see a variation on this idea used to enter in the high-score in the pong game in the next section of this chapter.

Graphical LCDs

The G12032 serial LCD from Scott Edwards Electronics costs about $100, but it offers a wide array of text and graphics options. The LCD can display 4×20, 4×10, 2×20, or 2×10 in text mode. You can also treat the LCD as a 120×32 pixel graphics array. You can even mix graphics and text on the same screen.

To put this LCD through its paces, I built a simple pong-style game (see Figure 7.3). All you need is the LCD, a BS2, and two buttons wired to ground with pull-up resistors. When you start the game, it shifts the LCD into a large font and displays a splash screen. When you press one of the buttons, you'll see your paddle appear. A little later, the puck starts coming towards you. You have to bounce it between the walls, the far wall, and your paddle. When you hit the ball, your score will increase (indicated in the far right corner). When you miss, the game is over.

Figure 7.3   The pong game.

If you have the high score, you'll get to put your initials in (stored in EEPROM of course). Either way you'll see the high score before the game restarts.

Programming the LCD for text is very simple. You just use SEROUT to write to it like a terminal. It recognizes several commands to display reverse text, change fonts, etc.

The fun part is when you start using graphics. The LCD can store several predefined graphics in its EEPROM. You can also define custom fonts. For the game, it is simple to just plot points. The LCD can also graph lines easily.

Details

The display normally just writes out ASCII text. It also recognizes the usual control characters like carriage-return, line feed, etc. Table 7.3 shows the commands.

Table 7.3   G12032 commands.

^A	Home cursor
^B	Inverse start
^C	End inverse
^H	Backspace
^I	Tab
^J	Line feed
^K	Up one row
^L	Clear screen
^M	Carriage return (auto line feed; ignores redundant line feeds)
^N	Backlight on
^O	Backlight off
^P	Position cursor
^R	Right align

When a command expects a numeric argument, you can send it as plain ASCII text (e.g., 10). However, you may find it easier to send the binary number plus 64 (assuming the number is less than 192 because 191 + 64 = 255). This allows you to send most numbers as a single byte, taking up less space in the Stamp and executing faster.

For graphics, you send ESC followed by a letter and perhaps some data. The graphics commands appear in Table 7.4.

There is one point that took me awhile to figure out. Sometimes when I would start the program, the player's paddle would be missing until you started moving it. It turns out that when the Stamp restarts, it might have been in the middle of doing something with the LCD. If that something had the ink set to white, the paddle wouldn't show up initially. The same problem can keep the screen from clearing if the ^L occurs when the LCD is expecting other input.

Because there is no arbitrary reset for the LCD, I found it useful to clear the screen three times and set the ink to black at the start of the program. While this probably isn't foolproof, for this program it did prevent the LCD from getting confused. Later Scott Edwards pointed out that a more efficient way to do this is to send the byte 64 ("@") four times followed by a clear screen. Either way works in this case, but the three clear screens takes more time than sending four characters.

Table 7.4   Graphics commands.

ESCA	Set screen address
ESCB	Write bit pattern
ESCD	Download graphic
ESCE	Show EEPROM graphic
ESCF	Set font or page
ESCI	Set ink color
ESCL	Plot a line
ESCM	Set/reset XOR mode
ESCP	Plot a point
ESCR	Reverse lines
ESCT	Plot a line starting at end of last line
ESCV	Set vertical origin
ESCW	Save to EEPROM
ESCX	Capture screen to EEPROM

The code for the pong game appears in Listing 7.2. The code isn't terribly complicated. The main loop calls advpuck to advance the puck (the moving ball). Then it calls drawpuck to actually display the ball in motion. A call to hittest determines if the puck hit the paddle or a wall and makes the appropriate adjustments. At the end of the loop, the code checks to see if the user is moving the paddle and adjusts it accordingly. (Discussion continues on page 337.)

Listing 7.2   The pong game.

```
' Pong - push button version
' Al Williams

leftkey var in8
rightkey var in9
lbutton con 8
rbutton con 9
baudrate con 16468
lcdport con 6
misses con 1   ' # of misses before game is over
```

Listing 7.2 The pong game. (Continued)

```
player var word   ' player's position (X)
tick var byte     ' tick count through the loop
puckx var word    ' puck x and y position
pucky var word
deltax var word   ' deltax and deltay
deltay var word
accx var word     ' error accumulators for x & y
accy var word
lastx var word    ' last drawn position for erase
lasty var word
rword var word    ' random word
sign var word     ' direction of delta
hitct var byte    ' number of hits
miss var byte     ' number of misses


' The high score stuff needs
' variables but not at the same time
' so we will reuse them
hiscore var player.lowbyte
init1 var rword.lowbyte
init2 var rword.highbyte
init3 var miss
letter var player.highbyte
begin:
tick=0
pause 100  ' wait for LCD to catch up
' repeat in case we reset in the mid of graphics
serout lcdport,baudrate,[12,12,12,14] ' clear screen & backlite on
' Should select black ink just in case
serout lcdport,baudrate,[27,"I",65]

serout lcdport,baudrate,[27,"F",66] ' big font
serout lcdport,baudrate,[2,"   Pong by AWC!   ",3,"   Press a key"]
gosub keywait
hitct=0
```

Listing 7.2 The pong game. (Continued)

```
miss=0
gosub clslcd
for player=0 to 9
serout lcdport,baudrate,[27,"P",player+64,31+64]
next
player=0  ' initial pos

top:
pause 20
tick=tick+1
if tick<>150 then noinit
gosub puckinit
noinit:
if tick<150 then nopuck
tick=150  ' no use letting it roll over
gosub advpuck
gosub drawpuck
gosub hittest
nopuck:
if leftkey=0 then left
rword=rword+1         ' randomize
if rightkey=0 then right
rword=rword+2
goto top

' move player right 2 spaces
' this makes player move faster than puck
' this is in 2 steps so we are sure we
' don't roll over the edge
' if you want a more challenging game
' remove one move below
right:
gosub rightmove
gosub rightmove
goto top
```

Listing 7.2   The pong game. (Continued)

```
' move player left 2 spaces
' this makes player move faster than puck
' this is in 2 steps so we are sure we
' don't roll over the edge
' if you want a more challenging game
' remove one move below
left:
gosub leftmove
gosub leftmove
goto top



' Actual right move logic
rightmove:
if player>=108 then rightret
serout lcdport,baudrate,[27,"I",64]
serout lcdport,baudrate,[27,"P",player+64,31+64]
serout lcdport,baudrate,[27,"I",65]
serout lcdport,baudrate,[27,"P",player+10+64,31+64]
player=player+1
rightret:
return

' Actual left move logic
leftmove:
if player=0 then leftret
serout lcdport,baudrate,[27,"I",64]
serout lcdport,baudrate,[27,"P",player+9+64,31+64]
serout lcdport,baudrate,[27,"I",65]
serout lcdport,baudrate,[27,"P",player-1+64,31+64]
player=player-1
leftret:
return

' Initialize puck parameters
puckinit:
```

Listing 7.2   The pong game. (Continued)

```
   puckx=1
   pucky=1
   deltax=1
   deltay=1
   accx=0
   accy=0
   return

drawpuck:
' Don't erase player!
   if lasty=31 and lastx>=player and lastx<player+10 then noclear
' Set ink to white and erase puck
   serout lcdport,baudrate,[27,"I",64]
   serout lcdport,baudrate,[27,"P",lastx+64,lasty+64]   ' clear old puck
' Set ink to black again
   serout lcdport,baudrate,[27,"I",65]
noclear:
' Draw puck
   serout lcdport,baudrate,[27,"P",puckx+64,pucky+64]
' Remember where
   lastx=puckx
   lasty=pucky
   return
' Advance puck
' Since X and Y may not increase each time
' the puck's speed depends on its angle
' To make the speed constant, you'd need
' to know which was changing more rapidly: X or Y?
advpuck:
   accx=accx+1
   accy=accy+1
   if accx<>abs(deltax) then noxadv
   sign=1
' Note: can't say deltax<0 because compare is unsigned
   if deltax<$8000 then xsgn
   sign=-1
```

Listing 7.2   The pong game. (Continued)

```
xsgn:
  puckx=puckx+sign // 120
  accx=0
noxadv:
  if accy<>abs(deltay) then noyadv
  sign=1
  if deltay<$8000 then ysgn
  sign=-1
ysgn:
  pucky=pucky+sign // 32
  accy=0
noyadv:

return


hittest:
 if pucky=0 then hit   ' bounce off top
' Hey the player hit it!
 if pucky=31 and puckx>=player and puckx<=player+10 then hit
' bounce off sides
 if puckx=0 or puckx>=119 then bounce
' Not close to player yet
 if pucky<>31 then nohit
' missed!
miss=miss+1
if miss=misses then gover   ' end game?
 pucky=0   ' wrap around
 return
bounce:   ' bounce off sides by reflection
 deltax=-deltax
 if puckx=0 then x1
 puckx=118
 goto x118
x1:
 puckx=1
```

Listing 7.2 The pong game. (Continued)

```
x118:
 accx=0
 return

' Player hit or hit top
hit:
 ' need to reflect puck
 deltay=-deltay
 if pucky=0 then y1     ' top hit
 pucky=30
' player hit it so count it
 hitct=hitct+1
' Show score
' Note -- the puck erases this score as it
' moves through it -- could make a bounce
' around the score, or omit completely
 serout lcdport,baudrate,[16,64+20-3,dec3 hitct]
' Add some random english to the puck
 random rword
 deltay=deltay ^ (rword & 3)
' If you make deltax a constant at 1
' (remove next 2 lines) the game is faster
 random rword
 deltax=deltax ^ (rword>>2 & 3)
' Disallow x=0 y=0 so we don't get caught
 if deltax<>0 then dxnz
 deltax=1
dxnz:
 if deltay<>0 then dynz
 deltay=1
dynz:
 goto y31
y1:
 pucky=1
y31:
 accy=0
```

Listing 7.2   The pong game. (Continued)

```
nohit:
 return


' GAME OVER!
gover:
  gosub clslcd
  serout lcdport,baudrate,["Game over",13,"Score=",dec hitct]
' check saved hiscore
  read 0,hiscore
  gosub keywait
  serout lcdport,baudrate,[27,"F",64] ' norm font
' This guy is not king of the hill so say who is
  if hiscore>=hitct then showhs  ' no high score
' Big winner -- get his name
  serout lcdport,baudrate,[12,"High score!",13,"<- change -> accept",13]
' reuse variables (see top of code)
  init1="A"
  init2="A"
  init3="A"
' Don't clear the button workspace
' inside GetLet or the 2nd and 3rd calls will not work
' right
  accx=0   ' used as button workspace

  letter=init1  ' Get all 3 letters (could use an array)
  gosub getlet
  init1=letter
  letter=init2
  gosub getlet
  init2=letter
  letter=init3
  gosub getlet
  init3=letter
' Write high score info
  write 0,hitct
  write 1,init1
```

Listing 7.2 The pong game. (Continued)

```
   write 2,init2
   write 3,init3

' Show high score
showhs:
  read 0,hiscore
  read 1,init1
  read 2,init2
  read 3,init3
  serout lcdport,baudrate,[12,"High score: ",dec hiscore,13," by
",init1,init2,init3]
  gosub keywait
  goto begin  ' start over

' Wait for a key
keywait:
  if leftkey=0 or rightkey=0 then keywait
kw22:
  if leftkey=1 and rightkey=1 then kw22
kwait3:
  if leftkey=0 or rightkey=0 then kwait3
  return

' Get a letter arcade style
getlet:
  serout lcdport,baudrate,[letter]
getlet1:
  pause 5  ' some time for button loop
  button lbutton,0,100,50,accx.highbyte,1,nxtlet
  button rbutton,0,255,0,accx.lowbyte,1,nxtslot
  goto getlet1
nxtlet:
  letter=letter+1
  if letter=$21 then LetA   ' A follows Space
  if letter<="Z" then letdisp  ' Space follows Z
  letter=" "
```

Listing 7.2 The pong game. (Continued)

```
    goto letdisp
letA:
  letter="A"
letdisp:
  serout lcdport,baudrate,[8,letter]
  goto getletl

nxtslot:
  return

clslcd:
  serout lcdport,baudrate,[12]   ' clear game
  return
```

One of the more interesting parts of the code is the portion that handles the high score. If you get the high score, the Stamp lets you use one button to cycle through letters and the other button to accept the current letter. You can enter three letters and the Stamp stores them and the score in the EEPROM. The getlet routine does all the work and could easily be reused if you needed a similar function in another program.

The other interesting part of this code is that there are not enough variables for the high score code to use. However, it is easy to see that most of the variables in the program are not needed while entering the high score. Likewise, the high score variables are not needed during the rest of the program.

It is easy to share variables between different parts of the code when you use the predefined variable names (like B1 and W5, for example). However, this program allows the Stamp software to automatically allocate variables. If you want to share variables in this case, you have two options. First, you can just use the same variable names. This might be acceptable if you have generic variable names like I or loopctr.

It is a bad idea to reuse the names player and miss for the high score and an initial. Instead, the program creates aliases for the high score variables:

```
hiscore var player.lowbyte
init1 var rword.lowbyte
init2 var rword.highbyte
init3 var miss
letter var player.highbyte
```

You could make many enhancements to this game. Sound would be fun, although you might need external hardware to keep the game from slowing down too much. Another idea would be to interface a variable resistor to the Stamp and use the RCTIME command to set the position of the player. You might also use a switch-type joystick like the one that comes with a Sega Genesis game system. These controllers happen to use a standard DB-9 connector, so they are easy to work with.

Summary

LCDs and keypads can provide a professional appearance to microcontroller projects. If you have the I/O pins and code space to spare, driving LCDs directly is an inexpensive option. If you want to get something going in a hurry that uses a single pin and virtually no program space, opt for a serial LCD.

Although a keypad is the most common input device, you may want to consider the benefits of using several separate push buttons and a simplified interface instead. This isn't as attractive as a full keypad, but it typically takes much less I/O and program space to realize.

Another way to accommodate a larger keypad is to use analog techniques to read the keypad using one pin. With careful component selection this method can be quite reliable. While it does consume some program space, you can hardly complain because it only requires one I/O pin.

Exercises

1. Using a keypad or discrete push buttons, build an analog keypad like the one in Figure 7.2. Write a program that reads the keys and prints them on the debugging terminal as you press them. Be sure that the program only reports each key press once and that it always reports the correct key.

2. Using the keypad from exercise 1, write a simple RPN calculator that can at least perform addition and subtraction. (RPN is the same style used by Hewlett Packard calculators.) To enter 5 + 3, you actually press: 5, Enter, 3, Plus on the keyboard.

3. If you have access to an LCD that uses the Hitachi drivers, rewrite the code in Listing 7.1 to use 8-bit mode instead of 4-bit mode.

For answers to the exercises, see the Answer Key, page 441.

Chapter 8

A Remote Control Robot: Motors

Ever since Capek wrote a play entitled *Rossum's Universal Robots* (in the 1920s, if you can believe it), robots have been a staple in fictional literature, television, and movies. *Silent Running, Star Wars,* and Michael Crichton's *WestWorld* are just a few of the movies that have robots as main characters (I'll ignore *Robot Monster* with its diving-helmeted gorilla robot).

In truth, robots are everywhere — just not how authors imagined them. Today's robot doesn't really look like Yul Brenner or R2D2. Instead, they have bodies particularly suited for their job. Any modern factory is full of robots that cut materials, drill holes, weld, and do many other tasks.

Most modern robots don't move around except in a specific area. However, there is a tremendous desire to build full-featured robots like C3PO — or at least like R2D2. Even if you don't want to build a moving robot, there are many other computer projects that require motion.

Although there are a few alternatives, serious robotic motion today requires a motor. At first glance, you might think that a motor would be a simple device to interface to a Stamp. Like a light bulb, you could just turn it on with a transistor, right? In the simplest case, that's all you need to drive a motor. However, in practice, you need more control over the motor. You may need precise control over the motor's position or speed. Also, practical motors tend to require significant drive current. You may not be able to use the simple driver circuits you've encountered in earlier chapters.

Complete control of motors, not to mention robotics, is beyond the scope of this book. But armed with a little information, there are many motorized projects you can easily handle with the Basic Stamp. In this chapter, you'll learn:

- how to use DC, stepper, and servo motors,
- what issues to consider when creating motor drive circuits, and
- how to control the BoeBot.

While this chapter won't enable you to create the next C3PO, it will give you enough foundation to undertake some beginning robotics projects.

DC Motors

Standard DC motors (often sold as hobby motors) are what most people think of when they want to use a motor in a project. These motors often operate from 12V and have extremely high RPMs. What good is a motor that turns 10,000 times per second? That's probably of no use to you at all. The key is that the motor has very little torque. When you try to make the motor's shaft turn a wheel or a track, it will slow down somewhat. Even then, with all but the lightest loads, the motor will stop and simply get hot.

When you want to use a motor practically, you will use some combination of gears (similar to a car's transmission) to slow the motor down to a usable speed while also increasing the torque, and therefore the allowable load. Some motors have gears built in and are often called *gearhead motors*. Motors that turn at precise rates (often used in clocks or old-fashioned cam timing systems) are known as *timing motors*.

Often hobby shops will sell small transmissions that will gear down motors for use in model cars and other vehicles. You can also fashion your own with small gears stolen from a toy, tape recorder, or other motorized electronic device. You can, of course, use pulleys and belts to accomplish the same thing, but gears are probably a bit more rugged.

Don't forget that a DC motor usually requires a good bit of current. If you buy your motor, it will probably have specifications that tell you how much current it may draw. If you are liberating motors from old junked equipment, you may have to be a bit more creative. An ohm meter can tell you the resistance of the motor's coil. Using Ohm's law, you can get a good idea of how much current it will draw.

Practically any DC motor you find will require more circuitry than just a Stamp pin to drive it on or off. A 2N2222 driver (as you've seen in earlier chapters) will only handle about 100mA (and even then, you should heat sink the transistor).

You can find specific ICs designed to drive motors directly, or you can use a power transistor in a darlington configuration (see Figure 8.1). Be sure to use a diode, just like you would with a relay. A motor is nothing more than a coil with some bits of magnetic metal around it, so you can destroy transistors with reverse EMF quite easily.

Figure 8.1   A darlington transistor.

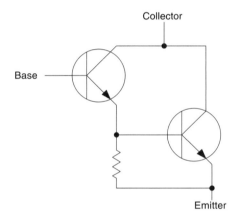

You can buy darlington transistors in one case or make them from individual transistors. Exactly which transistors you'll use depends on the amount of current you expect to handle. Don't forget that a darlington transistor will lose some voltage between the collector and the emitter. For power transistors, this may be a higher loss than you are used to seeing on small transistors like 2N2222s. You may deliver 1V or 2V less to the motor than you put in.

A popular motor driver is the ULN2803A (available from several sources including Motorola and Allegro). These chips have eight darlington transistors that can handle 500mA each. If you need more current-handling capacity, you can parallel more than one transistor. The IC has internal protection diodes, so you can drive a motor (or other inductive load) without external diodes. Built-in base resistors means you can drive the bases directly with 5V logic outputs.

Another popular choice is to use a MOSFET switch. Many companies (e.g., Fairchild, International Rectifier, and Harris) make MOSFETs that you can easily drive with a logic-level output. These transistors can switch 5A to 20A with practically no current required on the gate. You can even find the IRF-510 at Radio Shack (although they are often mislabeled as IFR-510s on the Radio Shack package). Even with 5V on the gate, it can handle about 1A. If you put 12V on the gate (maybe using a 2N2222 driver), you can switch around 10A.

You can find a simple MOSFET driver in Figure 8.2. The 1M resistor makes sure the gate has a path to ground. This is a good design practice to prevent gate damage from static electricity, although it isn't strictly necessary if the Stamp pin will always drive the gate high or low. An extra capacitor bridging the draw and source of the MOSFET can filter the noise the motor generates. It will also buffers the motor a bit against high frequency changes (for example, if you use PWM to control the motor speed).

Figure 8.2   Using a MOSFET.

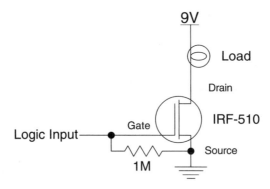

TIP

Motor-induced resets

If you try a circuit like that in Figure 8.2, you may find it behaves erratically. The motor may sound like it is revving up and down periodically. If this happens, it is likely that noise from the motor is resetting the Stamp. This can be a particular problem if you have the programming cable attached because the program cable will often pick the noise up and feed it into the ATN line where it triggers a reset.

A temporary solution may be to remove the programming cable. However, a better remedy is to put a 0.1µF capacitor from the ATN line of the Stamp or programming cable to ground.

If you suspect your program is resetting, try adding a debug statement (or making an LED blink) at the beginning of your program. Then you'll know if the program resets because the message appears more than once.

Of course, for very crude applications, you can always use a relay to switch the voltage to the motor on and off. This doesn't give you a lot of control, however, and is best suited for very crude motion with large motors.

No matter how you switch the motor on and off, you'll find that most of the time, you'll need to do more than just run the motor. You'll want to control the motor's speed or position as well.

Power supplies for motors

Ever notice that many toy cars take two batteries? Usually there will be four C or D cells, and then one or two smaller batteries (a 9V cell or a pair of AA batteries). That's because motors tend to draw lots of current and this is hard on the batteries. A voltage dip that won't really hurt the motor may drop the voltage below what the logic circuits (like the Stamp) require.

Mind your grounds

Motors can create lots of noise that can interfere with any electronic circuit including the Stamp. Be sure you have a heavy ground wire to the motor. Also, if you are using two power supplies, don't forget to connect their grounds together. Finally, you may have to place capacitors between the power and ground lines very close to your logic circuits to filter noise. In very heavy cases, you may want to use a ferrite core or bead on the power lines going to the motor. Depending on the type you get, you'll snap the bead around the wire, or wrap a few turns of wire around the ferrite. This will raise the inductance of the wire and therefore increase its impedance to high-frequency noise.

Using PWM

The Stamp can generate PWM and in previous chapters, you've seen projects that use this to generate voltages. However, another interesting use for PWM is to control motor speed.

You might initially think that you could feed a motor a lower voltage to slow it down. This is true to a point, but it is difficult to vary the drive voltage while supplying so much current. Also, below a certain voltage, the motor will probably just stop spinning. A better idea is to feed the motor a train of pulses. The *duty cycle* (that is, the amount of time the pulse is high versus the length of time it is low) will control the motor's speed.

Again, you must drive enough current to spin the motor, so don't plan on connecting a Stamp pin directly to the motor. You'll need to use a switch of some kind to provide the actual motor drive.

The Stamp's PWM is not especially suited to driving motors because it is proportionally generated. This is good for charging capacitors, but can cause noise when applied to motors. There are dedicated chips that produce PWM specifically for motor control. For example, the PAK-V chip from AWC generates eight channels of PWM. You can also use a MC34060 from Motorola.

The H Bridge

Another problem with the motor drives you've seen so far is that they only run the motor in one direction. The common way to drive the motor both forwards and backwards is an H bridge.

Again, you can find H bridges in an IC package ready to use (like the LMD18200, the L293D, or the MPM3002). You can also roll your own. The idea is simple (see Figure 8.3). Each side of the motor has two switches. One switches positive voltage to the motor and the other switches the ground connection. If the top switch is supplying voltage and the bottom switch is to ground, the motor will spin in one direction. If the top switch goes to ground and the bottom switch provides power, the motor will spin in the opposite direction.

Figure 8.3   An H bridge.

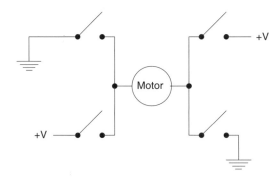

This seems simple, and it is. You'll usually use two transistors for the top and two at the bottom. When you draw this schematically (Figure 8.3), it resembles a letter H, which is where it gets its name. Of course, the details can be a problem.

It is very important that only the top switches or the bottom switches are on at one time. Turning on both switches on either side would result in a short circuit. It goes without saying that the transistors you use must be beefy enough to handle the motor current too.

You can use any sort of switch that can handle the current to build an H bridge. A bipolar transistor or a MOSFET will work. You might even use the ULN2803A — it has eight transistors — more than enough to build an H bridge.

TIP

Double jeopardy
When using an H bridge, the drive voltage passes through two switches at all times. If you have a darlington drive transistor that drops 1V, you will lose 2V to the motor because each transistor will contribute.

If you need to control a motor's speed and direction, you can replace the drive voltage with a PWM source. Again, the PWM signal must be stout enough to drive the motor, so a successful design will need at least four switches for the H bridge plus another to drive the PWM line.

About Stepper Motors

In addition to ordinary DC motors, there are several other kinds of motors that you might find useful in microcontroller projects. The first of these is the *stepper motor*. Stepper motors are often used to position heads in disk drives, and in fact, old floppy disks are a primary source for these motors.

The advantage of the stepper motor is that it is very precise. The motor responds to a series of pulses. The pulses will result in an exact position change in the motor's shaft. Many motors step 3.6°, for example. Other common step sizes are 1.8° and 7.5°. You can also step the motor in a half step for even greater control.

There are several different types of stepper motors. Bipolar steppers are not very common. They require you to reverse voltages on their coils using some arrangement similar to an H bridge. Unless you have no choice, you'll want to avoid using this type of stepper.

It is much easier to work with the more common unipolar stepper. These usually have five or six leads. In a five-wire motor, one lead will be the common connection between four coils (numbered 1 through 4). The other wires will connect to the other side of each coil (see Figure 8.4). On a six-wire unipolar stepper, there are two wires connecting to the common.

Figure 8.4 A stepper motor.

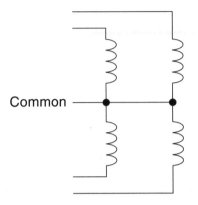

TIP

Reverse engineering a stepper

If you have an old floppy disk drive, you can easily remove the stepper motor from it. Look for a flat motor with five or six wires coming out of it. The problem is: how do you know how to wire it up?

The first thing to do is measure the resistance between all the terminals (or pins). You'll notice that one pin reads about half of the resistance that you see between the other pins. This pin is the common. When you measure the common pin's resistance to another pin, your meter only "sees" one coil. When measuring the other pins, the meter "sees" two coils.

Once you know which pin is common, connect it to a power supply that can supply the rated voltage (probably stamped on the back). Be sure it can provide enough current (the voltage divided by the coil resistance). Ground one of the other pins, and call it coil 4's pin. What if it isn't coil 4? It doesn't matter. What drives the stepper motor is the sequence of pulses on the coils. Any coil could be coil 4, so long as you number the other coils appropriately.

With coil 4 grounded, ground one of the other pins. If the motor does nothing, you have found coil 2. If the motor shaft jerks clockwise, you have coil 3. If the shaft jerks counterclockwise, you are grounding the pin for coil 1. Repeat until you find all the coils.

Like a regular motor, the stepper motor's coils require a lot of current, so you'll need a drive transistor of some sort. Unlike a regular motor, you don't just apply current to make the stepper run. Instead, you apply current in a particular pattern.

Table 8.1 shows a sequence that will cause the motor to take four steps. You can reverse the direction of the step by reversing the order of the steps. An alternate sequence appears in Table 8.2. This sequence consumes about twice the power (because it drives two coils at once). However, it is not as smooth as the first sequence. Why use it? It generates about 1.4 times the torque compared to the first sequence. Table 8.3 shows the sequence that will step the motor using half steps.

Keep in mind that a 1 in these tables means the coil is energized. If the common motor lead is connected to the power supply, you will actually ground the coil lead to energize it. Of course, using a transistor to switch to ground will invert the Stamp's output, so an output of 1 may ground the coil lead. It would be just as valid to ground the motor common and switch voltage to the individual coil wires — if you wanted to do it that way.

Table 8.1 The normal sequence for stepping.

Step	Coil 1	Coil 2	Coil 3	Coil 4
1	0	0	0	1
2	0	0	1	0
3	0	1	0	0
4	1	0	0	0

Table 8.2 A higher-torque sequence.

Step	Coil 1	Coil 2	Coil 3	Coil 4
1	0	0	1	1
2	0	1	1	0
3	1	1	0	0
4	1	0	0	1

Table 8.3 Half steps.

Step	Coil 1	Coil 2	Coil 3	Coil 4
1	0	0	0	1
2	0	0	1	1
3	0	0	1	0
4	0	1	1	0

Table 8.3   Half steps. (Continued)

Step	Coil 1	Coil 2	Coil 3	Coil 4
5	0	1	0	0
6	1	1	0	0
7	1	0	0	0
8	1	0	0	1

Obviously the speed of the motor will depend on how fast you step it. As you repeat one of the sequences above, the motor will continue to turn, advancing the specified number of degrees with each step. However, when you use a stepper you are often not as concerned with speed as you are with the position of the shaft. Steppers are used in disk drives, printers, plotters, and other devices that require precise positioning.

If you have the appropriate transistors on the Stamp, it is simple to produce the correct sequence. Stamp Application Note #6 (in the Stamp Manual on the CD-ROM) shows a clever way that only requires two pins and very little code.

This scheme takes advantage of a simple observation — with the high-torque drive, there are only two coils active at one time, and the coils operate in pairs. That is, if coil 1 is on, coil 3 is off (and vice versa). Coils 2 and 4 operate the same way. The design in the application note uses two bits to control the stepper and then passes each bit through two sections of a ULN2003 driver. Not only does this allow the Stamp to supply enough current for the motor, it also provides complimentary outputs. That is, one output will be true while the other output is false. Of course, this design limits what kind of steps you can perform with the motor because you can't individually control each coil.

The code you'll find in the Stamp application note calculates the step. This is clever, but you might just as well look up the step using the LOOKUP command.

Servos

Servos are most often used in remote control applications. However, they are very easy to use with the Stamp.

You supply a servo power via one lead, and a control signal through another lead. The control signal consists of a varying-width pulse. The servo has a range of motion that it follows (often 90–180°). When the input pulse is 1.5mS in length, the motor will move to its center position. As the pulse lengthens or shortens, the motor will move to one side of its travel to the other. A typical servo will travel to its limits when the pulse is 1mS or 2mS in length.

One advantage to a servo is that it does not require high drive on the control input. The electronics are built into the servo itself. However, servos do not spin like a conventional motor, so they are only useful when you want a particular range of motion.

Another key advantage of servos with the Basic Stamp is that a simple `PULSOUT` command is perfectly capable of controlling the servo. Just make sure you output a pulse between 1mS and 2mS about 50 times a second, and the servo will work just fine.

A servo is really a motor with a variable resistor connected to the shaft. The resistor controls a pulse generator. The servo's internal circuitry compares this pulse to the external pulse to decide how far off the shaft is from the desired position and moves the motor accordingly.

Because servos are made to move significant objects, they contain powerful, geared-down motors. Because of this, many people modify servos so that they can achieve full rotation. You can open the servo up and remove all the electronics. Then you'll wind up with a geared-down motor. Of course, then you have to drive it like a normal DC motor using some sort of driving switch, and possibly an H bridge.

Another popular modification is to remove the feedback resistor and replace it with two fixed resistors that simulate the feedback value at the servo's midpoint. Now if you send a 1.5mS pulse, the servo will not move. A wider pulse will cause the servo to spin in one direction (and not stop because the feedback resistor can't change its value). A narrower pulse will make the servo motor spin in the opposite direction.

The BOEBot

Parallax took their popular Board of Education and married it to an aluminum robot chassis. The result is the BOEBot which is available from Parallax. You can also find the plans for the entire thing on their Web site if you are handy enough with metal fabrication to build one yourself. Figure 8.4 shows a BOEBot with some extra circuitry attached to it.

The BOEBot uses two modified servo motors. Instead of replacing the servo's pot with fixed resistors, the Parallax instructions direct you to remove the gear that couples the servo's shaft to the servo pot. Then you can adjust the pot to the midpoint. This isn't as accurate as using fixed resistors, but it is typically good enough and is very easy to accomplish.

The BOEBot's two servo motors are back to back (a third ball-like wheel is not driven, but keeps the robot stable). Since they are back to back you have to spin them in opposite directions to go forwards (or backwards). If you spin the motors in the same direction, the robot will turn in place (either clockwise or counterclockwise, depending on the motor's direction).

Here's a simple subroutine to move the BOEBot forward a bit (assuming the servos are on pins left_wheel and right_wheel):

```
go_forward:
for x=1 to 20
pulsout left_wheel,650
pulsout right_wheel,850
pause 20
next
return
```

This code is for the BSII, which uses units of 2µS for the PULSOUT command. Since 1.5mS is 1,500µS, a PULSOUT of 750 would — in theory — hold the servo still. In this case, I've set one motor to 650 and the other to 850. That's 100 units (200µS) away from the center in both directions.

In theory, this should make the robot move forward (or backwards, depending on what you think the front of the robot is). Since the adjustment is not exact, you might have to fudge that number a bit to make it go straight. Small differences in the motors, the pot, and other factors may cause the robot to veer right or left.

The bigger the difference between the values and the center position, the faster the robot will go (up to a point). You might write:

```
go_forward:
for x=1 to 20
pulsout left_wheel,750-speed
pulsout right_wheel,750+speed
pause 20
next
return
```

Now you can adjust the speed variable to control the robot's velocity.

It is easy to write a subroutine to move the robot backwards, or turn it in either direction. For example:

```
go_left:
for x=1 to 10
pulsout left_wheel,650
pulsout right_wheel,650
pause 20
```

```
next
return

go_right:
for x=1 to 10
pulsout left_wheel,850
pulsout right_wheel,850
pause 20
next
return
```

Control

Armed with these subroutines, it is easy to program any sequence you like into the BOEBot. Soon, though, you get tired of downloading a new program every time you want to change the robot's path.

I decided I wanted to take an old Sony remote control and make the BOEBot respond to it. The electronics required to make this work is not difficult at all. You can get a special IC that has all the electronics required for a buck or two. I used a Panasonic PNA4602M, but there are many other IR sensors that will work.

What you don't want to use is an ordinary IR phototransistor. Remote controls don't just shoot ordinary IR beams out. If they did, your TV might react to IR from other sources like warm bodies or fluorescent lights.

When you press a button on a remote control it sends out a burst of pulses. Each pulse is made up of infrared light modulated at some frequency (usually 38kHz). A regular IR phototransistor would receive this 38kHz signal along with any other IR signals floating around the room. The special ICs like the Panasonic unit have a photodetector, but they also have the circuitry required to detect the 38kHz signal and convert it into a clean digital signal.

The Panasonic device is easy to hook up. It has three pins. Pin 1 is the digital output for the Stamp, pin 2 is ground, and pin 3 is the 5V supply. Like any IC, it is a good idea to use a bypass capacitor (say a .1µF unit) close to the IC between power and ground.

The Challenge

Reading the remote with a sophisticated IR sensor should be easy, but it isn't. The remote starts each signal with a long IR pulse. Then it sends a 1 as a medium-sized pulse and a 0 as a short pulse. Most remotes work in a similar fashion (although some measure the space between pulses instead of the pulse itself).

To read the data, the Stamp has to measure several pulses in sequence. Ideally, you'd read a pulse, see if it was a long pulse, and if not, go back and try again. Once you detected the long pulse, you'd simply read each pulse to determine the corresponding bit.

Unfortunately, the Stamp's execution speed is too slow to read the pulses, do significant processing, and then read another pulse without missing pulses. The Stamp's CPU is actually fast enough. However, the Stamp reads your program from a serial EEPROM which is not nearly as fast as the Stamp's CPU and this is the limiting factor.

The BSII is just fast enough to read the pulses, store them, and examine them later.

```
Consider this bit of code:
irsense con 0    ' pin 0 is the IR sensor
irinput var in0
irthreshold con 450    ' less than this is a zero, more is a one
irstartlow con 1100    ' minimum start pulse
irstarthi con 1300     ' maximum start pulse
value var byte   ' result

raw var word(7)    ' holding area
dummy var word     ' dummy value
start var word          ' tenative start bit

read_ir:
  if irinput=0 then noir   ' Already in the middle of a pulse so skip it
  pulsin irsense,0,start     ' hope we are in a start bit
  pulsin irsense,0,raw(0)
  pulsin irsense,0,raw(1)
  pulsin irsense,0,raw(2)
  pulsin irsense,0,raw(3)
  pulsin irsense,0,raw(4)
  pulsin irsense,0,raw(5)
  pulsin irsense,0,raw(6)
' Could comment these out
  pulsin irsense,0,dummy
  pulsin irsense,0,dummy
  pulsin irsense,0,dummy
```

```
    pulsin irsense,0,dummy
    pulsin irsense,0,dummy
' test for good start bit
    if (start<irstartlow) or (start>irstarthi) then noir
' build byte
    value=0
    for dummy=6 to 0
      value=value*2
      if raw(dummy)<irthreshold then ir0
      value=value+1
ir0:
    next


    return
noir:
    value=-1  ' didn't get it
    return
```

You could call this routine and if it happens to sync on a start bit, it will return the IR code. If it doesn't then it will return –1. Each key, of course, will have a unique code. It seems hit or miss to hope you'll synchronize with the start bit, but it practice it works well. That's because remotes continue to beam the same code over and over as long as you hold down the key.

So armed with the subroutine to read the remote and subroutines to control the motor, everything should be fine, right? If you design your program properly, everything is fine. However, there is one more hidden peril waiting ahead.

Look back at the IR remote reading subroutine. If codes are streaming out of the remote, we may or may not synchronize on them, but eventually the code will happen to catch a start bit and work correctly. It is also easy to see that if the subroutine is waiting for a start bit and the user presses a remote key, the code should work flawlessly.

However, what happens if the user doesn't press a key? Each PULSIN command will have to time out before the subroutine can continue. With 13 PULSIN commands, the total time out is over 1.7 seconds!

Understanding this is crucial to the design of the robot. Suppose you want to press the 2 button to go forward. Then the robot would continue to move forward until you pressed the 5 button to stop. In a similar fashion the 8 key would start the robot moving in reverse.

That makes good sense, but the timeout will cause problems. The Stamp only does one thing at a time. So when you call one of the motor subroutines, the motors will turn a bit, and the IR routine will block any further motion for nearly two seconds. Then the motors will turn a bit more, and then everything goes to sleep again for two seconds.

The best way to handle this is to design the interface so that the user pushes the button to move the robot. When there is no button push there is no motion. This way when there is no IR activity, the Stamp doesn't have to do anything but listen for the remote.

This is the approach taken by the code in Listing 8.1. The Sony codes have key 1 as code 0, so the commands in the program are:

2	Forward
4	Left
6	Right
8	Back

Listing 8.1 Remote control BOEBot.

```
' Remote Rover by Al Williams
irsense con 0
irinput var in0
irthreshold con 450
irstartlow con 1100
irstarthi con 1300

value var byte  ' result

raw var word(7)
start var word
dummy var word
x var byte

right_wheel con 3 ' right servo motor
left_wheel con 15 ' left servo motor
i var byte
```

Listing 8.1 Remote control BOEBot. (Continued)

```
top:
  gosub read_ir
  if value=1 then forward
  if value=7 then back
  if value=3 then left
  if value=5 then right

  goto top

forward:
  gosub go_forward
  goto top

back:
  gosub go_reverse
  goto top

left:
  gosub go_left
  gosub go_left
  goto top

right:
  gosub go_right
  gosub go_right
  goto top

read_ir:
' The problem here is that the gap between bits
' is about 500uS and the Stamp may miss bits unless
' you read everything in one swoop. So you can't
' read this in a loop or even test the start bit
' until you are finished.
  if irinput=0 then noir  ' Already in the middle of a pulse so skip it
  pulsin irsense,0,start
  pulsin irsense,0,raw(0)
```

Listing 8.1 Remote control BOEBot. (Continued)

```
  pulsin irsense,0,raw(1)
  pulsin irsense,0,raw(2)
  pulsin irsense,0,raw(3)
  pulsin irsense,0,raw(4)
  pulsin irsense,0,raw(5)
  pulsin irsense,0,raw(6)
' Could comment these out
  pulsin irsense,0,dummy
  pulsin irsense,0,dummy
  pulsin irsense,0,dummy
  pulsin irsense,0,dummy
  pulsin irsense,0,dummy
' test for good start bit
  if (start<irstartlow) or (start>irstarthi) then noir
  value=0
  for dummy=6 to 0
    value=value*2
    if raw(dummy)<irthreshold then ir0
    value=value+1
ir0:
  next

  return
noir:
  value=-1
  return

go_forward:
  for x=1 to 20
  pulsout left_wheel,650
  pulsout right_wheel,850
  pause 20
  next
  return
```

Listing 8.1 Remote control BOEBot. (Continued)

```
go_reverse:
  for x=1 to 20
  pulsout left_wheel,850
  pulsout right_wheel,650
  pause 20
  next
  return

go_left:
  for x=1 to 10
  pulsout left_wheel,650
  pulsout right_wheel,650
  pause 20
  next
  return

go_right:
  for x=1 to 10
  pulsout left_wheel,850
  pulsout right_wheel,850
  pause 20
  next
  return
```

Feedback Loops

Advanced motor projects may require some kind of feedback. Exactly what kind depends on if you are more interested in speed or position. Determining the speed of a motor requires some sort of tachometer. Some motors even have built-in tachometers.

You can add a tachometer to any motor. The idea is to count the number of revolutions per some unit time. One common method to do this is to use an optical sensor to read a dot on the shaft. You can also affix a magnet to the shaft and sense its passing with a Hall effect sensor or (if your speed is not too great) a reed relay.

Position determination is easy with a servo. Of course, you could homebrew a servo using the same sort of mechanism a real servo uses. Because a tachometer also tells you when the shaft passes a certain position, you may be able to use the same circuitry if all you need to know is when the motor passes a reference point.

Another approach to position determination is to use a shaft encoder. These may be optical or mechanical, and it is possible to homebrew your own. The idea is to use a disk attached to the shaft and an array of sensors. In a mechanical encoder, the sensors are a set of brushes (essentially wires that touch the disk). The disk has cut outs that allow the sensors to read the shaft's position.

As a simple example, consider a system with three sensors. This will allow you to determine the shaft's position to 45°. When the disk contacts all three sensors, the encoder will read 000. As the disk turns, an opening will appear under one of the sensors, so the encoder will read 001.

A problem occurs if a mechanical encoder tries to change two bits at once. The nature of mechanical things prevents precise alignment of the brushes and disk cut outs. In the previous example, suppose the disk turns to read 010. This would require the cut out under the first brush to close and another cutout to open under the second brush. If these don't occur exactly at the same point, the encoder will briefly read 011 or 000 before settling on the correct state.

To prevent this, mechanical encoders often use gray code. *Gray code* is a code that only permits one bit to change at a time. A possible gray code sequence appears in Table 8.4.

Optical encoders use the same technique except that the sensors are phototransistors and the disk contains clear and dark areas. Some optical encoders also use gray code to prevent problems with disk alignment.

Table 8.4   3-bit gray code.

Position	Code
0	000
1	001
2	011
3	010
4	110
5	111
6	101
7	100

Cannibalizing Motors

If you really want to build a robot, you might consider cannibalizing an existing toy robot, car, tank, or other mechanized toy. You can take two approaches here. The first is to open the toy and identify the motors. You'll often be able to locate an H bridge circuit or IC and drive it directly with a Stamp.

There is another alternative if the toy has a remote control. You can simply use the Stamp to control the switches on the remote control. The switches probably connect to ground, so a 2N2222 can easily simulate the switch closure. This approach is very simple to implement. If the control is wireless, there is another advantage. You can leave it connected to the PC while developing the robot. Then when you want the robot to operate, you can let it carry its own remote with the Basic Stamp circuit attached. If you design the switch replacements correctly, you can even control the robot manually when you need to do something yourself.

Of course, the details for this will differ depending on exactly what toy you use and what you want to do. There are no hard and fast rules. You'll just have to experiment to find what is best for you.

Radio Shack had the ideal toy robot a few years back. The real part of the robot was a small black plastic box about 12 inches per side. The entire thing sat about 3 inches tall. Not very impressive for a robot, right? To make it more exciting, they put velcro on the top and attached a 4- or 5-foot tall balloon shaped like a robot. A remote control (wireless) let you move it forward or turn it (move one wheel only).

They don't have them anymore, but you can find similar items around and you may still find the one I have at a garage sale or toy resale. You don't care about the balloon, just the perfectly usable base. Even if you can't find this particular robot, you'll see how easy it is to hack just about any of these cheap robots.

The Inside Story

There are two ways you can Stamp control a robot like this. First, you can make the Stamp control the motors onboard the robot, or you can use the Stamp to switch the remote control buttons. Then the Stamp doesn't even need to be onboard. I wanted to be able to add sensors and other items to the robot, so I wanted to control the robot directly and just discard the remote control.

Just about all of these cheap robots have a single chip to handle the remote control function and a simple H-bridge that you'll be able to easily recognize (see Figure 8.5). My first thought was to disconnect the existing controller and drive the H-bridge directly. However, after a little probing, I decided to try a different approach.

Using a scope, logic probe, or voltmeter you can probe the control IC while pushing the remote control buttons. You should find a pin that either goes high or low when you push a button on the remote. My remote had two buttons, so I found two pins. I thought about cutting the PC board trace and wiring the pins to the Stamp's inputs and wiring the Stamp's outputs to the cut trace. However, I wanted to keep it simple at first, so I just decided to piggy back on the remote. The remote would still work, but the Stamp could also direct the motors.

Figure 8.5   This Radio Shack toy robot base makes an excellent motor platform for Stamp control.

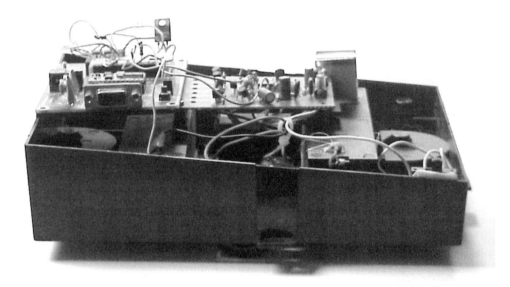

I simply soldered two wires to the chip and soldered 1K resistors to the other ends of the wire (to prevent the Stamp and the controller from shorting each other out). Figure 8.6 shows the IC with the modifications. I cut the resistor leads short and used them to plug into a regular breadboard.

The Stamp uses its own 9V battery and the robot uses four D cells. That means you need a common ground. I soldered the wire to the battery holder for the robot and connected it to the Vss terminal of the breadboard. I didn't permanently attach the breadboard, but double-sided carpet tape did the trick.

Listing 8.2 shows some simple code that will run the robot. This code simply moves or turns the robot. Of course, with a big breadboard, you can add light sensors, bump sensors, or anything else you can design.

Figure 8.6 Closeup view of the modifications.

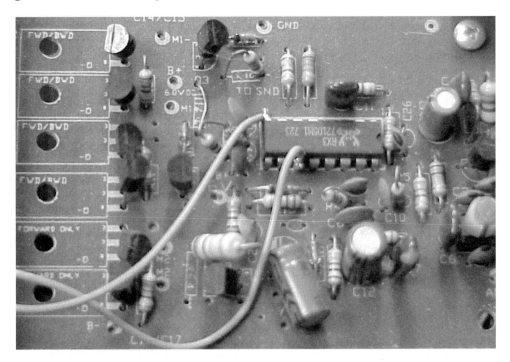

Listing 8.2 Driving the robot.

```
FWD con 14  ' pin for moving forward
TURN con 13 ' pin for turning
LOW FWD
LOW TURN
start:
HIGH FWD   ' move forward
PAUSE 5000 ' for 5 seconds
LOW FWD
HIGH TURN  ' turn
PAUSE 1250
LOW TURN
PAUSE 15000
GOTO start
```

If you were really adventurous, you might try a more sophisticated modification. If you carefully cut the control traces, you could have the Stamp drive the outputs like I did. However, you could also wire the now open IC pins to two Stamp input pins. Then you could use the remote to send commands to the Stamp and the Stamp could control the robot.

Summary

Adding motors to a project is a complicated task. Motors consume more power than most components you usually use. Also, motors can generate lots of noise that will play havoc with your other circuitry.

Still, if you need motion in your project, it is hard to beat a motor. You can find muscle wires that contract when you heat them, but they are not as useful as motors in most cases. They also require a great deal of current to heat them so they will contract. While these are a great novelty, most projects that need motion still need motors.

Once you decide you want a motor, you have to decide what kind you'll use. There are ordinary DC motors, stepper motors, gearhead motors, and servo motors. Each of these have a place depending on what you want to do.

Exercises

1. Build the circuit in Figure 8.2. Use it to control the speed of a DC motor. Can you make the motor operate at $^1/_{256}$ of its rated speed?
2. Using the same DC motor from exercise 1, control the speed with a potentiometer. If you wanted to homebrew a servo motor, could you do it using this circuit and special software?
3. Find a toy car or robot with a wired or wireless remote control. Outline a plan to operate the toy with a Stamp and implement it.

For answers to the exercises, see the Answer Key, page 446.

Chapter 9

Morse Code Projects

I just about failed shop in high school. The only reason I didn't was that there was one unit on electricity. To tell the truth, I'm an old-school engineer and I'm still more comfortable sketching designs for someone else to build. Luckily, I've gotten better at the mechanical part of this work over the years, but I'm still no match for the average handyman when it comes to drilling panels, cutting up sheet metal, and the like.

One of the problems with shop was that they told you what you had to make and how you had to make it. I couldn't really understand why I wanted to a make a key holder shaped like a key. The metal doorstop seemed silly, too. I did a little better in the plastics unit. Maybe that was because you could build whatever you wanted. I started out making an acrylic cross, but after a mistake, it became a number 7.

Maybe my experience with shop is why I don't like useless projects. However, when you are trying to learn, it is hard to start with full-blown projects. Still, the previous chapters have had a few useful items — the Merlin game, the PC-based frequency counter, the power supply, and the homebrew A/D converter are all substantial projects.

By now, you should have a good understanding of the Stamp and its associated software. In this chapter, I'll show you a selection of projects that you can build or use as a starting point for similar projects of your own. All of these projects have one thing in common: they use Morse code to output (or sometimes input) their results. Since I've been a amateur radio operator for over 25 years, I like Morse code. However, even if you aren't interested in Morse code *per se*, you'll still see how to interface external memory, use a PC keyboard, and a few other tricks in these projects. There are no exercises for this chapter — just build a project or two!

Morse Code IDer

I mentioned I'm an amateur radio operator. The FCC requires many unattended transmitters (like repeaters) to ID using Morse code at a certain interval. Hams know this, of course, but even other services have this requirement. You've probably noticed this if you own a scanner, for example.

This project transmits a message in code repeatedly with a programmable delay. Construction is simple. Just use a Stamp II with a speaker wired to pin 7 (see the FREQOUT page, page 117, in Chapter 2). Also wire an LED to pin 8 and +5V and pin 9 and +5V. If you are using ordinary LEDs, you'll need to include a dropping resistor.

The LEDs represent the Morse code output (pin 8) and the signal to key the transmitter (pin 9). In real life, you might use a simple transistor switch to key the transmitter. You could use pin 8 to drive a CW transmitter. For FM or other audio transmitters, you'd use the audio from the speaker instead.

The code is simple (see Listing 9.1). The id string is made up of dots, dashes, and spaces. The Stamp immediately sends the string and then pauses for five minutes. Of course, the longest delay you can achieve with a single pause is about 65 seconds. That means to pause for five minutes, the code has to pause for one minute five times.

If you want more memory, be sure to check out the ID project in Chapter 6 that uses an external EEPROM to hold more characters.

Listing 9.1 Morse code ID.

```
' CW Ider by WD5GNR
spkr con 7
key con 8
ptt con 9
mindelay con 5  ' 5 minutes
pttdelay con 50 ' delay to let transmitter key
ditlen con 100  ' set morse code speed
f con 1000      ' frequency for speaker
addr var byte
dotdash var byte
i var byte
output spkr
```

Listing 9.1   Morse code ID. (Continued)

```
' Code to send (end with zero byte)
id data "-.. .  .-- -.. ..... --. -. .-.",0
high ptt    ' unkey xmit
high key    ' unkey cw keying
top:
addr=id
low ptt    ' key transmitter
pause pttdelay  'wait for xmit to settle
loop:
read addr, dotdash    ' get code element
addr=addr+1
' element must be 0 (end), blank, dot, or dash
if dotdash=0 then wait1
if dotdash=" " then cspc
if dotdash="-" then dash
low key
freqout spkr, ditlen, f
high key
goto elspc
dash:
low key
freqout spkr, ditlen*3,f  ' dash is 3*dit
high key
elspc:         ' space each element
pause ditlen
goto loop
cspc:          ' space between characters
pause ditlen*4
goto loop
wait1:         ' done! wait for next time
pause pttdelay
high ptt
for i=1 to mindelay
  pause 60000           ' 60 seconds
next
goto top                ' do it again!
```

Morse Code Keyer

Of course, the ultimate Morse code project would be a keyer. In the movies, you often see radio operators tapping on old-fashioned keys to form Morse code. In reality, very few professional operators use this method for forming the dots and dashes that make up Morse code.

Most real radio operators use an electronic keyer. A keyer uses two switches (known as paddles) that you operate with your thumb and forefinger. One switch (usually your thumb) generates dots at a constant speed. The other switch generates dashes at the same speed. This allows you to easily generate machine-precise code at higher speeds than most people can operate a regular key.

The keyer is simple to build having only one IC (the Stamp), two transistors, and a handful of resistors and capacitors. Unlike other keyers in its price range, this one is field programmable. You can change the firmware in the keyer to program the features you want.

Because the keyer is programmable, you can add nearly any feature you want to it. Some of the possible features include:

- Full iambic operation
- Dit and Dah memories
- Sidetone
- Separate input for a straight key
- Straight key operates even if the microprocessor malfunctions or has incorrect software
- Programmable function key
- PC-programmable memory keyer plays back a predefined message when your press the function key

The schematic for the GNR keyer is in Figure 9.1 and a PC board layout in Figure 9.2 (page 369). Because this project is a bit more complex than the others, you might want to refer to the parts list in Table 9.1. IC1 is a Basic Stamp BS1-IC microprocessor. If you prefer to power the chip from an existing 5V-regulated supply, you can feed 5V into pin 5. Then you would omit J1, S1, and C3 from the assembly.

Pins 9 and 10 read the status of the attached paddle. R2 and R3 serve as pull-up resistors so that the inputs read high when the paddles are open. When a paddle switch closes, it grounds the pin so that the stamp reads a 0. It is important that the paddles only switch ground because many accessory devices will assume that they can simulate a paddle closure by grounding the input.

Figure 9.1   The keyer.

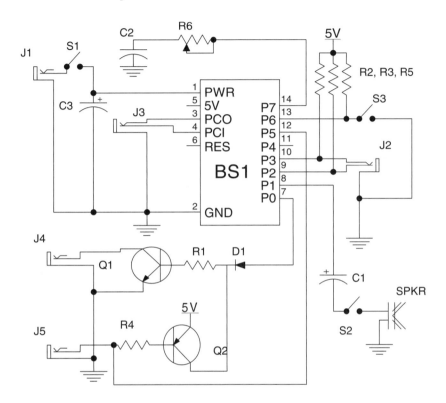

Table 9.1   Parts list for the keyer.

Part	Description
	Printed Circuit Board
C1	10µF Electrolytic Capacitor
C2	0.1µF Capacitor
C3	100µF Electrolytic Capacitor
R1	680 Ω $^1/_2$W Resistor
R2, R3, R5	10K Ω $^1/_4$W Resistor
R4	1K Ω $^1/_4$W Resistor
D1	1N4148 Diode
Q1	2N2222 NPN Transistor

Table 9.1   Parts list for the keyer. (Continued)

Part	Description
Q2	2N3904 PNP Transistor
IC1	Basic Stamp BS1-IC Microprocessor
	14-Pin SIP Socket for IC1
R6	*10K Potentiometer* *
J1	*Power Connector 6-15V*
J2	*Paddle Connector*
J3	*Programming Connector (suggested: $^1/_4$" stereo phone jack)*
J4	*Jack to Transmitter Key*
J5	*Straight Key Connector*
S1	*Power Switch SPST*
S2	*Sidetone Switch SPST*
S3	*Function Key SPST Momentary*
	Enclosure
	Power Supply or Battery

*   Note: Items in *italics* will vary depending on your specific requirements.

Pin 7 drives the transmitter's keying input via a small network of components. A straight key hooks up to J5 where it grounds the base of Q2 through R4. This saturates Q2 passing nearly 5V to the base of Q1 through R1. This saturates Q1 keying the transmitter. When the straight key is keying the transmitter, D1 is off preventing IC1 from sinking current through pin 7. If the straight key is up, IC1 can drive pin 7 high. This will cause current to flow through R1 again saturating Q1. IC1 can also read the status of the straight key on pin 12. This line is pulled up by the combination of Q2's base-emitter junction and R4. It is useful for IC1 to read the straight key if you want to generate sidetone for the straight key.

S3 is a function key that the program can use as it wishes. The basic firmware uses this as a Tune button. When you press it, it keys the transmitter. The advanced firmware uses S3 as a cue to play back a prerecorded message.

R6 is a pot that IC1 can read. The firmware can use this input for anything, but typically it is a speed control. A special command in the firmware charges C2 via R6 and measures the time it takes to charge to a logic-level 1. This time is proportional to the value of R6. Firmware could use this control for other purposes. For example, you might make it set weighting (the ratio between a dot and a dash) if S3 is depressed.

Figure 9.2   The PC board layout.

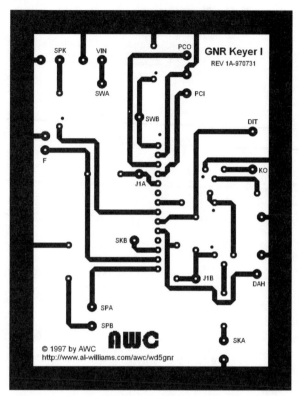

Pin 8 of IC1 generates the sidetone output. The tone is actually a square wave which C1 and the speaker filter into a rough sine wave.

Programming the chip is done by connecting pins 2, 3, and 4 of the stamp to pins 25, 11, and 2 on a printer port. Listing 9.2 and 9.3 contain the code for the basic and advanced keyer firmware. Here are some important points:

- Bring Pin 7 (known as pin0 in software) high to key the transmitter.

- Use the pot command to read R6.

- It is tempting to use the Sound command to provide sidetone, but it doesn't work well. Why? Because the Sound command locks up the processor the entire time it is beeping. That means you can't implement dot and dash memories. The existing code creates the sound "manually" on pin 8 (pin1 in the software), which means the tone is fixed (and determined by the speed of the stamp chip). However, on each cycle of the sound, the program can sample the dot and dash levers.

- Pins 9 and 10 (pin2 and pin3 in the program) are equal to 0 when the corresponding paddle lever is on.

(Discussion continues on page 376.)

Listing 9.2 Basic keyer firmware.

```
' BSIC Keyer - WD5GNR
' Features: Iambic, Dit/Dah memory, adjustable speed
'            Built in sidetone
' Still to add: weight control, manual key input (w/sidetone)
' Preprogrammed memory playback maybe


' Register usage
' W0 - using Bit0 and Bit1
' W1 - Available
' W2 - B4 used B5 available
' W3 - Used
' W4 - Used
' W5 - Available
' W6 - Used by GOSUB

Symbol  potport = 7
Symbol  potscale = 27
Symbol  pot_reading = b4
Symbol  length = w3
Symbol  loopctr = w4
Symbol  Ditswitch = pin2
symbol  Dahswitch = pin3
Symbol  ditmem = Bit0
Symbol  dahmem = Bit1
Symbol  keypin = 0    ' right now coded for active low
Symbol  spkrpin = 1

dirs=$f3
pins=$FF
ditmem=0
dahmem=0
loop:
pot potport,potscale,pot_reading
length=pot_reading*3/2+100
```

Listing 9.2   Basic keyer firmware. (Continued)

```
length=length*9
length=length/9 ' make even divisible by 9
' sense input
if Ditswitch=0 or ditmem=1 then dodit
ditcontinue:
' dodah... campfire girls sing their songs...
if Dahswitch=0 or dahmem=1 then dodah
dahcontinue:
goto loop

dodit:
ditmem=0
gosub dit
goto ditcontinue

dodah:
dahmem=0
gosub dah
goto dahcontinue

Dit:
low keypin
for loopctr=1 to length step 9
toggle spkrpin
toggle spkrpin
dahmem=DahSwitch ^ 1 | dahmem
next loopctr
high keypin
for loopctr=1 to length step 9
low spkrpin ' equalize loop time
low spkrpin
dahmem=DahSwitch ^ 1 | dahmem
next loopctr
return

Dah:
```

Listing 9.2   Basic keyer firmware. (Continued)

```
low keypin
for loopctr=1 to length step 3
Toggle spkrpin
Toggle spkrpin
ditmem=DitSwitch ^ 1 | ditmem
next loopctr
high keypin
for loopctr=1 to length step 9
low spkrpin ' equalize
low spkrpin
ditmem=Ditswitch ^ 1 | ditmem
next loopctr
return
```

Listing 9.3   Advanced keyer firmware.

```
' BS1C Keyer - WD5GNR
' Features: Iambic, Dit/Dah memory, adjustable speed
'            Built in sidetone, preprogrammed memory playback
' Still to add: weight control, manual key input (w/sidetone)

' Register usage
' W0 - using Bit0 and Bit1
' W1 - Available
' W2 - Used
' W3 - Used
' W4 - Used
' W5 - B10 used; B11 available
' W6 - Used by GOSUB

Symbol  potport = 7
Symbol  potscale = 27
Symbol  pot_reading = b4
Symbol  length = w3
Symbol  loopctr = w4
Symbol  Ditswitch = pin2
symbol  Dahswitch = pin3
```

Listing 9.3   Advanced keyer firmware. (Continued)

```
Symbol   ditmem = Bit0
Symbol   dahmem = Bit1
Symbol   keypin = 0     ' right now coded for active low
Symbol   spkrpin = 1
Symbol   mempin = pin6
Symbol   memcount = b5
Symbol   membyte = b2
Symbol   memmask = b10
Symbol   memvalue = b3


port=$73FF
b0=0  ' clear dit mem and dah mem in 1 stroke
loop:
pot potport,potscale,pot_reading
length=pot_reading*3/2+100
length=length*9
length=length/9 ' make even divisible by 9
' sense input
if mempin=0 then memplay
if Ditswitch=0 or ditmem=1 then dodit
ditcontinue:
' dodah... campfire girls sing their songs...
if Dahswitch=0 or dahmem=1 then dodah dahcontinue:
goto loop

dodit:
ditmem=0
gosub dit
goto ditcontinue

dodah:
dahmem=0
gosub dah
goto dahcontinue
```

Listing 9.3 Advanced keyer firmware. (Continued)

```
Dit:
high keypin
for loopctr=1 to length step 9
toggle spkrpin
toggle spkrpin
dahmem=DahSwitch ^ 1 | dahmem
next loopctr
low keypin
for loopctr=1 to length step 9
low spkrpin ' equalize loop time
low spkrpin
dahmem=DahSwitch ^ 1 | dahmem
next loopctr
return

Dah:
high keypin
for loopctr=1 to length step 3
Toggle spkrpin
Toggle spkrpin
ditmem=DitSwitch ^ 1 | ditmem
next loopctr
low keypin
for loopctr=1 to length step 9
low spkrpin ' equalize
low spkrpin
ditmem=Ditswitch ^ 1 | ditmem
next loopctr
return

memplay:
read 0,memcount   ' count
membyte=1
memmask=128
memloop:
if memcount=0 then loop
```

Listing 9.3   Advanced keyer firmware. (Continued)

```
read membyte,memvalue
bit2=memvalue/memmask
if bit2=1 then dahspace
gosub dit
memnext:  ' go to next command
if ditmem=1 or dahmem=1 then loop
memmask=memmask/2
if memmask<>0 then memloop
gosub advance
goto memloop
dahspace:
memmask=memmask/2
if memmask<>0 then read1
gosub advance
if memcount=0 then loop
read1: ' get 2nd bit
read membyte,memvalue
bit2=memvalue/memmask
if bit2=1 then space
gosub dah
goto memnext

space:  ' do a character space
for loopctr=1 to length step 2 ' odd weight
low spkrpin ' equalize loop time
low spkrpin
low spkrpin
next loopctr
goto memnext
advance:
memmask=128
membyte=membyte+1
memcount=memcount-1
return
```

Listing 9.3   Advanced keyer firmware. (Continued)

```
' Memory data
' CQ CQ CQ DE WD5GNR WD5GNR WD5GNR K
' This EEPROM line should be one line
' But it is too long for the page
eeprom 0,(24,$93,$A5,$F2,$74,$BE,$4E,$97,$C6,$F5,$71,$83,$A7,$34,$D5,$C6,
$0E, $9C,$D3,$D5,$C6,$0E,$9C,$D3,$97)
```

The advanced program uses a peculiar method to encode the message that the device plays when you press the user-defined button. This scheme uses a form of hoffman encoding. The first byte is the number of bytes that follow. In each byte, a 0 represents a dot. A sequence of 10 represents a dash and a 11 is a pause. You'll find a Windows program on the CD-ROM that helps you generate these patterns. If you have more dots than dashes and spaces, this allows you to store more characters than if you used a more straightforward encoding scheme.

If you build the PC board for this project, you'll find that it has several pads for connecting wires. You'll find a description of these pads in Table 9.2.

Although the GNR Keyer is meant to send Morse code, you could program it to do anything that requires two switch closure inputs, a readable pot, a speaker, and a switched output. What could you do? Perhaps you'll read limit switches via J2 and use J4 to turn off a rotator motor. S3 could provide a manual override. It isn't very power-efficient, but you could even use J2 as two outputs because the Stamp could easily drive R2 and R3 plus a small load attached to J2. Use your imagination..

Table 9.2   PC board pads.

Pad designator	Connection
VIN	Input Voltage
SWA	One side of power switch
SWB	Other side of power switch
SPK	Speaker
PCO	Programming Connection (pin 3)
PCI	Programming Connection (pin 4)
F	Function Key
J1A	Jumper 1 (Side A)
J1B	Jumper 1 (Side B)
DIT	Paddle Dit Switch

Table 9.2   PC board pads. (Continued)

Pad designator	Connection
DAH	Paddle Dah Switch
KO	Keyer Output
SKA	Straight Key
SKB	Straight Key (wired to the same place as SKA)
SPA	Speed Control Wiper
SPB	Speed Control (C2-side)

An Keyboard Keyer

If you aren't a Morse code wizard, you might prefer to type characters on a keyboard and have the Stamp generate the correct tones. That would probably require a PC, right? Not at all! You can connect a PC keyboard to the Stamp with an extra chip (the PAK-VI from AWC). This chip converts a standard keyboard to output RS232 suitable for use with a Stamp.

In addition to the code, the program will have several predefined messages and store your callsign and a custom message in the Stamp's EEPROM. Special keyboard keys allow you to play the predefined messages.

By default, the PAK-VI converts the keyboard's code to ASCII (keyboards use a strange code that doesn't relate to ASCII at all). This is what you usually want. However, if you want to, you can switch the PAK-VI to raw mode and take control yourself. This is useful if you are using the keys for something other than ASCII characters, or you want to read a PS/2 mouse (good for reading an XY position).

The PAK-VI works with Basic Stamp flow control so you don't have to worry about missing characters. The PAK-VI buffers 16 characters (or scan codes in raw mode) and the keyboard itself can usually buffer 16 more scan codes. If you are not in raw mode, operation is very simple. The PAK even controls the status LEDs (shift lock, caps lock, and scroll lock) for you. Extended keys (like the function keys) emit one byte which makes it very easy to process them using the Stamp.

For this application, the Stamp doesn't send many commands to the PAK (just a software reset command). However, there are commands to switch modes; set scroll, num, and caps lock; and send commands directly to the keyboard.

Figure 9.3 shows the schematic diagram (you'll find the parts list in Table 9.3). Y1 is the resonator included with the PAK-VI. The center leg of the device is ground. The two end leads are interchangeable.

Figure 9.3   The keyboard keyer.

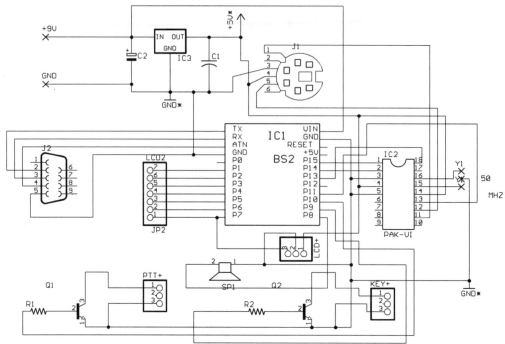

The PAK sends ASCII codes to the Stamp. It would be possible to not connect pin 15 of the Stamp since only a reset command is sent to the PAK. You can easily connect the PAK to a keyboard using a PS/2 motherboard socket. You can find these in computer stores for about $5. They allow you to connect a PS/2 keyboard to an ordinary motherboard that has pins for the keyboard. Just cut the header off and make your connections.

Table 9.3   Parts list for the keyboard keyer.

Part	Description
C1	.1µF 25V Ceramic Disk Capacitor
C2	10µF 35V Electrolytic Capacitor
IC1	Basic Stamp II
IC2	PAK-VI Keyboard Encoder
IC3	7805 Voltage Regulator
J1	6-position Right Angle Mini Din Receptacal (Singatron MDJ-004-6P)
J2	9-pin Right Angle DB Connector (Female)

Table 9.3   Parts list for the keyboard keyer. (Continued)

Part	Description
Q1, Q2	2N2222 Transistor
R1, R2	1K $^1/_4$W Resistor
SP1	Piezo Speaker
Y1	50MHz Resonator (Supplied with IC2)

The code (see Listing 9.4) operates in a loop. It reads each keyboard character and tests to see if it is one of the special commands in Table 9.4.

If the program finds one of these special codes it jumps to the correct routine. Otherwise, it processes the characters with the charproc subroutine.

Table 9.4   Special commands.

Command	Key	Definition
$91	Up arrow	Increase speed
$97	Down arrow	Decrease speed
$9A	Del	Switch to receive mode
$CA	Shift+F11	Set callsign
$CB	Shift+F12	Set custom macro

To handle a normal character, the code looks up two bytes from EEPROM. One is the number of elements (dits and dahs) in the character. The other is the actual dit/dah pattern. If the number of elements is $FF, the item is a space. Macro handling is interesting. There is a table that contains a pointer to each macro. The callsign macro is exactly long enough to hold a long U.S. callsign (e.g., WD5GNR/2). The custom macro appears at the end so it can grow as needed. The program limits the length of the custom macro to 50 characters.

Press enter when you are done setting either the callsign or custom macro. In the preprogrammed macros, you can use a $FF character to signal the program to send the callsign.

Because this is a substantial project, I've included a two-sided PC board layout (see Figure 9.4 for the top side and Figure 9.5 for the bottom side). The board has extra connections to allow you to connect other devices (such as LCDs) to perform other experiments with the keyboard. You'll also find the layout on the CDROM. (Discussion continues on page 387.)

Figure 9.4 The top side PC board artwork.

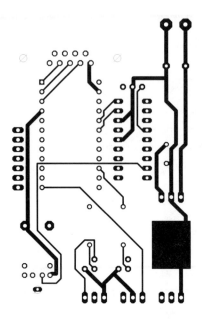

Figure 9.5 The bottom side PC board artwork.

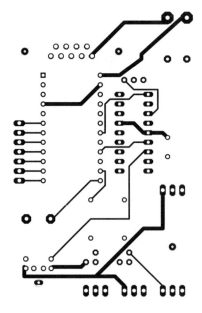

Listing 9.4   The keyboard keyer.

```
'  CW Keyboard using BS2 and PAK6

pakout con 15
pakin con 14
baud con 84
fpin con 13
ptt con 10
key con 9

' sidetone
spkr con 8
freq con 1000

dot var word
dash var word
notx var bit
keyin var byte
taddr var word
maddr var word
len var byte
didah var byte

notx=0
dot=100
dash=300
dotmin con 10
dotmax con 1000

high fpin
low ptt
low key

serout pakout,baud,[$FF]
pause 500
top:
' read character
```

Listing 9.4   The keyboard keyer. (Continued)

```
serin pakin\fpin,baud,[keyin]

debug hex2 keyin
' check for commands (Del=Rx,up=speed+,dn=speed-)
if keyin=$CA then setcall
if keyin=$CB then setmac
if keyin=$91 then speedup
if keyin=$97 then speeddn
if keyin=$9A then rx

high ptt    ' ptt on
gosub charproc
goto top

rx:
  low ptt
  goto top

speedup:
  dot=dot-1
  goto speed
speeddn:
  dot=dot+1
speed:
  if dot>=dotmin then minok
  dot=dotmin
minok:
  if dot<=dotmax then maxok
  dot=dotmax
maxok:
  dash=dot*3
  debug ?dot
  goto top

charproc:
if keyin<"a" or keyin>"z" then nouc
```

Listing 9.4   The keyboard keyer. (Continued)

```
keyin = keyin & $5F  ' force upper case
nouc:
taddr=keyin+ltbl
Read taddr,len
if len=0 then ret
if len=$FF then cspace
if len=$FE then wspace
if len>=$80 then macro
' ordinary char
taddr=keyin+ctbl
Read taddr,didah
cloop:
  gosub element
  didah=didah<<1
  len=len-1
  if len<>0 then cloop
cspace:
  pause dash' element space
  return

wspace:
  pause dash*2
  return

element:
  if notx then nokey0
  high key
nokey0:
  if (didah & $80)=$80 then dah
  freqout spkr,dot,freq
  debug "."
  goto elspace
dah:
  freqout spkr,dash,freq
  debug "-"
elspace:
```

Listing 9.4   The keyboard keyer. (Continued)

```
  if notx then nokey1
  low key
nokey1:
  pause dot
ret:
  return

macro:
  maddr=2*(keyin-$80)+macrotbl
  read maddr,taddr
  read maddr+1,maddr
  maddr=maddr*256+taddr
mloop:
  read maddr,keyin
  debug "Macro: ",keyin,cr
  if keyin=0 then ret
  if keyin<>$FF then norm
  gosub sendcs
  goto nextm
norm:
  gosub charproc
nextm:
  maddr=maddr+1
  goto mloop

csmacro:
  maddr=csmac
  goto mloop

csaddr var word
sendcs:
  csaddr = csmac
scsloop:
  read csaddr,keyin
  if keyin=0 then ret
  gosub charproc
```

Listing 9.4   The keyboard keyer. (Continued)

```
    csaddr=csaddr+1
    goto scsloop

setcall:
  notx=1
  csaddr = csmac
scl:
  if csaddr=csmac+8 then scfin
  serin pakin\fpin,baud,[keyin]
  if keyin<>8 then nobs
  if csaddr=csmac then scl
  csaddr=csaddr-1
  goto scl
nobs:
  if keyin<>13 then nocecho
scfin:
  write csaddr,0
  gosub sendcs
  notx=0
  goto top
nocecho:
  write csaddr,keyin
  csaddr=csaddr+1
  gosub charproc
  goto scl

setmac:
  notx=1
  csaddr = umacro
sumac:
  if csaddr=umacro+50 then smfin
  serin pakin\fpin,baud,[keyin]
  if keyin<>8 then mnobs
  if csaddr=umacro then sumac
  csaddr=csaddr+1
  goto sumac
```

Listing 9.4   The keyboard keyer. (Continued)

```
mnobs:
  if keyin<>13 then mnocecho

smfin:
  write csaddr,0
  notx=0
Debug "done",cr
  goto top
mnocecho:
  write csaddr,keyin
  csaddr=csaddr+1
  gosub charproc
  goto sumac


ltbl  data $00,$00,$00,$00,$00,$00,$00,$00,$00,$00,$00,$05,$00,$05,$00,$00
data $00,$00,$00,$00,$00,$00,$00,$00,$00,$00,$00,$00,$00,$00,$00,$00
data $FE,$00,$00,$00,$00,$00,$00,$00,$00,$00,$00,$06,$00,$06,$05
data $05,$05,$05,$05,$05,$05,$05,$05,$05,$05,$00,$00,$00,$05,$00,$06
data $00,$02,$04,$04,$03,$01,$04,$03,$04,$02,$04,$03,$04,$02,$02,$03
data $04,$04,$03,$03,$01,$03,$04,$03,$04,$04,$04,$00,$06,$00,$00,$00
data $00,$00,$00,$00,$00,$00,$00,$00,$00,$00,$00,$00,$00,$00,$00,$00
data $00,$00,$00,$00,$00,$00,$00,$00,$00,$00,$00,$00,$00,$00,$00,$00
data $80,$81,$82,$83,$84,$85,$86,$87,$88,$89,$8A,$8B,$00,$00,$00,$00
data $00,$00,$00,$00,$00,$00,$00,$00,$00,$00,$00,$00,$00,$00,$00,$00
data $00,$00,$00,$00,$00,$00,$00,$00,$00,$00,$00,$00,$00,$00,$00,$00
data $00,$00,$00,$00,$00,$00,$00,$00,$00,$00,$00,$00,$00,$00,$00,$00
data $00,$00,$00,$00,$00,$00,$00,$00,$00,$00,$00,$00,$00,$00,$00,$00
data $00,$00,$00,$00,$00,$00,$00,$00,$00,$00,$00,$00,$00,$00,$00,$00
data $00,$00,$00,$00,$00,$00,$00,$00,$00,$00,$00,$00,$00,$00,$00,$00
data $00,$00,$00,$00,$00,$00,$00,$00,$00,$00,$00,$00,$00,$00,$00,$00


ctbl  data $00,$00,$00,$00,$00,$00,$00,$00,$00,$00,$00,$B0,$00,$50,$00,$00
data $00,$00,$00,$00,$00,$00,$00,$00,$00,$00,$00,$00,$00,$00,$00,$00
data $00,$00,$00,$00,$00,$00,$00,$00,$00,$00,$00,$00,$CC,$00,$54,$90
data $F8,$78,$38,$18,$08,$00,$80,$C0,$E0,$F0,$00,$00,$00,$88,$00,$30
data $00,$40,$80,$A0,$80,$00,$20,$C0,$00,$00,$70,$A0,$40,$C0,$80,$E0
```

Listing 9.4   The keyboard keyer. (Continued)

```
data $60,$D0,$40,$00,$80,$20,$10,$60,$90,$B0,$C0,$00,$14,$00,$00,$00
data $00,$00,$00,$00,$00,$00,$00,$00,$00,$00,$00,$00,$00,$00,$00,$00
data $00,$00,$00,$00,$00,$00,$00,$00,$00,$00,$00,$00,$00,$00,$00,$00
data $00,$00,$00,$00,$00,$00,$00,$00,$00,$00,$00,$00,$00,$00,$00,$00
data $00,$00,$00,$00,$00,$00,$00,$00,$00,$00,$00,$00,$00,$00,$00,$00
data $00,$00,$00,$00,$00,$00,$00,$00,$00,$00,$00,$00,$00,$00,$00,$00
data $00,$00,$00,$00,$00,$00,$00,$00,$00,$00,$00,$00,$00,$00,$00,$00
data $00,$00,$00,$00,$00,$00,$00,$00,$00,$00,$00,$00,$00,$00,$00,$00
data $00,$00,$00,$00,$00,$00,$00,$00,$00,$00,$00,$00,$00,$00,$00,$00
data $00,$00,$00,$00,$00,$00,$00,$00,$00,$00,$00,$00,$00,$00,$00,$00
data $00,$00,$00,$00,$00,$00,$00,$00,$00,$00,$00,$00,$00,$00,$00,$00

macrotbl  data macro0&$FF,macro0>>8,macro1&$FF,macro1>>8
     data macro2&$FF,macro2>>8,macro3&$FF,macro3>>8
     data macro4&$FF,macro4>>8,macro5&$FF,macro5>>8
     data macro6&$FF,macro6>>8,macro7&$FF,macro7>>8
     data macro8&$FF,macro8>>8,macro9&$FF,macro9>>8
     data csmac&$FF,csmac>>8,umacro&$FF,umacro>>8


csmac   data "NOCALL/0",0
macro0  data "CQ CQ CQ DE ",$FF," ",$FF," ",$FF,0
macro1  data "DE ",$FF,0
macro2  data "QRZ? DE ",$FF,0
macro3  data "TNX UR 599",0
macro4  data "73 AND TNX DE ",$FF,0
macro5  data 0
macro6  data 0
macro7  data 0
macro8  data 0
macro9  data 0
umacro  data 0
```

Reading Code

It is easy to make Morse code keyers. But what about turning things around? Can a Stamp read Morse code?

Other micros can read Morse code — after all, there are numerous commercial products that do it. Why not the Stamp? If you are an amateur radio operator, you can imagine using a Stamp to read code off the air. However, you might also want to use Morse code as an input device to the Stamp. Another idea would be to create a Morse code trainer that shows text on an LCD and "listens" to you send it, telling you if it is correct or incorrect. For beginners, it could even show the dots and dashes on the LCD.

To simplify matters, I've assume that the Morse code input is clean and square on pin 0, with a 1 indicating signal present and a 0 indicating the key is "up." You can use a simple switch or Morse code key if your switch is relatively free from bounce. To copy signals off the air, you might investigate using a 567-tone decoder or a PLL to monitor the code's beep frequency (usually 700Hz or 800Hz on most receivers).

One problem with Morse code sent by hand is that it is irregular. The code tries to guess at spacing but this is not always reliable. If you were using code to send commands to the Stamp, you'd probably want some sort of echo/confirm sequence. In other words you'd send a command, the Stamp would indicate the command (perhaps on an LCD), and you'd do something to confirm the command. This would help prevent misunderstood commands from executing.

The software (see Listing 9.5) is simple enough, but it uses a novel scheme for decoding dots and dashes into characters. Each "character" begins with a 1. Subsequent elements shift the character to the left and add a 1 for a dash or a 0 for a dot. The initial one allows you to distinguish letters like S and H which only differ in length. So an S is %1000 and an H is %10000. A C (-.-.) is %11010.

Once the program detects a pause between elements, it looks the resulting number up in a EEPROM table using the READ command. In this example, the program just prints the character on the debug terminal.

Your first impulse might be to use the PULSIN command for reading the key. That was my idea too. However, with a mechanical key, the PULSIN responded too easily to bounces. By using a manual loop, you can reduce the noise sensitivity and have better control over timeouts as well.

You may want to experiment with the initial code speed and intercharacter delays to suit your purposes. The program attempts to autotrack the code speed by applying a weighted average of the dot lengths to determine the new dot length. Each new sample is weighted one-third into the average. Any key event that is less than 1.5 times this length is considered a dot. Longer events make up a dash.

Listing 9.5 Morse code reader.

```
' Morse code reader
' Williams
' debounced digital input on pin 0
key var in0
```

Listing 9.5 Morse code reader. (Continued)

```
keypin con 0
' time key was "down"
keyin var word
' Current idea of a dit length
dlen var word
' "pointer" into data table
ptr var word
' character
c var byte
' flag to prevent space chatter
sp var bit
' Look up table
' # means no opinion
' ~ AS
' * AR
' @ BT
data  "#"," ","E","T","I","A","N","M"
data  "S","U","R","W","D","K","G","O"
data  "H","V","F","#","L","#","P","J"
data  "B","X","C","Y","Z","Q","#","#"
data  "5","4","#","3","#","#","#","2"
data  "~","#","#","*","#","#","#","1","6"
data  "@","#","#","#","#","#","#","7","#","#"
data  "#","8","#","9","0"
dlen=100  ' guess
ptr=1
sp=0
top:
gosub readkey
if keyin=0 then endchar
if keyin<2 then top    ' ignore noise
if keyin<=(3*dlen/2) then dit
' dah
' better to not adjust speed on dashes
' because of poor manual weighting
ptr=ptr<<1+1
```

Listing 9.5 Morse code reader. (Continued)

```
goto top
dit:
dlen = (2*dlen + keyin)/3    ' weighted average
ptr=ptr<<1
goto top
' paused so figure this character and reset
endchar:
if ptr=1 and sp=1 then top   ' only 1 space
sp=1
if ptr=1 then dosp
sp=0
dosp:
read ptr,c
debug c
ptr=1
goto top
' Would like to use PULSIN here but
' PULSIN is too fast and times out unreliably
readkey:
keyin=0
rk0:
keyin=keyin+1
if keyin>(3*dlen) then rkz   ' letter space
if key=0 then rk0
keyin=0
rk1:
keyin=keyin+1
if key=1 then rk1
return
rkz:
keyin=0
return
```

Chapter 10

The Next Step

In the previous chapters you've seen that you can do plenty of things with a Basic Stamp — more things that you might have thought possible. Even though the Stamp has some limitations, it is possible — using clever design — to make it do many useful tasks. The advantage the Stamp has over practically all other microcontrollers is that it is easy to use.

However, it is easy to fall into a trap if you are not careful. There is an old saying that "when you only have a hammer, everything looks like a nail." I like the Stamp, but it isn't for every job. As you begin to build microcontroller projects, you'll eventually want to do things that the Stamp can't do easily. What then?

The answer is to switch to a more conventional microcontroller. There is no shortage of microcontrollers you can use. Motorola's 68HC11 is quite popular, so are several Intel micros like the 8051. There are many other processors available from a variety of vendors.

In this chapter, I'll show you how you can easily get started with the PIC microcontrollers from Microchip. Why Microchip? First, the PIC is the processor that the Basic Stamp uses, so it is a natural migration path for existing Stamp users. Second, the PIC has some interesting features that make it very easy to get started. PICs are very popular and there are wide array of free and low-cost tools that you can use — some of which are very Stamp-like.

Why Not Stamps?

With all you've been able to do with the Stamp, you might wonder why you'd ever want to use anything else. Certainly, the Stamp is easy to use, no matter how experienced you are. However, the Stamp falls short in a few key areas:

Speed   Even with the introduction of the faster Stamp II variants, the Stamp is not very speedy. This is mostly because the Stamp has to load its instructions from an external EEPROM. This EEPROM uses a serial protocol that can only go so fast.

Interrupts   There are many projects that need to know immediately when something happens. Perhaps you are counting rain drops, or monitoring a logic signal. These things won't wait for the Stamp to check them. Most microprocessors (but not the Stamp) have a way for external devices to interrupt the running program to handle special events. The Stamp IIP has a polling feature that can substitute for interrupts in some, but not all, cases.

Cost   The Stamp is moderately expensive if you are mass-producing a product. You have to balance the cost of development versus the cost of production. If you are building one or two units, the savings in development time is more than enough compensation for the cost of the Stamp hardware. However, if you are making 10,000 units, your development cost per unit will probably be low anyway. Then you'll want to minimize how much you spend building each unit.

I/O Flexibility   The Stamp requires external devices to keep the time of day, do serious analog I/O, and other functions. Many processors have the ability to perform these functions with few or no external parts.

The downside to using a PIC processor (or any other processor, for that matter) is that you'll need more support hardware and development tools. Debugging is not as easy as it is with the Stamp. For some PICs, you'll need to use a special ultraviolet light to erase the devices so you can reuse them.

What You Will Need

By far the easiest PIC to start with is the 16F84. This processor is reasonably fast, reasonably powerful, easy to get, and doesn't require much in the way of special equipment. You'll find a simple programmer in this chapter that can program a 16F84 and erase it, so you probably have everything you need to breadboard a programmer right now. Another common part to use is the 16F87x family (for example, the 16F873 or 16F877 device). These parts cost a little more but have more I/O pins, more memory, and they have special features like analog to digital converters and UARTs. Luckily, programming the 16F87x family is not much different than the 16F84 — the 16F87x has a slightly different memory layout and extra registers to support the new features, but otherwise the 16F87x is just an advanced 16F84. For the rest of this chapter, I'll only talk about the 16F84.

Obviously you will need at least one 16F84. These parts are available in different speed ratings. The 10MHz part is only a few pennies more than the 4MHz part and you'll get more use out of the 10MHz part, so that's what you'll want to buy. The PIC doesn't need much in the way of support hardware, but it does need a few things. First, it needs a 5V regulated power supply. Unlike a Stamp, you can't just connect a 9V battery to the PIC! A 5V power supply is easy enough to build (see Chapter 1). In a pinch, you could use the Stamp to produce 5V and power the PIC that way. This is especially useful if you use the Stamp-based programmer in this chapter because you'll have to use the Stamp anyway.

The other thing that the PIC needs is a clock. There are many ways to clock a PIC, but the easiest is to get a ceramic resonator with built-in capacitors. For a 10MHz PIC, you can use the ECS ZTT-10.00MT resonators which are very inexpensive and give good results. You can also buy resonators without built-in capacitors, but then you'd need to supply the capacitors. If you want to use a crystal, you'll need capacitors for that too. Best to stick with the resonator for your first projects.

It is no problem to operate a PIC at less than its rated speed. Many people will overclock slower PICs to higher speeds, but the price difference is so little, I hardly think it is worth it.

You can also find kits that have all the parts you need in one place from a variety of vendors. See "Hardware Shortcuts" on page 397 for an overview of PIC modules that are available.

Software

Once you have your parts on order, you have to wait, right? Wrong. While you are waiting for your hardware, you can start assembling your software. Better still, you'll be able to start experimenting right away using software emulation.

Your first stop should be the Microchip web site (www.microchip.com). You can download the 16F84 data sheet there. This data sheet explains all the assembly language commands and other details about the chip. You'll also want MPLAB — the development environment for all PICs. It is free to download, but it would be easily worth any reasonable price they wanted to charge for it.

MPLAB is an integrated environment that allows you to write PIC programs in assembly language. MPLAB also compiles that code into a HEX file. If you have a

Microchip programmer (or other microchip development hardware), MPLAB can send the hex file to the chip directly. If you use other programmers, you'll have to load the HEX file manually. The other function you'll find useful with MPLAB is that it can simulate the operation of the PIC in software. That means you can compile and execute your program on the PC and get it working completely. Then when you burn the program into a real PIC, you have a good idea that it will probably work.

Software simulation is a powerful idea. I have spent weeks working on programs without ever burning a real chip. When I finally burn the chip, everything works! Of course, you may have small problems that only show up in real time on real hardware, but you can certainly exorcise all the petty demons that show up in your code before you commit to hardware. MPLAB can even provide artificial stimulus to simulate the action of real hardware in your system (although is tedious to build complex stimulus files).

MPLAB is a complex piece of software. You have to build a project that represents your final device. You can set the project's device type (16F84 for this chapter) and associate your code with the project. Luckily, Microchip provides a manual and a tutorial that should get you started.

Other Software

Most PIC programmers work in assembly language (see Table 10.1). It isn't hard once you get used to it, and it provides you with the ultimate control over your program. However, if you just can't bear to write assembly, you might check out a language compiler. There are several Basic compilers that closely mirror the Basic Stamp's PBASIC language (I like the one from MicroEngineering Labs). There are also free and low-cost C compilers, Forth compilers, and several high-level languages that are unique for the PIC. You can find links to many of these in Chapter 11.

Table 10.1   PIC16F84 instructions.

Instruction	Meaning	Example
ADDWF	Add W to register F	ADDWF XYZ,F
ANDWF	And W with register F	ANDWF XYZ,W
CLRF	Register = 0	CLRF XYZ
CLRW	Clear W register	CLRW
COMF	Invert bits in registers	COMF XYZ,F
DECF	Result = Register − 1	DECF XYZ,W

Table 10.1 PIC16F84 instructions. (Continued)

Instruction	Meaning	Example
DECFSZ	Result = Register − 1, skip if 0	DECFSZ I,F
INCF	Result = Register + 1	INCF XYZ,W
INCFSZ	Result = Register + 1	INCFSZ XYZ,F
IORWF	Or W with register F	IORWF XYZ,F
MOVF	Result = Register	MOVFXYZ,W
MOVWF	Register = W	MOVWF XYZ
NOP	No operation	NOP
RLF	Result = Register shifted left	RLF XYZ,W
RRF	Result = Register shifted right	RRF XYZ,W
SUBWF	Result = Register − W	SUBWF XYZ,F
SWAPF	Result = Swapped nybbles in register	SWAPF XYZ,W
XORWF	Result = Register XOR W	XORWF XYZ,F
BCF	Clear bit in register	BCF XYZ,0
BSF	Set bit in register	BSF XYZ,7
BTFSC	Skip if register bit clear	BTFSC XYZ,4
BTFSS	Skip if register bit set	BTFSS XYZ,3
ADDLW	Add constant to W	ADDLW 0x30
ANDLW	And constant with W	ANDLW 0x80
CALL	Subroutine call	CALL aLabel
CLRWDT	Clear watchdog timer	CLRWDT
GOTO	Jump to new location in program	GOTO aLabel
IORLW	Or constant with W	IORLW 1
MOVLW	Load W with constant	MOVLW 0xFF
RETFIE	Return from interrupt	RETFIE
RETLW	Return with value in W	RETLW 0xAA
RETURN	Return from subroutine	RETURN
SLEEP	Enter low-power mode	SLEEP
SUBLW	Subtract W from constant	SUBLW 0xF
XORLW	Exclusive or W and constant	XORLW 0xFF

Assembler Survival Guide

This book isn't really about PIC assembly language — that's another entire book. However, the PIC16F84 datasheets (available from Microchip's website) can help you get started.

If you want to wade through the listings in this chapter, you'll find Table 10.1 useful. It shows the commands you can use with the 16F84. Just remember that the W register is a temporary register that is involved in nearly everything. Every time you do any math or logical operation, one of the arguments will be in the W register. You can usually store the result in the W register, or into the other register involved.

As an example, consider the ADDWF command. This instruction adds the W register to a specified register. You'll usually give the register a name, so think of it as a variable. If you say:

```
ADDWF XYZ,F
```

The result winds up in the XYZ register. However:

```
ADDWF XYZ,W
```

places the result back in the W register, leaving the XYZ variable undisturbed. You might wonder why the MOVF instruction has this format. Why would you want to say:

```
MOVF XYZ,F
```

Won't this just put the contents of XYZ back into XYZ? Yes. But it will also set the STATUS register's Z flag if the XYZ variable is equal to 0.

There are several registers that have special functions. For example, STATUS contains bits that tell you if the last operation resulted in a zero result, an overflow, and other related information. Other special registers include PCL, FSR, and EEDATA. The PORTA and PORTB registers reflect the I/O pin status and the TRISA and TRISB registers act like the Stamp's direction registers. However, you should know that a 0 in one of the TRIS registers sets the corresponding pin to an output (unlike the Stamp, which requires a 1 for an output bit).

This chapter uses the Microchip assembler instructions that most people use today. However, if you search the web you may find some PIC programs that appear to be in a different language. These probably use the Parallax instruction set. Parallax used to sell a PIC programmer (now sold by Tech Tools) that used a different assembler (SPASM). This assembler uses instructions that more closely resemble Intel 8051 instructions. The generated code, of course, is the same. However, some Parallax commands generate more than one instruction word, which can make skip instructions not operate properly if you are not careful.

Hardware Shortcuts

If all this sounds daunting, you might want to consider a few shortcuts. There are two ways you can take some shortcuts to moving to the PIC if you don't mind spending some money.

1. **The PICStic** — MicroMint offers the PICStic which is nothing more than a 16F84 PIC, a 4MHz crystal, and a voltage regulator in the exact same form factor as a Basic Stamp I. These chips are pricey, but they prevent you from having to deal with the extra PIC hardware. Also, if you have an existing design that uses a Stamp I, you can directly replace it with a PICStic. There are enhanced PICStics (that cost more) that include A/D converters and real time clocks. MicroMint sells a development kit for the PICStic that includes a programmer and a Basic Compiler. However, you don't have to buy the kit — any 16F84 programmer can program the PICStic.

2. **The SimmStick** — The SimmStick is similar to the PICStic idea, but it is much more flexible and less expensive. The SimmStick integrates a PIC, a ceramic resonator, a voltage regulator, and slots for other parts (like an RS232 level converter, EEPROM, etc.) on a 30-pin SIMM PC board (like an old-fashioned PC memory chip). The SimmStick is a kit, so you can put what you want on it and leave off the rest. You can plug it into a SIMM socket, or you can solder a right angle header into the provided holes and make a module out of it. You can even get SimmSticks for other brands of processors. In the United States, you can buy these from Wirz Electronics. Again, you don't need the development kit unless you just want their programmer and accessories.

3. **Interpreter Chip** — Another way you can save money is to buy just the Stamp's interpreter chip from Parallax. This is just a PIC with the correct software programmed into it. You add a EEPROM, a crystal or resonator, a voltage regulator, and a few other parts.

    How is this better than using a Stamp? The chips themselves are less expensive (about half the price of the entire Stamp). If you already have, for example, a regulated source of 5V, you don't need another voltage regulator. You might be able to use the same clock to run other devices in your projects. If you aren't using port 16 for serial I/O (and you have a way to program EEPROMs), you could omit the serial port hardware, too. You can find the schematics for the Stamps, by the way, in the Stamp manual. This is a good place to start if you want to roll your own.

Building the SimmStick kit

One of the best ways to get started with PICs is with the SimmStick. This clever board has the exact form factor of a 30-pin SIMM. The board has a place for a PIC, an RS232 level converter, a regulator, a EEPROM, a real time clock, and an A/D converter! You buy the SimmStick as a kit, so you can customize it if you want. For example, you can change the clock speed and type of PIC to fit your needs. You don't have to add the EEPROM or any of the other pieces if you don't need them.

The kit is easy to put together and the board is high-quality, but the instructions are sparse, and there are no sockets for the ICs. A quick trip to Radio Shack or your junk box will supply the sockets. When I first saw the SimmStick, I wondered how hard it would be to work with SIMM sockets. You can, in fact, mount the finished board in a SIMM socket and the company provides several "motherboards" that contain several SIMM sockets. However, for most purposes, all you do is solder the supplied right-angle header in the holes above the SIMM contacts. This gives the module 30 single-inline pins that make it look like a large Stamp I.

If you are using RS232 communications with the SimmStick, here is a trick: Take a DB9 connector and shorten the fifth pin from the back of the connector (just trim it flush with the connector body). Align pin 2 of the DB9 with pin 1 of the right angle header on the SimmStick. Solder pins 2 and 3 of the DB9 to pin 1 and 2 of the header. Pin 4 will touch the header at pin 3 (which is not connected) — solder it for mechanical stability. Next, carefully solder a wire to what's left of the fifth pin on the DB9. Run this wire to a ground point on the SimmStick and solder. Now you have a built-in DB9 for RS232 communications.

(Discussion continues on page 402.)

Listing 10.1 The APP-I Stamp software.

```
' PICPGM - APP-1 Software
' This file is V1.0 for Stamp I
' There is virtually nothing in this file you
' should change unless you are certain you
' understand what it means.
' http://www.al-williams.com/awce.htm

symbol pcinput=2    ' Input from PC
```

Listing 10.1 The APP-I Stamp software. (Continued)

```
symbol pcoutput=3    ' Output from PC
symbol baudrate=4    ' Must be 4 (1200) to match PC S/W
symbol clearpin=0    ' Bring this pin high to reset PIC
symbol datapin=7     ' PIC data pin
symbol clk=6         ' PIC clock pin
symbol progdelay=10  ' program cycle delay (ms)
symbol resetdelay=10 ' reset delay (*10uS)
output pcoutput
output clk
output datapin
output clearpin
pulsout clearpin,resetdelay
top:
serin pcinput,baudrate,b1,b2,b3
branch b1,(wcmd,ccmd,rcmd,rstcmd,pcmd,pcmd,lcmd,lcmd)
errout:
serout pcoutput,baudrate,("E")
goto top
intread:
  b2=4
  if bit8=1 then icmd
  b2=5
icmd:
  gosub doccmd
  gosub dorcmd
  return
lcmd:
gosub intread
incout:
b2=6
gosub doccmd
goto outout
pcmd:
w3=w1
gosub intread
if w4=w3 then  incout
```

Listing 10.1 The APP-I Stamp software. (Continued)

```
b2=2
if bit8=1 then ppcmd1
b2=3
ppcmd1:
gosub doccmd
w1=w3
gosub dowcmd
b2=8
gosub doccmd
Pause progdelay
goto lcmd
ccmd:
gosub doccmd
okout:
serout pcoutput,baudrate,("!")
goto top
doccmd:
b10=1
for b5=1 to 6
  high clk
  b3=b2&b10
  if b3=0 then d1
  high datapin
  goto d0
d1:
  low datapin
d0:
  b10=b10*2
  low clk
next
  high datapin
  return
rcmd:
gosub dorcmd
outout:
serout pcoutput,baudrate,("!",b8,b9)
```

Listing 10.1 The APP-I Stamp software. (Continued)

```
goto top
dorcmd:
input datapin
w4=0
w5=1
for b5=1 to 16
   pulsout clk,1
   if pin7=0 then nozi
   w4=w4+w5
nozi:
   w5=w5*2
next
w4=w4/2&$3FFF
output datapin
return
wcmd:
gosub dowcmd
goto okout
dowcmd:
w1=w1*2
low datapin
w5=1
for b5=1 to 16
   high clk
   w4=w1 & w5
   if w4=0 then dz
   high datapin
   goto dnz
dz:
   low datapin
dnz:
   w5=w5*2
   low clk
next
low datapin
return
```

Listing 10.1 The APP-I Stamp software. (Continued)

```
rstcmd:
low datapin
low clk
low clearpin
if b2=0 then pulselow
high clearpin
pulselow:
pulsout clearpin,resetdelay
goto okout
```

Getting Started

Once you have all the hardware and software ready, you'll need a programmer. There are several designs for programmers on the web (see Chapter 11). There are an equal number of companies that will sell you a programmer. My favorite free programmer is a little gem known as the "LudiPipo programmer." This is a handful of resistors and a 5V zener diode to regulate 12V from your serial port down to 5V. You can find plans for the LudiPipo on the web. Just be sure your serial port really generates 12V and don't use very long serial cables.

Figure 10.1 shows the APP-I programmer. This programmer uses a Stamp I or II to do all the work. You can find the Stamp software on the CD-ROM, or the Stamp I version in Listing 10.1. Also on the CD-ROM is the PICAWC84 program that will operate this programmer or the LudiPipo programmer. You'll find more details about the APP-I in Appendix B.

For your first PIC project, start simple. For example, consider building the circuit in Figure 10.2. If you are using a PICStic, or SimmStick, you won't need the support circuitry (but you will need the LEDs).

Figure 10.1 APP-I programmer.

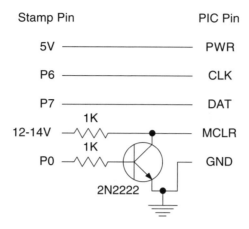

Figure 10.2 Test PIC circuit.

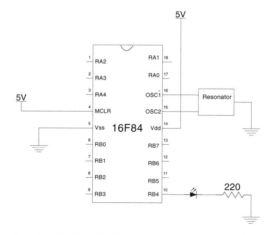

Here's how to make the LED blink using MPLAB and the APP-I programmer:

1. Program a Basic Stamp I with the program in Listing 10.1, or use the BSII version on the CD-ROM with a Basic Stamp II. If you use a BSIIX or BSIIP, you'll need to adjust the serial port and pulse timing parameters.
2. Run MPLAB.
3. Select Project | New Project.
4. Select a directory you want to use and enter TEST.PJT. Click OK.

5. A dialog will appear, allowing you to set the project options.

6. Click the TEST[.HEX] entry in the Project Files box. Click Node Properties.

7. You don't absolutely need to change any entries here, but you may want to make sure that the Case sensitivity check box is set to Off so that you can use upper- and lowercase names interchangeably (you might also prefer to make the standard radix decimal instead of hex). Click OK.

8. Click Add Node and enter TEST.ASM as the file name

9. Verify that the Development Mode selection is MPLAB-SIM, 16F84; If not, click Change and adjust the settings.

10. Click OK to dismiss the dialog box.

11. Select File | New and enter the program in Listing 10.2.

12. Select File | Save As and save the file as TEST.ASM.

13. Press F10 to build the program; ignore the warning about the TRIS instruction.

If the build doesn't work, you can double click the error message to jump to the offending line. Once you have a complete build, you could use your programmer to burn a PIC. But first, try these steps to simulate your program:

1. Select Window | Special Function Registers.

2. Select Window | File Registers.

3. Press F8 to step through each line of the program; observe PORTB, W, and locations 0x10 to 0x11 in the register windows.

If you get tired of waiting for the delays to step through, try right-clicking on a source line to set a breakpoint or cause the program to run to the indicated line. If you open the Stopwatch window (on the Window menu), you can even see how long the loop will really take at a given clock speed. Of course, the simulation is much slower than the actual execution.

One thing that takes some getting used to with the PIC is that there are no IF statements like there are in Basic. Instead, certain instructions will skip the next instruction if some condition is true. For example, suppose you want to see if the variable X is equal to 10. If it is, you'd like to jump to label X10. Otherwise, you want execution to continue as normal. In Basic, this is trivial:

```
IF X=10 THEN X10
```

With a PIC, you'd write the same thing like this:

```
MOVLW D'10'      ;  W=10
SUBWF X          ; W=X-10
BTFSC STATUS,Z   ; If Z bit is set, the W is equal to 0, so X is equal to 10
GOTO X10         ; so go to X10
; Continue here if STATUS,Z was clear
```

Listing 10.2 TEST.ASM

```
                PROCESSOR 16F84
                __CONFIG 0x3FF2          ; HS, PWT, no WDT

                INCLUDE <P16F84.INC>     ; 16F84 definitions
            org 0
delay           equ 0x10                      ; memory locations
delay1          equ 0x11  ; (variables)
            clrf delay
            clrf delay1
            clrw
            tris PORTB      ; port B to output
top:        movwf PORTB     ; 0 or FF -> PORTB
            xorlw 0xFF      ; make 0 -> FF and vice versa
; Delay
; about 79ms at 10MHz
; about 197ms at 4MHz

dloop:
            decfsz delay,F   ; delay=delay-1, skip if 0
            goto dloop
            decfsz delay1,F  ; delay1=delay1-1, skip if 0
            goto dloop
            goto top

            end
```

The Real Thing

Once you are satisfied that your program operates properly, you are ready to try it for real. With the 16F84, this isn't a big commitment because you can always reprogram the part. If you use a PIC that is ultraviolet erasable (they have a JW in their part number), you'll have to spend a few minutes erasing the PIC. Many ordinary PICs are OTP (One Time Programmable). Once you program them, you can't make changes.

Exactly how you burn the HEX file that MPLAB generates into a PIC depends on the programmer you are using. If you want to use the APP-I programmer from this chapter, you'll need to run the PICAWC84 program from the CD-ROM. Here are the steps:

1. Make sure the programmed Stamp is connected to the PC and the Stamp software is not running. If you use the DOS version of the Stamp software, close the DOS window too. Connect the PIC as shown in Figure 10.1.
2. Run PICAWC84.
3. Click View | Setup; select APP-I and High-Speed APP-I options; choose the correct COM port (the one you have the Stamp connected to); press OK.
4. Select File | Open; navigate to the TEST.HEX file you created earlier and load it.
5. Pick 16F84 in the combo box near the bottom of the program — the other options should not require changes.
6. Push the Program button — this will take a little while.
7. Remove the PIC and place it in the circuit you'll find in Figure 10.2.
8. If you have LEDs connected to any port B pin, they should blink.

That's it! You've programmed your first PIC and made it work. From here you can start out in small steps and build bigger programs.

Beyond PICs

Another easy-to-use processor is the Scenix SX processor. This device is similar to a PIC16C54, but has many extra features. One big feature is that it can operate up to 50MHz and use a single cycle for each instruction. This is roughly equivalent to a 200MHz PIC! If you don't mind running at 4MHz or less (which is still like a 16MHz PIC), you don't even need an external clock.

Like the 16F84, the SX is electrically erasable. Unlike the 16F84, the SX uses a 12-bit instruction word which makes it a little different to use (the PIC 16C54 uses the 12-bit instructions also).

There are inexpensive SX programmers available from vendors (including Parallax) and a few free designs on the web. However, if you are willing to spend a few hundred dollars, you can get the SX-Key programming system from Parallax. The SX-Key is a small device that connects to your PC via the serial port.

The key can program the SX part, but it can also put the chip into a special debug mode. In this mode, you can run the chip at full speed, while monitoring its execution. You can set a breakpoint, view and modify registers, and single step through your program. This makes debugging your code much more pleasant. You can get similar emulators for the PIC, but they require special PIC devices and cost three to five times the amount that the SX-Key costs.

There are many other processors available that are more capable than the PIC. However with the large user community, availability of free tools, and wide variety of PIC devices, the PIC is an excellent next step into the world of microcontrollers.

TIP

PIC pitfalls

Moving from Basic to assembly can have a few pitfalls. Here are some common problems people have:

• **Banking** — Registers on the 16F84 are in two banks. To address register 0x80 and above, you must set the RP0 bit in the STATUS register. For example, to access register 0x81 (OPTION), you really access register 1 (TMR0) but with RP0 set instead of clear. Some registers (including all the user-defined registers) exist in both banks. The assembler will warn you when you try to access registers in bank 1, so you can ensure that you have the RP0 bit set properly.

• **Hex numbers** — By default, MPLAB sets your project up so that it uses hex numbers. This can cause confusion if you are used to thinking in decimals. You can force any number to be a hex number by using the 0x prefix (like 0xFF) or the H'' notation (as in H'FF'). You can use D'' for decimal (D'255') or B for binary (B'11111111').

• **Harvard architecture** — The PIC uses a Harvard architecture which means there is separate storage for program and data. The program word is 14 bits long (on the 16F84, anyway) while the data word is eight bits. You can't directly read data from the program memory. It is also hard to remember that location 10, for example, is different from variable location 10.

Stamps + PICs?

Of course, the Stamp is still much easier to use than a PIC. Is there any way to get the best of both worlds? You can do your development on the Stamp and then use a Basic compiler to transfer your program to a PIC. The Micro Engineering Labs

PicBasic compiler is quite adept at doing this. The base-level compiler functions much like the Basic Stamp I's language.

The PicBasic Pro (PBP) compiler is close, but not exactly like, the Basic language you'll find on the Stamp II. It is usually easy to transfer your code with just a few changes. PicBasic Pro also has several special features that you won't find on the Stamp. For example, PBP allows you to mix assembly language into your Basic program. You can also handle interrupts, access an external LCD, use external EEPROMs, and even read X10 commands (the Stamp can only transmit X10 commands).

PBP is somewhat expensive. However, it can more than pay for itself in development time saved if you are moving from the Stamp to the PIC.

You can test PBP online at www.compilespot.com. If you prefer to manually convert your code, you might find the information at www.dontronics.com/see.html interesting — it shows Basic Stamp I instructions and the equivalent PIC instructions.

A Sample PBP Program

Listing 10.3 shows a simple phone dialer application using PBP. The program uses SERIN2 instead of the Stamp's usual SERIN command (SERIN2 more closely mimics the Stamp II's SERIN command).

Listing 10.3 Sample PBP program.

```
Digit var byte
OUTPUT PORTA.1
OUTPUT PORTA.2
Loop:
SERIN2 PORTA.1, 3313, [DEC1 Digit]
DTMFOUT PORTA.2,[Digit]
GOTO Loop
```

This program looks like the equivalent Stamp II program except that it uses SERIN2 and also uses pin names (PORTA.1, for example) instead of the predefined Stamp I/O pin names. Of course, this program is simple; there are other compatibility differences you might encounter in a larger program. For example, there are no nybble variables in PBP. PBP also processes math expressions in the usual way. While the Stamp thinks that $5 + 2 \times 3 = 21$, PBP will find the answer 11, which is the standard way to order calculations.

Of course, another difference between normal Stamp Basic and PBP is raw speed. The Stamp has to fetch instructions from EEPROM. PBP programs run directly on the PIC. Also, compiled programs don't have the same overhead that the Stamp has.

After all, the Stamp has to examine your program and take the steps you want. A PBP program just does what you want directly. This all combines to result in programs that can literally run hundreds of times faster on a PIC than a Stamp.

When you execute PBP, it generates an ASM file and then automatically runs the assembler to generate a HEX file. PBP has its own assembler that you can use, or you can configure it to use MPLAB. You can also add PBP to MPLABs tools so that you can debug your Basic programs in MPLAB (using assembly language, unfortunately).

Summary

One day you'll find a project that you can better solve with a more powerful processor than a Stamp. That day may be some time in coming, however. Although this chapter can't do more than whet your appetite, you'll find moving to a 16F84 relatively painless if you follow the steps given here.

The PIC16F87x family of processors have another feature — they can program themselves (known as a *bootloader*). The idea is that a small program in the PIC accepts commands and data from a PC and uses the data to program other areas of the PIC's memory. Unfortunately, to program a bootloader, you need an ordinary programmer at least to begin. The other alternative is to buy a PIC preprogrammed with a bootloader (for example, see `http://www.al-williams.com/awce/app2.htm`). The advantage over a normal programmer is a bootloader lets you compile, program, and test your code in the same way you do with a Stamp. Some bootloaders also have rudimentary debugging support.

Fair warning: the extra speed and power afforded by using a traditional microprocessor can be addictive. Even then you'll find yourself wishing for the Stamp's simple I/O commands. Don't forget with a PIC, you'll have to write a lot of code just to do simple things like generate tones or debounce buttons. Perhaps the best of both worlds is to use a PIC with a Basic compiler.

Exercises

1. Download MPLAB as described in this chapter. Follow the directions to load `TEST.ASM` and build the hex file. Using the MPLAB simulator and the stopwatch window, how long will the delay take if you used a 3.58MHz clock? (Note: 3.58MHz is a common crystal frequency used in color television sets.) Hint: Change the clock frequency on the `Options | Processor Setup | Clock Frequency` menu.

2. Modify the code in TEST.ASM to provide half the delay time. Notice that currently, the DELAY and DELAY1 variables start at 0 and count down to 0 again for 256 total cycles. Use the stopwatch to verify the results.

3. The TRIS instruction in Listing 10.2 is considered obsolete. It would be better to use the TRISB register instead. To do so, you must set the page bits in the STATUS register correctly. Make this change and verify your work using the MPLAB simulator.

For answers to the exercises, see the Answer Key, page 448.

Chapter 11

On Your Own

If you've made it this far, congratulations! By now you should have a solid grasp of how the Stamp works both at a hardware and software level. By now you should have a head full of ideas for projects. If you are like me, you'll be lucky to find the time to do a third of them.

Microcontrollers can be projects unto themselves, but they can also add a whole new dimension to traditional electronic projects. Why build a simple volt meter when you could build a Stamp-based volt meter with RS232 I/O, and LCD display, range alarms, and the like? With the appropriate hardware, Stamps can measure, control, and communicate with the outside world. Nearly any project can benefit from the addition of a microcontroller. After all, almost everything you buy today has a microprocessor in it; why not what you build too?

If you still don't have enough ideas, there are thousands of projects on the web. There is also a mailing list where over 1,000 Stamp users interact for ideas and guidance. In fact, one of the things that makes the Stamp so useful is the very active user community that supports it.

The Parallax Mailing List

There is a very active mailing list that Parallax sponsors to allow Stamp users to interact with one another. Go to http://groups.yahoo.com/group/basicstamps to subscribe. Be warned: this list often generates 100 or more messages a day. If you can set your e-mail software to filter the messages into a separate folder, you'll be happier. If you can't do that you might consider signing up for a free e-mail account (for example at `www.hotmail.com`) and use that address to receive messages.

Web Sites

There are thousands of web sites that have something to do with Basic Stamps or other microcontroller projects. Here are a few of my favorites, in no particular order. This is by no means a complete list. But these links should keep you busy for awhile. Besides, most of these sites have links to even more pages!

Generally useful:	
The Stamp FAQ	`www.al-williams.com/wd5gnr/stampfaq.htm`
	I maintain an unofficial Stamp FAQ. There is a snapshot of it on the CD-ROM, but the most current version is on the web.
The LOSA	`www.hth.com/filelibrary/txtfiles/losa.txt`
	This is a list of applications developed with the Stamp. Many of them have source code and schematics available on the web. Be sure to report your own creations here.
Stamp Project of the Month	`www.al-williams.com/awce/som.htm`
	My famous Stamp project of the month.
Parallax	`www.parallaxinc.com`
	Parallax has many useful areas on their site including free downloads of the Stamp software and manuals. You can also search the mailing list archives.
Stamps Archive	`www.jamesrusso.com/stamp/`
	James Russo maintains a search engine that lets you find things from the old Stamp mailing list.
Nuts & Volts	`www.nutsvolts.com`
	This magazine is a great general electronics magazine and has a column each month about the Stamp.
Bob Blick	`www.bobblick.com/bob/stamp/index.html`
	Bob Blick has many interesting Stamp projects including a roll-your-own H-bridge and more.
Tracy Allen	`www.emesystems.com`
	Unique insights into Stamp math and quirks.

Other vendors:

Arrick Robotics	www.robotics.com/arobot/
	A fellow Texan with a Basic Stamp robot.
AWC	www.al-williams.com/awce
	My company produces many tools for the Stamp and PIC developer including floating point math coprocessors, PWM processors, and prototyping tools.
HVW Technologies	www.hvwtech.com
	A Canadian source for Stamp gear, robotics, and more.
Peter Anderson	www.phanderson.com
	Peter is a professor at Morgan State University. His site has many "white papers" and also some products for sale.
RTN	www.nollet.com.au
	An Australian Parallax distributor, Ronald has a lot of information here.
Scott Edwards	www.seetron.com
	Scott makes serial LCDs that are well-suited for Basic Stamp use.
Solutions Cubed	www.solutions-cubed.com
	Solutions Cubed makes modules for keeping time and controlling motors.
Wirz Electronics	www.wirz.com
	Motor controllers, serial LCDs, and a U.S. source for SimmSticks

PIC-related web sites:

Microchip	www.microchip.com
	The maker of the PIC. Download datasheets and tools from here.
PicList	www.piclist.com
	Web site for the large PIC mailing list.
Tech Tools	www.tech-tools.com
	This company now produces what used to be the Parallax PIC programmer.
Dontronics	www.dontronics.com
	This Australian firm has many resources for moving from Stamps to PICs including sample PIC code for all the Basic Stamp I commands.
Micro Engineering Labs	www.melabs.com
	Makers of the PIC Basic compilers.
SimmStick	www.simmstick.com
	Home for information about SimmSticks.
MicroMint	www.micromint.com
	Home of the PICStic.
FastForward	pw2.netcom.com/~fastfwd/index.html
	A great set of Q&A about the PIC.

General electronic part sources:

Digikey	www.digikey.com
Mouser	www.mouser.com
Newark	www.newark.com

Surplus electronic part sources:

All	www.allcorp.com
Alltronics	www.alltronics.com
Electronics Goldmine	www.goldmine-elec.com
HSC	www.halted.com

About the CD-ROM

On the accompanying CD-ROM, you'll find the source code for each chapter. In addition, you'll find the Stamp manuals, application notes, and software courtesy of Parallax. The APP-I programmer software is also on the CD along with the Basic Stamp I Simulator.

About the Stamp I Simulator

BS1 is an emulator for the Basic Stamp I. It is being released as complimentary software to the Basic Stamp community. As such, there is limited support and you may or may not find the emulator useful to you. This is a Beta release, therefore, you can expect to find things that do not work.

How Do I Use It?

Write your program using the STAMP.EXE editor (from Parallax). Then add a line anywhere in your program that reads: BSAVE. Download the program (even if you don't really have a Stamp hooked up — you don't even have to own a Stamp). This places a file in the current directory called CODE.OBJ. You can rename the file if you like, but keep the .OBJ extension.

Next, start BS1. It will bring up a dialog where you can pick what file you want to open. After you open the file, the main screen will appear. At the top of the window are 8 LEDs that show your outputs (black is 0, red is 1, and hollow means the pin is an input). Below that are 8 buttons that represent your inputs. Black is a zero input and green is a one input. Below that are several special I/O locations (see the following section). Below that are all the W and B registers along with the PORT register. You can modify the W registers by typing over the numbers already there. At the very bottom of the screen, you will see a decoding of the next statement to execute (which may look a little odd, compared to your original source, but you'll be able to figure it out).

There are three buttons: Run, Step, and Step Over. The Run button causes the program to execute as fast as possible (about 1 instruction per millisecond). Step executes one line of code. Step Over executes a line of code too, but if it is a GOSUB, the debugger stops when it hits the corresponding RETURN. When you press RUN, by the way, the button changes to STOP and you can press it to go back to single step mode.

Special I/O Locations

In the center of the screen are three boxes: LastPWM, Pot Input, and Pulse In. The LastPWM box shows the result of the last PWM command (to any pin) as a fraction of 5 volts. You can't change this value and the next PWM will write over it.

The Pot Input and Pulse In boxes let you specify input values for any POT or PULSIN command regardless of the pin specified in the program. If you leave the boxes blank, BS1 will prompt you for a value (which is not handy when you are in RUN mode). If you use more than one POT or PULSIN pin, you'll probably want to leave these boxes blank when you run at full speed.

Unsupported Constructs

In this release, DEBUG is not functional (it is ignored). BUTTON, SEROUT, and SERIN are not functional and will cause BS1 to reset.

Quirks

Disassembling BS1 statements is difficult because much of the information you supplied at runtime is already gone. Some statements (notably FOR/NEXT) do not disassemble completely, but they function correctly. Others like SOUND and BRANCH will have an extra comma in the list — which is harmless.

Of course, you will not see any comments or symbol information. Addresses are shown in Hex, which probably doesn't mean anything to anyone.

Specifics

`LET, LOOKDOWN, LOOKUP, HIGH, LOW, INPUT, OUTPUT, TOGGLE, REVERSE`	No notes.
`GOTO, BRANCH, END`	No notes.
`PWM`	The `PWM` command shows its output in the `Last PWM` box. It changes the I/O state of the pin correctly, but you won't see any change to the digital state of the output.
`POT`	The `POT` command will read from the special input box, if possible. You should enter the final answer you expect from the CD-ROM reading (0–255).
`PULSOUT`	`PULSOUT` doesn't really pause for the correct number of 10µS periods, but it does attempt to flash the digital output visually and leaves the pin in the correct state.
`PULSIN`	`PULSIN` reads from the special input box, if possible. Enter the period in 10µS units.
`FOR`	As noted, the `FOR` statement doesn't disassemble correctly, but it does function properly. You will only see the variable and the inital value as in: `FOR B1=10`
`NEXT`	It would be possible to show more information for the `NEXT`, but in this release, the simulator does not provide any additional information.
`READ, WRITE`	EEPROM reads and writes are not paced to account for their slow execution.
`GOSUB`	There is a 16 `GOSUB` limit. `GOSUB` writes zeros to W6 so that you know not to use it (as in the real BS1) but the execution details are not the same! In other words, a real BS1 program will store something else in W6.
`RETURN`	Same notes as for `GOSUB` (W6 is destroyed even though BS1 doesn't really use it).
`PAUSE`	`PAUSE` attempts to wait the correct interval in `RUN` mode although this is not a sure thing.
`NAP`	`NAP` attempts to wait the correct interval in `RUN` mode.
`SLEEP`	`SLEEP` attempts to wait the correct interval in `RUN` mode.
`RANDOM`	`RANDOM` probably uses a different algorithm to generate numbers than the real Stamp. However, starting with the same seed should give you the same numbers in BS1 (but that may be different from a real Stamp).

SOUND	Windows 95 and 98 make the same sound for any note value. Windows NT generates the approximate tones.
IF	The IF statement shows a little arrow next to it if the jump will be taken.
DEBUG	Unimplemented and ignored.
BUTTON, SERIN, SEROUT	Unimplemented in the Lite version.

The Non-Lite Version

At this time there is no non-lite version. Some features I've thought about including are:

- Real serial I/O via the PC's serial port or simulated to a terminal window
- Unlimited Pot and PulsIn pin simulations
- Better disassembly corresponding to original source file
- Viewing of entire program at once
- Bounds checking on READ/WRITE; W6 usage, etc.
- Better SOUND emulation
- Emulation of BUTTON
- Allow for intermittent I/O (push buttons)
- Allow for reversing sense of switches/LEDs
- Breakpoints and Watchpoints

Disclaimers

This software is provided free and is "as-is." AWC makes no warrantee as to its fitness for any purpose whatsoever. Basic Stamps are a product of Parallax Inc. AWC is in no way affiliated with Parallax.

Appendix B

The APP-I PIC Programmer

In Chapter 10, you saw how the APP-I PIC Programmer could use a Stamp to burn a PIC. This appendix will provide you with a bit more details on the construction of the APP-I.

What's Needed?

- A 12-14V DC power supply
- If you want to omit the power supply, you may be able to use the PC's serial port. However, this is not always reliable. If you wish to omit the power supply, you'll need a 1N914 or 1N4148 diode.
- A 2N2222 transistor
- Two 1K resistors
- The PICAWC84 programming software
- A Basic Stamp II
- A 16C84, 16F84, or PICStic
- A PC running Windows 95, 98, or NT with a free serial port
- The standard Stamp software

- Something to generate PIC code (e.g., MPLAB discussed in Chapter 10) — any tool that generates 8-bit Intel hex files should work.

Building It

Refer to the schematic (Figure B.1) to determine the parts placement. Note that P0 on the Stamp II is physically pin 5.

Figure B.1   The APP-I programmer.

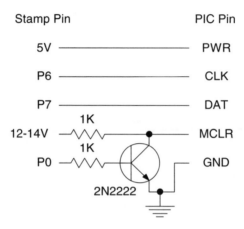

Notice there is no pinout given for the PIC. Use the following table to determine the pin numbers to connect for the type of PIC you are programming:

Name	16C84/16F84 Pin	PICStic Pin
PWR	14	5
GND	5	2
MCLR	4	6
DAT	13	14
CLK	12	13

Software

The APP-I requires software on the Stamp and on your PC. Run SETUP from the \Listings\Chap10\APP1V1 directory of the CD-ROM. In the same directory, you will find `PICPGM.BS2`. Connect the ASP-1 to the PC and download the file using the Parallax software. You only need to do this once unless you reprogram the Stamp.

Next, run PICAWC84. Use the View | Setup menu to select the appropriate COM port. Also select the high-speed option.

PICAWC84 allows you to load 8 bit Hex files (produced by most development tools including Microchip's free MPLAB and MPASM). If you want to use Parallax tools, be sure to suppress the special Parallax Hex records. By default, the software drives the APP-I programmer (via COM1), but you can make other selections on the View | Options menu. By changing the configuration, PICAWC84 can also drive a LudiPipo programmer (which operates on a different principle than the APP-I).

That's it! You can now program PICs and PICStics easily. If you are using a PICStic, you can move R1 so that it connects MCLR to 5V and the program will run. Other PICs require an external clock before the program will execute.

Troubleshooting

If you encounter difficulties, check the following:

1. Are you connected to the COM port that PICAWC84 is using?
2. Is the Stamp programmed with the correct software?
3. Can you program the Stamp at all?
4. Do you have long test leads connected to MCLR? (This can cause odd behavior.)

PICAWC84 Controls

Although they aren't labeled, the fuse configuration controls on the PICAWC84 screen are easy to decypher. If your HEX file contains the correct configuration, you shouldn't need to change these anyway. To the far left, the check box marked Protect turns code protection on and off. The drop down list next to that selects the device type. Knowing the device type allows PICAWC84 to correctly set and decode the fuse word. The next list is the oscillator selection (use XT for a PICStic). The next box allows you to select the Power Timer (PWT), the Watchdog Timer (WDT), both, or none.

The five boxes for ID words are related. The four top boxes allow you to enter hex numbers. The bottom box contains the ASCII text of the low 8 bits of the ID words. When you change any of the numbers, the text updates and vice versa.

Don't forget to set the program up for your COM port and programmer type (select Setup from the View menu). You'll find more tips for using PICAWC84 in Chapter 10.

Using the COM Port as a Power Supply

In some cases, it may be possible to use the COM port as a power supply. AWC does not recommend this due to the large variance in COM port voltages. However, if you would like to try it, here's how:

1. Using a voltmeter, measure the ATN line on the Stamp while it is connected to the PC and no software is trying to talk to the Stamp. If the absolute value of the voltage is less than 12 volts, this procedure probably will not work.

2. Break the connection between the Stamp and the ATN line. How you do this depends on how you have the Stamp connected. The Stamp should already be programmed before you do this.

3. Connect a 1N914 (or 1N4148) diode to the wire that used to connect to the ATN line. The banded end of the diode goes towards the PIC and away from the Stamp.

4. Connect the banded end of the diode to the MCLR resistor where the schematic shows the resistor connecting to the external power supply.

5. Start PICAWC84 and in the setup screen (from the View menu) be sure that the COM Port Power check box is selected.

Appendix C

Making Cables

The Stamp programming software is free, but you still need a way to connect the Stamp to your PC. There are several commercial solutions including the Parallax carrier board and the AWC ASP-II. However, it is easy enough to build your own cables. This is especially useful when you want to integrate in a programming cable connector into a project.

Stamp I

The easiest way to make a Stamp I cable is to buy a cheap PC printer cable. One end will have a male DB25 connector. The other end will have a large Centronics-style connector. Cut the cable near the Centronics end and throw that part away.

Strip the wires exposed at the end and use an ohmmeter to find pins 2, 11, and 25. Pin 25 is a ground pin, so it may be shorted to the other ground pins which is no cause for alarm.

Once you have the wires in place, you need a way to connect wire 2 to pin 4 of the Stamp, wire 11 to pin 3, and wire 25 to pin 2. Exactly how you do this will depend on your setup and your ingenuity. You can use a pin header like the Parallax carrier board, but you may find strain relief to be a problem. The CW keyer project in Chapter 9 uses a 1/4" phone jack to make these connections. By soldering a plug on the cable, and soldering the Stamp pins to the jack, it is a simple matter to reprogram the keyer at a moment's notice.

Stamp II, IISX, IIE, and IIP

All members of the Stamp II family use an identical programming cable. You can build a serial cable using solder-type or crimp-style connectors that are available almost everywhere. Here's the connections you'll need to make:

DB9 pin	DB25 pin	Stamp Pin
2	3	1
3	2	2
4	20	3
5	7	4

In addition, the Stamp software needs to know what port you are using. You can manually set this, of course, or you can short the DSR and RTS pins so the Stamp software can automatically find the Stamp. If you are using a DB9 connector, short pins 6 and 7 on the connector. For a DB25 connector, short pins 4 and 6.

When you program the Stamp, the software uses the ATN line (pin 3 on the Stamp) to initiate programming mode. However, this can interfere with using the same serial cable with the SERIN or SEROUT commands in your program. For this reason, you'd like to have a way to break the ATN line with a switch or jumper so that it is not connected to the serial cable unless you are programming. You can also place a 0.1µF capacitor between the serial cable pin 3 to get the same effect. If you do use the capacitor, you might want to put another 0.1µF capacitor between the ATN pin and ground to filter any noise the cable may pick up.

Answer Key

Chapter 1 Answers

1. 128 + 32 + 16 + 1 = 177
    128 + 64 + 32 + 16 = 240
    128 + 64 + 32 + 16 + 1 = 241
    128 + 328 + 2 = 170
2. $FA, $19, $64, $40
3. %10000101, %01100011, %11111010, %01010101
4. Without a dropping resistor, the LED will appear to be practically a short to the 5V supply, and will draw current until the LED fails or the power supply trips a fuse, circuit breaker, or other component.
5. Total drop across two LEDs = 2.4V
    Desired drop across resistor = 5 – 2.4 = 2.6V
    Current through resistor = .020A (current is equal in series)
    Resistor Value = $^{2.6}/_{.02}$ = 130Ω
6. A pull-up resistor provides a default path to the positive supply so that an input pin will be in a logic 1 state unless a connected output sets the pin's state to a 0. A pull-down resistor provides a default path to ground, making sure the pin's state is 0, unless a connected output explicitly sets a high state on the pin.

Chapter 2 Answers

1. x=10 (on the Stamp II, you must write it this way)
2. SEROUT is used to communicate with RS232 devices asynchronously. Data flows at a predetermined speed (the baud rate) whenever the sender elects to transmit. It signals the beginning of a transmission with a start bit, and signals the end with a stop bit. SHIFTOUT, communicates synchronously. That is, it uses a clock that the receiver uses to synchronize with the transmitter. This allows the speed to vary, and makes a start and stop bit unnecessary.
3. 4, 3, and 5
4. Change the process routine like this:

```
process:
gosub bsyled
. . . . ' Some processing
goto notbsy
```

Chapter 3 Answers

1. Reverse the polarity of the LEDs instead of reversing the bits. Of course, if you are using the Parallax Stamp activity board, this is practically impossible.
2. You could get the same effect by counting from 15 to 0 and not inverting the bits. This gives the same results, but takes less code and runs faster (of course, speed isn't an issue in this program).
3. The BUTTON command uses the temporary workspace to track debouncing and repeat cycles for each button. If you use the same variable for both switches, you won't be able to rely on correct debounce and repeat operation.
4. You can find the Stamp II version of the Merlin game in Key Listing 1.

Key Listing 1   The Merlin Program
rewritten for the Stamp II.

```
' This version can be used with the Stamp Activity Board
' The problem is that the speaker and SW3 are on the
' same I/O pin which makes the game behave a little funny
' If you breadboard this, just put the speaker on
' a different pin and it work fine.
```

Key Listing 1   The Merlin Program
rewritten for the Stamp II. (Continued)

```
' Merlin 1.0 - A game like Simon  (c) 1997 by AWC. All Rights Reserved.
' Uses a Basic Stamp I with 4 switches and LEDs on P0-P3 and a speaker
' on P4.
' Play: Press P0 to start game, Merlin plays a note and lights an LED.
' You must press the corresponding switch. Next, Merlin adds a note
' and you must match him until you can play 16 notes in a row
' You get a raspberry if you lose and all the lights come on if you
' win.


temp var byte       ' temp storage
maxstep var byte    ' tones in sequence
i var byte          ' loop counter
current var byte    ' current tone #
cstep var byte      ' offset in byte of current tone
ctone var word      ' current tone
delay con 40       ' general delay
tlen con 240       ' length of tone
tone1 con 1000
tone2 con 1100
tone3 con 1200
tone4 con 1300
on con 0           ' state for an "on" switch or LED
off con 1          ' state for an "off" switch or LED
allon con 0
alloff con 15
SwPort var inc
LEDPort var outc
SPKRPort con 11
SW0 var in8
SW1 var in9
SW2 var in10
SW3 var in11
outdir con %1111100000000  ' Dir mask to make outputs
```

Key Listing 1   The Merlin Program
rewritten for the Stamp II. (Continued)

```
baselow var word
basehigh var word


restart:                ' Wait for start button (1st button)
  basehigh=basehigh+1            ' randomize number
  baselow=baselow+2
  if SW0=off then restart
restart0:
  if SW0=on then start  ' wait for release of button
  goto restart
start:
maxstep=0             ' reset stuff
random basehigh               ' further randomize numbers
random baselow

agn:
dirs=outdir     ' set outputs
pause 1500            ' let player "reset"
gosub display            ' display sequence
gosub readsw             ' wait for user input
maxstep=maxstep+1        ' he got it, so bump up and go
if maxstep<16 then agn ' 16 is a winner
dirs=outdir
LEDPort=allon   ' all lamps on
freqout SPKRPort,tlen,1600
freqout SPKRPort,tlen,0
freqout SPKRPort,tlen,1600
LEDPort=alloff ' all off
goto restart

' Display current sequence
display:
  for i=0 to maxstep
```

Key Listing 1   The Merlin Program
rewritten for the Stamp II. (Continued)

```
    pause delay      ' inter tone delay
    gosub geti       ' get current pattern
    lookup current,[14,13,11,7],temp  ' turn on one light
'    lookup current,[1,2,4,8],temp     ' use this if on=1
    LEDPort=temp
    freqout SPKRPort,tlen,ctone              ' make tone
    LEDPort=alloff  ' all lamps off
  next
  return


' This takes the current value of i and find
' the pattern (current) and the tone (ctone)
' would be easier with arrays
geti:
    cstep=i/4        ' which byte?
    temp=cstep*4     ' which two bits in the byte?
    temp=i-temp
    current=basehigh.lowbyte
    ' load current with correct byte (b8-b11)
    if cstep=0 then getishift
    current=basehigh.highbyte
    if cstep=1 then getishift
    current=baselow.lowbyte
    if cstep=2 then getishift
    current=basehigh.highbyte
 getishift:
    if temp=0 then getimask   ' if 1st bits, mask off
    current=current/4         ' otherwise shift right 2 places
    temp=temp-1               ' bump the count
    goto getishift            ' and try again
getimask:
    current=current&3         ' chop off last two bits
    lookup current,[tone1,tone2,tone3,tone4],ctone  ' convert to tone
    return
```

Key Listing 1   The Merlin Program
rewritten for the Stamp II. (Continued)

```
' Read user's input
readsw:
    dirs=0                  ' change to inputs
    for i=0 to maxstep
      gosub geti            ' get pattern
readloop:
      if SW0=on then hit0   ' wait for a switch
      if SW1=on then hit1
      if SW2=on then hit2
      if SW3=on then hit3
      goto readloop

hit0:
    freqout SPKRPort,tlen,tone1      ' make correct tone
    if current=0 then readswok ' go if correct
    goto readswbad               ' not correct
hit1:
    freqout SPKRPort,tlen,tone2
    if current=1 then readswok
    goto readswbad
hit2:
   freqout SPKRPort,tlen,tone3
    if current=2 then readswok
    goto readswbad
hit3:
    freqout SPKRPort,tlen,tone4
    if current=3 then readswok
readswbad:
    if SWPort<>alloff  then readswbad  ' wait for switch to open
    freqout SPKRPort,1000,600   ' lost!
  goto restart

' Success!
```

**Key Listing 1   The Merlin Program
                     rewritten for the Stamp II. (Continued)**

```
readswok:
    if SWPort<>alloff  then readswok  ' wait for switch to open
  next   ' keep going
' Got 'em all
  return
```

Chapter 4 Answers

1. Assuming the PWM hardware is on pin 0:

```
I var BYTE
Rate con 20
Top:
FOR I = 0 to 255
  PWM 0,I,Rate
NEXT
FOR I=0 to 255 STEP -1
  PWM 0,I,Rate
NEXT
GOTO Top
```

2. Here is the organ code for three buttons and a Basic Stamp II.

```
bt1 con 8
bt1i var in8
bt2 con 9
bt2i var in9
bt3 con 10
bt3i var in10
spkr con 11
bt1v var byte
bt2v var byte
bt3v var byte

output spkr  ' speaker
```

```
loop:
' really don't have to use button here
  button bt1, 0, 1, 1, bt1v, 1, t1
  button bt2, 0, 1, 1, bt2v, 1, t2
  button bt3, 0, 1, 1, bt3v, 1, t3
goto loop

t1:
  freqout spkr,10,4000
  if bt1i=0 then t1
  goto loop

t2:
  freqout spkr,10,5000
  if bt2i=0 then t2
  goto loop

t3:
  freqout spkr,10,6000
  if bt3i=0 then t3
  goto loop
```

3. See Key Figure 1. This circuit uses two op amps. The first op amp adds 1V to the input. The second multiplies the output by 2. The three potentiometers allow fine-tuning of the circuit. The 10K pot generates the 1V to add to the input. The 50K pot controls the summing circuit. With 0V in, you should adjust the 50K pot until the output of the first op amp is 1V. The 100K pot on the second op amp controls the gain for the final stage. Since the input resistor is 47K, the pot should be adjusted to about 94K to achieve a gain of two.

Key Figure 1 Circuit for 2–11V output.

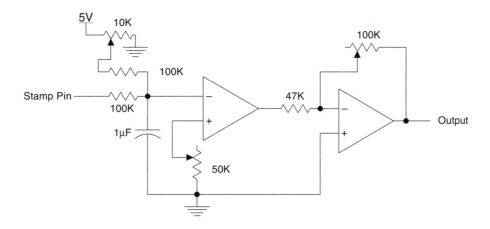

Chapter 5 Answers

1. One possible answer is to use a voltage divider (two resistors) to scale the input voltage to 0 –5V. Of course, the resolution goes down proportionately. Be sure to use precision resistors for best results.

2. Here is one possible solution set up for the Stamp II and the Stamp Experiment Board:

```
potpin con 7
led0 con 11
led1 con 10
led2 con 9
led3 con 8
pos var word
output led0
output led1
output led2
output led3

top:
  High potpin
  pause 10
```

```
    rctime potpin,1,pos
 ' pos = 1 to about 5800 for my setup
    if pos>4400 then 13
    if pos>3000 then 12
    if pos>2600 then 11
 ' light led 0 - remember bits are inverted
    outc=$7
    goto top
11:
    outc=$B
    goto top
12:
    outc=$D
    goto top
13:
    outc=$E
    goto top
```

3. See Key Figure 2. Each section of the comparator measures a 1V range.

Key Figure 2   A comparator checks an input voltage.

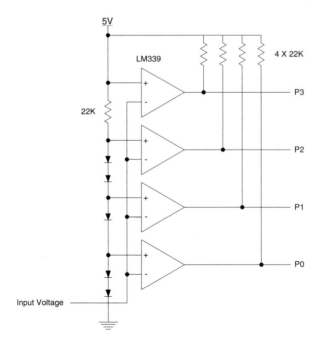

Chapter 6 Answers

1. Here is a suitable replacement for each SHIFTIN and SHIFTOUT call that reads or writes a byte in Sodata:

```
Socount var byte
Sodata var byte
MyShiftOut:
      OUTPUT datap
      FOR Socount=0 to 7
            LOW datap
            If (Sodata & $80) <> $80 then So0
            HIGH datap
      So0:
            Sodata=Sodata<<1    ' Shift left 1 bit
            PULSOUT clk,5
      NEXT
      RETURN

MyShiftIn:
      INPUT datap
      Sodata=0
      FOR Socount=0 to 7
      Sodata=Sodata<<1          ' Shift left 1 bit
      Sodata=Sodata | in 15
      PULSOUT clk,5
      NEXT
      RETURN
```

2. The Stamp software will require two changes: (1) the SEROUT command will require an inverted baudmode (e.g., 16,468) and, of course, (2) the new pin number. The PC software shouldn't require any changes. However, if the Stamp code received data from the PC, you'd need to take into account that when you aren't using port 16, there is no echo of received data. In this case, the Stamp only transmits, so this isn't a problem.

3. You can find a possible solution below. Notice that the maxad variable contains the highest address you've set. The line that causes this to happen is:

```
maxad = maxad MIN ptr
```

While this seems incorrect, it actually works. The MIN keyword returns a value that is at least as high as its second argument (but could be higher). MAX has the opposite effect. Another point of interest: when the program requests data using SERIN, you might be tempted to use the HEX2 modifier. However, this won't tell you when the user simply presses enter, so the program reads the data as a string and then converts it to hex using a simple-minded algorithm.

```
' Pattern generator
SinPort con 16
SoutPort con 16
BaudRate con 84
scl con 1
sda con 0
sdain var in0
sclin var in1

i2cackbit var bit   ' Ack bit -- should be 0
i2carb var bit      ' Arbitration -- should be zero
i2craw var byte     ' I2C in or out byte
i2ci var nib        ' I2C bit counter
eeadr var word      ' EEPROM address
eedata var byte     ' EEPROM data in or out

' main variables
line var byte(4)
ptr var word
byt var byte
maxad var word
maxad=0
top:
' read command
    serout SoutPort,BaudRate,["(",hex3 maxad ,") Command:"]
    serin SinPort,BaudRate,[line(0)]
    serout SoutPort,BaudRate,[CR]
    if line(0)="L" or line(0)="l" then loadee
    if line(0)="G" or line(0)="g" then go
    if line(0)="D" or line(0)="d" then dump
    serout SoutPort,BaudRate,["Unknown command",CR]
```

```
goto top

loadee:
  serout SoutPort,BaudRate,["Address:"]
  serin SinPort,BaudRate,[hex3 ptr]
dloop:
  serout SoutPort,BaudRate,[CR,hex3 ptr," Data:"]
  serin SinPort,BaudRate,[str line\2\CR]
  if line(0)=0 then top
  if line(0)>"9" then atof0
  byt=line(0)-"0"
  goto ckdigit1
atof0:
  byt=(line(0)&$5F)-"A"+10   ' A-F uppercase -"A" + 10
ckdigit1:
  if line(1)=0 then bytdone
  byt=byt*$10
  if line(1)>"9" then atof1
  byt=byt+line(1)-"0"
  goto bytdone
atof1:
  byt=byt+(line(1)&$5F)-"A"+10   ' A-F uppercase -"A" + 10
bytdone:
  maxad= maxad min ptr
  eeadr=ptr
  eedata=byt
  gosub eewrite
  ptr=ptr+1
  goto dloop

go:
' Drive top 8 pins as output
 dirs=$FF00
 for eeadr=0 to maxad
   gosub eeread
   outh=eedata
 next
```

```
  goto go

dump:
 for eeadr=0 to maxad
   gosub eeread
   serout SoutPort,BaudRate,[hex3 eeadr,":",hex2 eedata,CR]
 next
goto top



' Use these routines to simulate external
' eeprom if you don't have any
eeread1:
  read eeadr,eedata
  return

eewrite1:
  write eeadr,eedata
  return

' Begin I2C Code

' Set up a start condition
' Sets i2carb=1 if busy
i2cstart:
  input sda
  input scl
  i2carb=0
  if (sdain & sclin)=1 then i2crdy
i2cnoarb
  i2carb=1
  return
i2crdy:
  low sda
  low scl
  return
```

```
' Set up stop condition
i2cstop:
  low sda
  input scl
  input sda
  return


' Read ack bit
i2cack:
  input scl
i2cawait:
  if sclin=0 then i2cawait  ' wait for clock stretch
  i2cackbit=sdain
  low scl
  return


' Write 8 bits to I2C bus
i2cwrite:
  for i2ci=1 to 8
    if (i2craw & $80)<>0 then i2conewr
    low sda
    goto i2cwrbit
i2conewr:
    input sda
    if sdain=0 then i2cnoarb ' arbitration lost!
i2cwrbit:
    input scl
i2cwrclk:
    if sclin<>1 then i2cwrclk  ' wait for clk sync
    low scl
    i2craw=i2craw<<1
  next
  input sda
  return


' Read 8 bits from I2C bus
```

```
i2cread:
  i2craw=0
  for i2ci=1 to 8
    input scl
i2crdclk:
    if sclin<>1 then i2crdclk  ' wait for clk sync
    i2craw=(i2craw<<1)+sdain
    low scl
  next
  return


' Begin EEPROM address
' Set EEPROM address -- common to read and write
eesetadr:
  gosub i2cstart
  if i2carb=1 then eesetadr  ' if we lose arbitration, try again
  i2craw=$A0 | ((eeadr>>7) & $E)
  gosub i2cwrite
  gosub i2cack
  if i2cackbit=1 then eeerr
  i2craw=eeadr & $FF
  gosub i2cwrite
  gosub i2cack
  if i2cackbit=0 then eeret
eeerr:
  ' NACK error -- what to do?
eeret:
  return


' Write byte to EEPROM
eewrite:
  gosub eesetadr
  i2craw=eedata
  gosub i2cwrite
  gosub i2cack
  if i2cackbit=0 then writeok
  ' NACK error
```

```
writeok:
  goto i2cstop  ' hidden return


' Read byte to EEPROM
eeread:
  gosub eesetadr
  gosub i2cstart   ' Abort write command
  i2craw=$A1 | ((eeadr>>7) & $E)
  gosub i2cwrite
  gosub i2cack
  gosub i2cread
  eedata=i2craw
  gosub i2cack
  goto i2cstop  ' hidden return


' Check for write complete
eecheck:
  gosub i2cstart
  i2craw=$A0
  gosub i2cwrite
  goto i2cack    ' hidden return


' Wait for write operation to complete
eepoll:
  gosub eecheck
  if i2cackbit=1 then eepoll
  return
```

Chapter 7 Answers

1. You'll find the essential parts of the code for this exercise in Key Listing 2 (the solution for exercise 2). The main program loop can simply call GETKEY and display the results. Of course, your numbers may vary depending on your exact circuit. These numbers worked with a keypad using 1K resistors and a 0.2µF capacitor (actually, two 0.1µF capacitors in parallel.

2. See Key Listing 2. This code uses 14 keys. This allows you to enter the 10 digits, plus, minus, enter, and clear. A 16-key array could easily add multiply and divide as well.

3. This requires minimal changes to the code if you move E and RS to the top eight bits of I/O. This frees the entire lower eight bits for talking to the LCD. There is little advantage to this approach because it uses four more bits, isn't very much faster, and doesn't require much less code.

```
i_LCD:
  outL = 0 ' Clear the output lines
  LOW E
  LOW RS
  dirL = %11111111 ' set outputs.
  pause 200 ' Wait 200 ms for LCD to reset.
' force 8-bit op - repeating to be sure it resets
  outL = %00110011
  pulsout E,pw
  pulsout E,pw

  char = 14 ' non blink cursor
'  char = 15  ' blinking cursor (use 14 for non-blink)
  gosub wr_LCD '
char = 6 ' Turn on cursor and enable l-r
wr_LCD:
  outL =  char
  pulsout E,pw ' Blip enable pin.
  return
```

Key Listing 2   The RPN calculator.

```
KPIN con 8
kavg var word
kraw var word
key var byte
tmpkey var byte
i var nib
j var nib
lift var bit
```

Key Listing 2   The RPN calculator. (Continued)

```
xy var word(4)
xyptr var nib
op var byte

clear:
Debug CR,"Clear",CR
xy(0)=0
xy(1)=0
xy(2)=0
xyptr=0
lift=0
xy1z:
xy(3)=0
debug ">"
top:
  gosub getkey
  if key=0 then top
  if key="C" then clear
  if key="+" then plus
  if key="-" then minus
  if key="=" then enter
  debug key   ' echo numbers
  if lift=0 then nolift
  gosub _enter
  lift=0
nolift:
  xy(xyptr)=xy(xyptr)*10+key-"0"   ' build number
  goto top

plus:
  if xyptr=0 then underflow
  xy(xyptr-1)=xy(xyptr-1)+xy(xyptr)
  op="+"
stackprint:
  xyptr=xyptr-1
```

Key Listing 2 The RPN calculator. (Continued)

```
  lift=1
  debug op,cr,dec xy(xyptr),cr,">"
  goto top

underflow:
  debug cr,"Stack underflow",CR
  goto top

minus:
  if xyptr=0 then underflow
  xy(xyptr-1)=xy(xyptr-1)-xy(xyptr)
  op="-"
  goto stackprint

enter:
  debug cr
  gosub _enter
  goto xy1z

_enter:
  if xyptr=3 then enter1
  xyptr=xyptr+1
  xy(xyptr)=0
  return
enter1:
  xy(0)=xy(1)
  xy(1)=xy(2)
  xy(2)=xy(3)
  xy(xyptr)=0
  return

getkey:
gosub getkeyraw
tmpkey=key
for j=1 to 2  ' make sure we get 3 in a row
  gosub getkeyraw
```

Key Listing 2   The RPN calculator. (Continued)

```
   if tmpkey<>key then nogetkey
next
' Wait for key to rise (could do repeat logic here)
keydown:
  gosub getkeyraw
  if tmpkey=key then keydown
  key=tmpkey
return

nogetkey:
key=0
return


getkeyraw:
kavg=0

for i=0 to 3    ' average 4 counts
  HIGH KPIN
  pause 1
  RCTIME KPIN,1,kraw
  kavg=kavg+kraw
next
kavg=kavg/4
key=0
if kavg>=1700 then nokey
' NOTE: the next two lines are really one line!
LOOKDOWN  kavg,>[1560,1450,1350,1220,1080,970,820,720,580,
  470,340,220,100,0],key
LOOKUP key,["=","C","0","1","2","3","+","6","5","4","7","8","9","-"],key
nokey:
  return
```

Chapter 8 Answers

1. Assuming pin 0 is the control pin, you need only generate PWM for the correct duty cycle. For example, to operate the motor at half-speed, you can write:

```
top:
PWM 0,128,1000   ' 1 second of 1/2 cycles
GOTO top
```

If you try to set the duty cycle to 1, you'll probably find that it won't work from a dead stop. That's because the small pulse won't provide the motor with enough torque to overcome its initial inertia. However, if you start the motor at a higher speed and then slow it, it may work because the inertia is working for you instead of against you. This is the same reason you can operate a car on the highway in third or fourth gear, but you have to start out in first gear. Here's a possible program:

```
      PWM 0,128,100  ' get started
top:  PWM 0,1,1000    ' slowwww down
      GOTO top
```

2. If you are using a Stamp I, use the POT command. If you are using the Stamp II, you can use RCTIME (see the Stamp manual for the connections you'll need). The exact values you'll need to use depend on the exact components you select. The idea will be to scale the minimum and maximum count values to range between 0 and 255. Then you can use this to drive the PWM command.

   You might start with this simple program (for the Stamp II):

```
RCLOOP:
      HIGH 1     ' Pot on Pin 1
      PAUSE 1
      RCTIME 1,1,W2
      DEBUG ?W2
      PAUSE 1000
      GOTO RCLOOP
```

Now you can easily see the values you'll get from the components you've selected. Suppose that your components output values from 0 to 9,270. You might write code like this:

```
RCLOOP:
    HIGH 1
    PAUSE 1
    RCTIME 1,1,W2
    W2=W2/37      ' range from 0 to 250
    PWM 0,W2,1000
    GOTO RCLOOP
```

The 37 in the program above is $9,270/256$, rounded up to an integer value. This results in a duty cycle that will range from 0 to 250 (because of the rounding). If you really needed full range, you might use the $*/$ operator (Stamp II only) or trim the resistor or capacitor to give you an even multiple of 256. You could also spread the counts using an algorithm that makes sense for your application.

3. Your exact solution to this problem will depend on exactly what toy you select. However, here are a few ideas:

    •   Open the remote control and locate the buttons that operate the toy.

    •   Use a volt meter to measure the voltage on each side of each button. One side of the button will probably read 0V, and the other will read a higher voltage.

    •   Most likely, the high voltage will drop to 0V when you push the button. If this is the case, you can use a simple 2N2222-type switch to ground that node and operate the device.

    •   It is possible, but not likely, that the 0V side of the button will rise in voltage when you push the button. Then you'll need to use a PNP transistor to drive the button, but this is very unusual.

    •   If all else fails, you might consider using a CMOS transmission gate (like a 4066 IC) or a MOSFET to operate as an electronic switch across the mechanical one. This is hardly ever necessary.

    •   Once the Stamp can control the buttons, the rest is easy.

    •   You'll find some inexpensive toys only have two buttons. For example, some robots can go forward or turn in one direction. Many toy cars go forward or reverse and turn at the same time. However, often these toys have complete H bridges inside, but the remote control is the limiting factor. In these cases, you might want to tear directly into the toy and control it directly.

- If you do experiment with direct control, try operating the device with a clip lead supplying ground connections (or power connections) to the transistors you want to drive. Only when you are sure you understand what is going on should you connect your $40 Stamp to the circuit. Be mindful that the Stamp may need help to drive motors and other high-current devices.

Chapter 9 *(No exercises)*

Chapter 10 Answers

1. The correct answer is 220.25mS. You can see MPLAB running the solution to this lab in Key Figure 3.

Key Figure 3 MPLAB simulating `test.asm`.

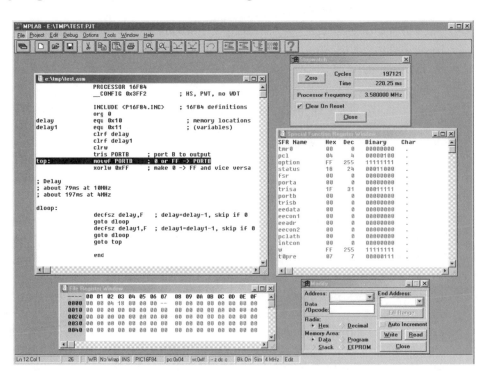

2. The easiest way (but not the only way) to do this is to set DELAY1 to 128 (0x80) so that the outer delay loop only runs half as many times as it did before. This is easy to do by placing these two statements before the dloop label:

```
movlw 0x80
movwf delay1
```

3. You can replace the TRIS command with the following code:

```
bsf STATUS,RP0
movwf TRISB
bcf STATUS,RP0
```

The assembler will warn you that TRISB is not in register bank 0. If you want to force the assembler to stop warning you, you could write:

```
bsf STATUS,RP0
movwf PORTB      ; PORTB is TRISB & 0x7F
bcf STATUS,RP0
```

or you might write:

```
bsf STATUS,RP0
movwf TRISB & 0x7F
bcf STATUS,RP0
```

It is a good idea to clear the RP0 bit after you store 7F in TRISB so that future register accesses will be in page 0 (even though for this program it doesn't really matter).

Chapter 11 *(No exercises)*

Index

Symbols

- 39, 44–45, 150
& 30, 40, 45, 161
&/ 30, 40, 162
* 30, 39, 45, 50, 150
** 30, 39, 45, 50, 151
*/ 45, 51, 152
+ 30, 39, 44–45, 150
/ 30, 39, 45, 150
// 30, 39, 45, 73, 153
<< 30, 45, 154, 160
>> 30, 45, 154, 160
^ 30, 40, 45, 161
^/ 30, 40, 162
| 30, 40, 45, 161
|/ 30, 40, 162
~ 30

Numerics

1488 282
1489 282
16F84 392, 394, 396, 406, 419–420
1-Wire 135, 141
276-075 198
2N2222 341, 359
2N2222A 177
2N3904 177, 179
2N3906 179
4016 178
4046 243
4066 180
68HC11 391
74C922 322, 324
74LS153 192
74LS165 192
74LS299 192

74LS595 192
7805 7
78L05 7
8051 391

A

A/D 228, 234–235, 239–241, 243, 250–251, 261, 286
ABS 30, 44, 156
AC loads 181
ActiveX 287
ADC 228, 232, 234, 237, 247
ADC08034 235
amplifiers 116, 214, 219, 226
    inverting 219
    noninverting 219
analog to digial converter
    See A/D or ADC
analog vs. digital 12
AND 15, 40, 81
annunciators 175
APP-I 402–403, 415, 419–421
    Stamp software 398
approximation
    successive 234
architecture
    Harvard 407
array 43, 57, 61
    button 325
    variables 43
ASCII 35, 56, 121, 326–327
ASP-II 6, 423
assembly language 393–394, 396, 408–409
asynchronous protocol 250–251

ATN 342, 422, 424
Automated Cable Tester 208
AUXIO 30, 136

B

base 10 13
base 12 13
base 16 15
baud rate 121, 124, 128, 196, 250, 280, 295
BELL 58
bilateral switch 178, 180
binary 14, 44, 58, 129
    numbers 13–14
bit 14, 40
BKSP 58
Board of Education 5
BOB (Break Out Box) 280
BOEBot 349
Boolean Algebra 15–16
Boolean operators 15–16
bounce 26, 106, 185
brads 158
BRANCH 30, 75, 84
breadboard 5, 173, 181, 217, 315
break out box
    See BOB
BS1EMU 9, 11
BSAVE 30, 64
BSR 108
bug 172, 201
BUTTON 30, 106–107, 185
buzzer 175, 212
byte 14, 40

Need to Upgrade Your Skills?

Let's compare your choices...

GO BACK TO SCHOOL...	OR	TAKE A CHALKBOARD COURSE...
$20,000 per semester	vs.	$200 average cost per course
today's technology	vs.	tomorrow's technology
finding parking	vs.	parking in your favorite chair
teaching assistants	vs.	world-leading instructors
using up gas	vs.	generating gas
notes on a whiteboard	vs.	a multimedia experience
bullies in the hallways	vs.	no bullies, no hallways
keeping up with the class	vs.	going at your own pace
dreary old buildings	vs.	portable classroom

Hey, it's your choice

The Chalkboard Network®

Online Training From The World's Leading Experts

www.chalknet.com

Get the resource that delivers
PRACTICAL, RELIABLE, and USEFUL C/C++
programming information

ONLY $19 95 for 12 issues

The only source that devotes 12 issues a year to C/C++ topics like:

- *Algorithms*
- *Debugging*
- *Graphics*
- *Windows*
- *Object-Oriented Programming*
- *Embedded Systems*
- *Software Tools*
- *And More*

PRACTICAL
C/C++ Users Journal translates advanced theory into working code month-after-month. Each article discusses issues of concern to professional C/C++ programmers.

RELIABLE
C/C++ Users Journal is always there, delivering feature after feature filled with advanced, useful information you need. Each issue brings you regular columns written by some of the most widely recognized experts in the field.

USEFUL
C/C++ Users Journal brings you tools and techniques you can use now — tools that will make you more productive and make your programs more reliable and useful.

Call TODAY for your FREE Issue!

C/C++ Users Journal™
Advanced Solutions for C/C++ Programmers

Special Book Buyer Discount

P.O. Box 52582
Boulder, CO 80322-2582

www.cuj.com/sub
Discount key code: 2CAQ

(Orders outside the U.S. must prepay. Canada/Mexico: 1 year - $46. Outside North America: $65 U.S. Funds)

New for 2002 ...

Your embedded reference library!

EmbeddedSystems
P R O G R A M M I N G

CD–ROM Library 7.0

The *Embedded Systems Programming* CD-ROM Library Release 7.0 contains columns, features, news items, editorials, and source code from the 1988 premiere issue through the December 2001 issue. This time-saver contains a powerful text search engine and is a must-have for veteran readers and for those new to *Embedded Systems Programming*, the preeminent source of embedded development for more than 13 years.

Features Include:

• Columns, features, and source code from the
  premier 1988 issue through the December 2001 issue

• More than 800 articles—columns and features

• A powerful text search engine

• The entire 2002 Buyer's Guide—more than
  1,500 products covered in detail

• Code you can copy directly into your designs

• Windows, Unix, Linux, and Mac compatibility

• Past and present author biographies

• Links to updated information on www.embedded.com

$89.95 new

2 ways to order:

online
www.embedded.com

phone
(800) 444-4881 U.S./Canada
(785) 841-1631 other countries

Order it
online today!

www.embedded.com

CMP
United Business Media

EmbeddedSystems
P R O G R A M M I N G

THE ONLY AUDITED MAGAZINE DEDICATED TO EMBEDDED DESIGN

Embedded Systems Programming has been providing invaluable information to the embedded industry for over 13 years. Our subscribers enjoy high-quality, practical articles on microcontroller, embedded microprocessor, DSP and SoC-based development month after month.

The industry magazine since 1988.

CMP
United Business Media

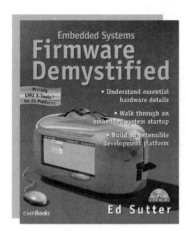

RD3934 $49.95

Embedded Systems Firmware Demystified

by Ed Sutter

Explore firmware development from cold-boot to network-boot. Investigate CPU-to-peripheral interfaces. Write a powerful CLI, flash drivers, a flash file system, and a TFTP client/server. The CD-ROM includes a cross-compilation toolset for 21 processors and source for an extensible firmware development platform. CD-ROM included, 366pp, ISBN 1-57820-099-7

DSP for Real-Time Systems

by Robert Oshana

This introduction to DSP development covers design principles from processor architectures and basic theory to the selection of appropriate languages and basic algorithms. You get practical guidelines, diagrammed techniques, and code templates for developing and optimizing DSP software. Project demonstrations illustrate how to develop an application, including integration and testing, development tools, and project management techniques. CD-ROM included, 464pp, ISBN 1-57820-098-9

RD3611 $49.95

Find CMP Books in your local bookstore.

Order direct 800-500-6875   e-mail: books@cmp.com
fax 408-848-5784   www.cmpbooks.com

CMP Books

TCP/IP Lean
Web Servers for Embedded Systems
Second Edition

by Jeremy Bentham

Implement dynamic Web programming techniques with this hands-on guide to TCP/IP networking. You get source code and fully-functional utilities for a simple TCP/IP stack that's efficient to use in embedded applications. This edition shows the Web server porting to the PIC16F877 chip as well as over an ethernet connection. Includes a demonstration port running on Microchip's PICDEM.Net demonstration board. CD-ROM included, 544pp, ISBN 1-57820-108-X

RD4293   **$59.95**

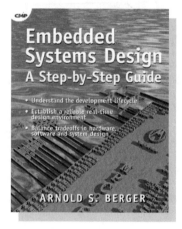

RD3689   **$34.95**

Embedded Systems Design
A Step-by-Step Guide

by Arnold S. Berger

Develop embedded systems from the ground up! This primer teaches the specialized aspects of writing software in this environment that are not covered in standard coursework for software developers and electrical engineers. It traces the software and hardware methodologies and the integration of the two disciplines. 236pp, ISBN 1-57820-073-3

Find CMP Books in your local bookstore.

Order direct 800-500-6875   e-mail: books@cmp.com
fax 408-848-5784   www.cmpbooks.com

CMP*Books*

RD3932 $74.95

MicroC/OS-II,
The Real-Time Kernel
Second Edition
by Jean J. Labrosse

Learn the inner workings of an RTOS! This release of MicroC/OS adds documentation for several important new features of the latest version of the software, including new real-time services, floating points, and coding conventions. It is a completely portable, ROMable, preemptive real-time kernel. Complete code is included for use in your own applications. Hardcover, CD-ROM included, 648pp, ISBN 1-57820-103-9

Practical Statecharts in C/C++
An Introduction to Quantum Programming

by Miro Samek

In the spirit of eXtreme programming, the author's quantum programming is a lightweight method that allows programmers to quickly hand-code working, real-time systems in C and C++ directly from UML statecharts. You get a cookbook with step-by-step instructions and complete source code to the state-oriented framework. CD-ROM included, 265pp, ISBN 1-57820-110-1

RD3935 $44.95

Find CMP Books in your local bookstore.

Order direct 800-500-6875   e-mail: books@cmp.com
fax 408-848-5784   www.cmpbooks.com

CMP Books

What's on the CD-ROM?

Microcontroller Projects Using the Basic Stamp, Second Edition, is accompanied by the companion CD-ROM which has all the source code for each chapter.

In addition, you'll find the Stamp manuals, application notes, and software courtesy of Parallax. The APP-I programmer software is also on the CD, along with the Basic Stamp I Simulator — an emulator for the Basic Stamp I. It is being released as complimentary software to the Basic Stamp community.

How do I use the Stamp I Simulator?

Write your program using the STAMP.EXE editor (from Parallax). Then add a line anywhere in your program that reads: BSAVE. Download the program (even if you don't really have a Stamp hooked up — you don't even have to own a Stamp). This places a file in the current directory called CODE.OBJ. You can rename the file if you like, but keep the .OBJ extension.

Next, start BS1. It will bring up a dialog where you can pick what file you want to open. After you open the file, the main screen will appear. At the top of the window are eight LEDs that show your outputs (black is 0, red is 1, and hollow means the pin is an input). Below that are eight buttons that represent your inputs. Black is a zero input and green is a one input. Below that are several special I/O locations. Below that are all the W and B registers along with the PORT register. You can modify the W registers by typing over the numbers already there. At the very bottom of the screen, you will see a decoding of the next statement to execute (which may look a little odd, compared to your original source, but you'll be able to figure it out).

There are three buttons: Run, Step, and Step Over. The Run button causes the program to execute as fast as possible (about 1 instruction per millisecond). Step executes one line of code. Step Over executes a line of code too, but if it is a GOSUB, the debugger stops when it hits the corresponding RETURN. When you press RUN, by the way, the button changes to STOP and you can press it to go back to single step mode.

For additional information on the CD-ROM, the Stamp I Simulator, special I/O locations, unsupported constructs, and so forth — see Appendix A on page 415.
